# The Roman Catholic Church

JOHN L. McKENZIE, S.J.

*Professor of Theology*
*University of Notre Dame*

HISTORY OF RELIGION SERIES

*General Editor: E. O. James*

Holt, Rinehart and Winston
New York    Chicago    San Francisco

SBN: 03-081021-3 Trade Edition
SBN: 03-081871-0 Text Edition
Printed in the United States of America

Imprimi Potest:    Robertus F. Harvanek, S.J.
                        Acting Provincial of the Chicago Province
Nihil Obstat:    Gall Higgins, O.F.M.Cap.
                        Censor Librorum
Imprimatur:    Joseph P. O'Brien, S.T.D.
                        Vicar General, Archdiocese of New York
                        May 14, 1969

The nihil obstat and imprimatur are official declarations that a book or pamphlet is free of doctrinal or moral error. No implication is contained therein that those who have granted the nihil obstat and imprimatur agree with the contents, opinions, or statements expressed.

# CONTENTS

# ILLUSTRATIONS
*(Between pages 144 and 145)*

## Acknowledgments
The publishers wish to thank the following for providing illustrations for this volume and for permission to reproduce them: United Press International, plate 1; Associated Press, plate 2; Catholic Herald, plate 20; Hirmer Fotoarchiv München, plate 3; Spanish National Tourist Office, plates 4 and 5; French Government Tourist Office, plates 6 and 17; Biblioteca Nazionale, Naples, plate 7; Musée Condé, Chantilly, plate 8; Peter Clayton, plate 10; Biblioteca Apostolica Vaticana, plate 9; National Monuments Record, plates 11 (by courtesy of the Reverend M. Ridgway), 12 and 13 (by courtesy of Her Majesty the Queen); Caisse Nationale des Monuments Historiques, plate 14; Anderson, plate 15; the Trustees of the British Museum, plates 16 and 18; the Mansell Collection, plate 19.

# PREFACE

It is a duty and a pleasure to acknowledge assistance received in the writing of this book. Recognition is due in the first place to Mr. Robert Engler, my graduate assistant at Notre Dame, who rendered essential assistance in the preparation of the footnotes and the bibliography. The Reverend Albert Schlitzer, then chairman of the department of theology, graciously allowed me the assistance of Mr. Engler during the entire period of writing. Mrs. Gillian Hughes of Weidenfeld and Nicolson and Mr. Joseph Cunneen of Holt, Rinehart and Winston, supervised the production of the book.

The Roman Catholic Church has surprised and bewildered members and others alike during recent years. Those who are interested are entitled to a more synthetic view of the church than they can obtain from journalistic pieces, many of them very well done. The publishers thought the synthetic view could be written, and they invited me to do it. It turned out to be an extremely difficult task, so difficult that I was tempted more than once to write the publishers and admit that the task I had accepted was impossible. The readers and the reviewers may tell me that my apprehensions were quite well founded, and I should have chosen the part of discretion. I merely want to assure them that no failure was ever achieved with greater effort.

John L. McKenzie, S.J.

University of Notre Dame
Easter Sunday, April 6, 1969

# INTRODUCTION

The problems of writing the history of a living religion are quite different from the problems of the history of a dead one. A dead religion can be described; it has had a beginning and an end, and its development has reached full term. He who treats of a living religion may state his observations and form his conclusions, but he runs the risk of seeing many of them falsified as soon as they are printed, and possibly even before they are printed. Up to 1962, few living religions appeared to be more stable than Roman Catholicism. The Roman Church had achieved a degree of stability which suggested to some, both within and outside its communion, that it had begun to ossify. The Second Vatican Council, however, introduced changes some see as revolutionary, others as threats to the very identity of the Church. Furthermore, the celebrated monolithic structure of Roman Catholicism is now recognized as an illusion. Divisions within the church have caused some apprehension of schism. The movements initiated by the Council seem to many to be full of promise, to others to be a headlong rush toward disaster. This book is being written at a moment of history when a knowledge of the past seems to indicate almost nothing of the future of Roman Catholicism.

The word *history* is not used here in its ordinary sense in the phrase "history of religion," and several approaches to the task are possible within this term. Some I excluded almost as soon as they came to mind. An outline of church history, useful as it may be, does not seem to fit the form and style of this series. It would of necessity be shallow, and whatever its quality might be, many other Roman Catholics are better able to prepare such a work than I am. An outline history of Roman Catholicism would be very nearly an outline history of Europe since the barbarian invasions. It would also be a history of the Papacy rather than of the Church, and one purpose of this book is to show that the Roman Church cannot simply be identified with the Papacy. A concentration upon this aspect of the history of the church would omit most of the elements which Catholics believe are vital in the reality of Catholicism.

The methods of the history of religion permit the approach which is followed here, an approach which is descriptive or phenomenological. The weakness inherent in phenomenological analysis is that it is very likely to be unhistorical, abstracting a certain moment from a history which is in constant flux. It is impossible, at least within the scope of this work, to avoid this weakness entirely. My effort is to describe Roman Catholicism as it exists at the time of this writing, with as much attention as possible given to the processes by which it became what it is. Depth in the historical analysis cannot be achieved, and the effort must be made to attend to those elements which are genuinely important. Selection here is a matter of personal judgment, reached by consulting the judgment of competent scholars; and the author must stand by a selection which he knows is open to criticism.

I have chosen to emphasize those features of Catholicism which seem to be peculiarly Roman; but what does this term mean? Roman Catholicism is one of many religious bodies which call themselves Christian. This Christian community implies a number of common features. The difference between the bodies implies some features which are not common. Other Christians do not refuse to profess Roman Catholicism because it is Christian or Catholic, but because it is Roman. There is a vague general agreement on what *Romanism* means; some features of this agreement are certainly due to misunderstanding, and it must be our purpose to avoid such misunderstanding. On the other hand, Roman Catholics believe that their Romanism is a reflection of the authentic Christianity of their church. This belief too may involve some misunderstanding, but it is impossible to discuss Roman Catholicism without admitting that Catholics accept their Romanism. Their acceptance may have reservations not generally known to other Christians, but Roman Catholics are not moving toward a non-Roman Catholicism.

I understand *Roman* Catholicism to begin with the conversion of Constantine. It would be false to say that the early church showed no Roman features before Constantine; but the conversion of Constantine was the first decisive factor in the series of events which was to give the Western church its Roman character. In the centuries following Constantine, the Greek church continued to move in a direction which resulted in its final secession from Rome. Between Constantine and Charlemagne, the Roman Church achieved its peculiar identity with Western Europe, the community of Christendom, and such Roman features as the Latin rite and the primacy of the Roman Pontiff became fixed, but it was not until the Reformation that the Roman Church was compelled to assert its Romanism in contrast to its Europeanism.

A glance at the table of contents will show that I have organized the description around certain obvious topics, as much to avoid overlapping as to compose a reasonably complete and orderly presentation. Even so, it has been impossible to avoid some repetition. The organization of the book does not follow the course of historical development. The primitive church was much more conscious of its worship and its works than it was of its structure and its beliefs. Of the four major headings, structure is the most recent development; but it is perhaps one of the more bewildering features of Roman Catholicism that its structure seems to develop with its belief. The two have evolved simultaneously in becoming more tight and rigorous. The structure of the Roman Church is one of its most evident features. The Protestant churches have refused to institute a similarly rigorous structure, and the theological implications of this difference reach far. It is precisely in the relations of structure to worship, beliefs, and works that repetition is inevitable in the treatment.

Where the volumes of this series are concerned with living religions, the editors have chosen a member of the religious body for the treatment. Obviously a believer is more likely to be sympathetic, and he has or ought to have a better chance of understanding the religion which he describes. This does not mean that he is secured from misunderstanding just by his membership. As I have remarked, Roman Catholicism is not as monolithic as both its members and others have been accustomed to believe. It is rather difficult to think of any one whose exposition would be accepted by the entire body of Roman Catholics as representative of their understanding and experience of their church. I do not think that the believer is any more likely to be prejudiced, misinformed, or dishonest than the unbeliever. He does not claim to be perfectly objective, and he doubts that any one else can truthfully claim to be. I do not conceive it to be my function to make value judgments about Roman Catholicism; on the other hand, it is impossible to speak about it at length without at least implying some value judgments. The Roman Church has been the center of deep and often bitter controversy for several hundred years. It is no longer necessary to write polemically about Catholicism, either in attack or in defense; but it would be unrealistic to pretend that Romanism arouses no feelings whatever. A description of Catholicism by a Roman Catholic may be regarded by some as an apology, even if the author did not intend it as such; indeed, he may write an apology without realizing it, but it should also be remembered that members of a church are able to criticize it in ways and in depth which the outsider cannot match.

I have already observed that Roman Catholicism stands at what may be the most critical point of its entire history, and that it is impossible to predict the direction of the future. Any assessment of the past must include those factors which made it possible for the Roman Church to produce such a crisis, for the crisis was not compelled by outside agents. The work should also include some analysis of the areas which seem open to development at present; this is a risky projection, but one could scarcely describe the phenomenon unless one made the attempt. Only recently a group of English Catholics collaborated in writing a book entitled *Objections to Roman Catholicism*.[1] Still more recently, one of the most respected Roman Catholics of the English-speaking world announced his severance from Romanism on the grounds that the Roman Church is corrupt.[2] Were these only isolated incidents, they could be treated as such; but in fact they are tokens of something larger. The Roman Catholic Church is passing into a crisis of authority and a crisis of faith; the two should be distinguished, but the fact of their confusion compounds the crisis. Both Catholics and others are perplexed by what is happening. Without pretending to explain it, this work must show how this unexpected turn arises from the existing reality of Roman Catholicism. In the plan of the work an attempt is made as each topic is developed to show how it is affected by the crisis and to indicate, where it is possible, the direction in which Romanism seems to be moving.

The crisis has shown itself most readily in the area of worship; the most massive changes yet made have occurred here. Their implications have not yet been seen fully. The area of works has shown less manifest change, but a number of profound and disturbing questions have been raised. Structure is not changeless in Roman Catholicism, but structural changes have occurred slowly in the history of the church. The possibility of radical structural changes is real, and we can at least identify some of the forces which move toward these changes. The area of belief is regarded by Roman Catholics as least open to change; but even here questions are raised, among them questions of the very nature of belief. One can scarcely do more at present than point out the questions and their roots.

HISTORY OF RELIGION

*The Roman Catholic Church*

# I. The Structure of
# Roman Catholicism

## 1. The Structure of Religion

Religion is a social phenomenon; that is, it is a function of man in society and not of the individual person. Personal or individual religion arises within the framework of a religious society; if it were purely personal and unconnected with a religious society, it would not be religion in the usual sense of the term. Religion is structured simply because it is social, but its social character does not predetermine it to any particular structure. Because all religions have the same basic concerns, there are basic similarities in religious structures, apart from borrowings. It will be seen that the structure of Roman Catholicism has adopted many structural features both from other religions and from secular societies.

The basic concern of religion is the attempt of a group to reach communion as a body with the deity in which the group believes. If the group, antecedently to its religious activity, already existed as a secular society, the structure of the secular society may impose itself upon the religion or may at least be of primary importance in determining the structure of the religion. Here one is speaking of the order of logic rather than of the order of time. The study of early religions does not disclose that existing secular societies adopted religion. Early man, as far as we know him, did not make the distinction between the sacred and the profane which modern civilized society makes. Because of this distinction, modern man may be a member of several secular societies which are not connected with his religious affiliation. Early man was a member of a single society which comprised both his secular and his religious activities. He knew nothing of a purely secular society. The family, the tribe, and the state were all religious groups. Indeed, the religious group seems at times to have given form to the secular group. The earliest city-states of Mesopotamia have been identified as temple communities.[1] The god was the owner and the ruler of the city, and the citizens were his slaves, tenants, and employees; they were all members of the staff of the temple. The rule of the god was exercised through his viceroy, the chief priest. The secularization of kingship and the state in Mesopotamia had begun at the opening of historic times, but the king never lost his sacred character entirely; he remained a religious official as well as a secular ruler. Even in Greece, the birthplace of rationalism, Socrates was prosecuted by the political society for an offense against the religion of the city.[2]

With the development both of politics and religion, two types of structure emerge, and the religious structure becomes more clearly defined as religious. The search for communion with the deity is always pursued through accredited persons, who mediate between the deity and the rest of the community. When religions are studied, attention naturally falls in the first place on this sacred personnel, because they show more clearly the distinct identity of the religion. It is safe to say that generally the sacred personnel are believed to be chosen both by the deity and by the community; there may be a tradition of a divine election of persons, accepted by the community, or an election by the community, ratified by the deity. The sacred personnel are distinguished from others by membership in chosen families, by costume, by some form of ritual appointment, or by some privileges and obligations peculiar to the class; in any case they are, because of their close relationship to the deity, not like other people, and the distinction must be preserved and manifested.

As religion develops, it is normal that the sacred personnel should increase in number and that their organization should become more complex. It is normal also that they should become more strictly professional religious persons. As was noticed, religious officers may also be secular officers; but the trend is always toward specialization. This is obviously associated with a multiplication of religious functions; one may say, I hope with due reverence, that Parkinson's law may be seen in operation here in that the number of religious functions is multiplied according to the number of persons available to perform them. In Mesopotamian religion, the titles of the priests were so numerous and so obscure that modern scholars cannot define and distinguish all of them. To some degree this complexification and specialization can be seen in all religions.

Whether with more specialization or with less, the sacred personnel have a peculiar competence and authority in religious activity. The sacred and the secular officers can and do clash in the definition of what is properly religious activity, but the principle of competence and authority is accepted in any society which recognizes religion. It is not too much to say that in religion the sacred personnel are active and the worshipers or believers are passive. The sacred personnel know the way to achieve communion with the deity. They know the proper performance of the rites of worship, and they are familiar with the complexity and rigidity which ritual worship always seems to develop. They are the possessors of religious knowledge, the knowledge of things about the deity; and this often means that they are the channels through which revelation or commands are transmitted to the worshipers. They pray and worship with a peculiar authority which the worshipers do not have, and they therefore pray and worship in the name of the community.

These general remarks are made here as a background for the consideration of Roman Catholic hierarchical structure. They indicate that the hierarchical structure, quaint as it may seem to many of our contemporaries, manifests in its general outline a universal feature of religion. It is not in these general qualities that the Romanism of the structure is seen. Each historic religion has its own variations on the general structure; the Roman variations are really without parallel. It is precisely in regard to its Romanism that the Roman structure is now to be examined and criticized; but this examination and criticism is not directed to the desacralization of sacred personnel nor to depriving the sacred personnel of its peculiar competence and authority in matters strictly religious.

## 2. *Apostolic Succession*

In Roman Catholic belief, the hierarchical structure of the church is the bearer of the sacred power which Jesus Christ committed to that group of his disciples who are called apostles. All Christian churches trace their origin to Jesus Christ through the apostles, and the Roman belief differs from other Christian beliefs less in affirming a legitimate succession from the apostles than in the nature of the hierarchical power which it claims to derive from them. The nature of this power as it is understood in Catholicism will be the object of our attention in many of the following sections. No Christian church denies that Jesus Christ intended to found and did found a permanent religious community; but what is the structure of this community? How much of the structure do Christians believe was directly intended by Jesus Christ? As we have observed, Christian churches believe in a ministry; but, except for the Roman Catholic,

Anglican, and Orthodox churches, they do not consider their ministers as successors of the apostles.

In the New Testament, an apostle is one who is personally commissioned by Jesus Christ to proclaim the gospel throughout the world.[1] The New Testament apostles include not only that group of disciples called the Twelve, who were the most intimate associates of Jesus, but also others who had the same commission. The best known of these is Paul, who clearly vindicated his claims to the title of apostle; it is not certain how many others made the same claim, but there were more than twelve apostles. In the strict sense, the apostles left no successors; that is, they left their own commission to no other apostles. The apostolic generation was unique in the Church. In Roman Catholic belief, however, the authority called apostolic was transmitted to others.

This apostolic authority, as we shall see in more detail, included the authority to preach the gospel, to administer the sacraments, and to rule the Church. Just as no one but Jesus could confer this authority on the apostles, so no one but the apostles could transmit the authority to successors. Thus in Romanism no one can bear authority in the Church unless he can trace his designation through legitimate succession from apostolic appointment. This is not a matter of historical proof, for historical evidence does not exist for the entire chain of succession of church authority. In practice, as we shall see in more detail, it has meant communion with the body of the church; that is, authority has been apostolic if it has been recognized as apostolic. But what is "the church"? In Romanism, the church has been identified by communion with the Roman Pontiff, who became the ultimate test of apostolic authority.

Apostolic authority is twofold: it includes the power of the priesthood and the power to rule. The strictly sacred power of the priesthood, which has as its major function the administration of the sacraments, is called the *power of orders*; that is, it is conferred by ordination. The power to rule is called the *power of jurisdiction*. We shall study each of these powers more closely. The power of orders is conferred by the imposition of hands, and the chain of imposition goes back to apostolic times. In Roman Catholic belief, a break in this succession deprives the church or a part of the church of sacred power. Because of the necessity of sacred power, the Roman Church holds that nothing breaks the succession except a lack of intention to confer sacred power or a distortion of the rite of ordination to such a degree that the rite no longer symbolizes the conferring of sacred power.

The Roman Church confers the power of jurisdiction by appointment. The modes of appointment have varied throughout the history of Catholicism, and the breaks which the Roman Church sees in legitimacy are not of the same character as the breaks in the chain of orders. Thus the Roman Church recognizes the orders of the dissident orthodox churches, but still refuses to recognize the orders of the Anglican Communion. In neither of these churches does the Roman Church recognize legitimate authority to rule. Disputes over legitimate authority appear very early in the history of the church; recognition was denied by the refusal of communion, the origin of the more recent "excommunication." These disputes sometimes involved the legitimacy of orders, but the two questions are entirely distinct; one who lacks orders is, of course, not a legitimate subject of jurisdiction. In the early centuries of the church, appointment to the episcopacy was usually granted by election within the diocese and recognition by the bishops of a region. In more recent times, all episcopal appointments in the Western church were made by the Roman Pontiff. Thus recognition of jurisdiction came to mean appointment by the Roman Pontiff, and this is the only way in which the Roman Church recognizes apostolic succession of jurisdiction. It is considered not only impossible for any one to refuse communion with the Roman See, but also impossible to refuse communion with a bishop appointed by the Roman See.

Apostolic succession is conceived as collegiate and not as individual. This means that a group succeeds a group and not a person another person. Succession is maintained by filling vacancies in the *college* and by expanding the college to meet the needs of the growing Church. The offices of proclaiming the gospel, administering the sacraments, and ruling the church are carried out by the college of bishops, but not in the sense that the entire college administers each diocese. As we shall see, the idea of episcopal power is not without complexity. Each bishop is supreme in his diocese, having no superior other than the Roman Pontiff, and this relationship must be explained later in more detail. A bishop has the power of supreme rule of a diocese only by acceptance into the college of bishops. Where he exercises his power is indifferent, even if a bishop is always appointed to a particular *see*. He can be transferred to another see. He does not, like the apostles, have the power to preach the gospel in the whole world. It is Roman Catholic belief that with the death of the apostolic group the apostolic power was there-after locally defined. It is impossible to trace this development in detail, but there is no doubt that Ignatius († A.D. 107) was Bishop of Antioch, and in his letters he speaks of the scope of his power in much the same terms in which a modern bishop would speak of his jurisdiction.

Apostolic succession of jurisdiction has reference only to the Roman Pontiff and to the bishops. Although for Roman Catholicism the priesthood and the diaconate are truly sacramental in nature, they are not essential to the ordinary jurisdiction of the church. In one way, the Roman understanding of the church is that it was founded as a hierarchical college; it is this which was instituted by Jesus. This understanding, without further qualification, does not give the complete picture of Roman belief, and it has been an historic point of contention between Roman Catholics and other Christian bodies. It could lead to the idea that the bishops are the church; and this is not what Roman Catholics believe. Nevertheless, the controversies in which episcopal authority has been defended have not encouraged a clear understanding of the church as a whole and of the place of other members in the church. One theological current which has been set in motion by the Second Vatican Council is directed to this problem. We shall discuss it at greater length subsequently.

## 3. The Papacy

The exposition of the details of the structure of the Roman Catholic Church begin with the Papacy, because it is the most obvious and distinctive feature of Roman Catholicism, to many the very symbol of Romanism. But in fact the relations of papacy and episcopacy are quite complex, and it should be noticed that there is really no parallel to these relations in any other structure of government, secular or religious. The Pope is called a *primate*, which is not simply the same thing as supreme officer. With this reservation, the office can be discussed as it exists in modern times, with some reference to the development of the office in history.

In Roman Catholic belief, the Pope is the successor of Peter as the head of the apostolic college, treated both in the preceding and in the following sections. This belief rests on two bases: the primacy of Peter as described in the New Testament, and the tradition of the Roman primacy within the church. Both of these bases have been denied by the dissident Eastern churches and by the Protestant churches and neither can be established without a complex process of argument. At one term of the Roman Catholic position stands the New Testament, and at the other the declaration of the Roman primacy of the First Vatican Council in 1870.

One needs little acquaintance with the New Testament and the practice of contemporary Catholicism to recognize that there are notable differences between the position of Peter in the apostolic group and the position of the Roman Pontiff in the Roman Church. The Roman thesis supposes a legitimate development of the primacy which must be validated by a study of the history of the papacy. When we speak of the structure of the church, we are not dealing with a written constitution such as the Constitution of the United States, nor even with unwritten constitutional traditions, such as those of the United Kingdom. Tradition here means what the church has accepted. Both Orthodox Christians and Protestants would say at once that "the church," of which they consider themselves a part, has not accepted the Roman traditions. The Roman response would be that the traditions were so long established by universal acceptance that neither the Orthodox nor Protestants were justified in rejecting them. No more is possible here than to set forth the two assertions.

It seems impossible to deny that Peter had a unique position in the apostolic group and that this position has to be described as leadership. A recent Protestant study of the question by Oscar Cullmann led to the conclusion that Peter was indeed the leader of the apostolic group, but that no one succeeded to his leadership.[1] Cullmann thus compares Peter to the other apostles: just as the apostles were not succeeded by other apostles, so Peter was not succeeded by another leader of the apostles. Roman Catholics affirm that just as the college of apostles was succeeded by the college of bishops, so the head of the college of apostles is succeeded by the head of the college of bishops. Obviously the argument cannot proceed on mere analogy.

In Roman Catholic theology, the primacy of Peter is based on several New Testament passages that demand a brief discussion. In Matthew 16:13–18, Peter is called the rock (the name Peter means "rock") upon which Jesus builds his church, the bearer of the keys of the kingdom of heaven, empowered to bind and to loose. The passage is not found in the corresponding context in Mark and Luke, and many critics exclude it from the authentic sayings of Jesus. This is not decisive; if the passage expresses the understanding which the apostolic church had of the mind and intention of

Jesus, and if it is in harmony with other passages, it is a witness of the position which Peter was thought to have in the apostolic group. In fact, it goes beyond other passages, but not so far beyond that it must be thought eccentric.

The word *church* occurs only twice in all four Gospels, both times in Matthew (here and 18:18); there is good reason for wondering whether Jesus ever designated the group of his followers as an "assembly" (Hebrew *qahal*, Greek *ekklesia*). This word, transferred from Jewish usage to Christianity, was employed very early and appears in the letters of Paul, the oldest writings of the New Testament. The bearer of the keys was the majordomo or master of the palace in ancient monarchies (*see* Isaiah 22:21–22); this certainly designates by metaphor some kind of authority within the household. "The kingdom of heaven" of which Peter holds the keys is elsewhere in Matthew the eschatological reign of God inaugurated by Jesus; it is thus roughly synonymous with "church," since the reign begins with the group of the disciples of Jesus. The power of binding and loosing has no biblical parallel, and indeed no contemporary echo except in Jewish rabbinical literature.[2] To *bind* was to give an interpretation of the Law which imposed an obligation, and to *loose* was to give an interpretation which freed from an obligation. Thus Peter is compared to a scribe, a comparison which is not used elsewhere in the New Testament, but which seems to suppose a development of the church to a point where its teaching included rules of conduct. The same power of binding and loosing is conferred upon the "church" in Matthew 18:18.

In Luke 22:31–32, Peter is bidden to confirm his brethren in faith. It is not at all obvious that this saying appears in its original context, which likewise has no parallel in Mark and Matthew. Nothing like it is addressed to any other of the Twelve.

In John 21:15–19, Peter is given the commission to act as shepherd of the flock of Jesus. The metaphor of shepherd signifies rule in the languages of the ancient Near East and the classical world; shepherd was a conventional title of kings. But in this context, particularly in John, the title must be understood in relation to the title of shepherd which Jesus gave himself (John 10:1–18); Jesus is the good shepherd who lays down his life for his sheep. The conferring of the title on Peter is followed by a prediction of the violent death of Peter.

Finally, there are the narratives of Acts 1–12 in which Peter exercises a kind of leadership in the Palestinian community. This is evident without discussion; it is also evident that when the author begins his account of the apostolate of Paul, Peter no longer appears except in Acts 15. It is also evident that Paul recognizes no "leader." On the other hand, Paul recognizes no one else as leader. No claims like those which can be made for Peter can be made for any other figure of the apostolic church.

It has been said that the New Testament gives Peter a unique position of leadership, and a reading of the pertinent texts leaves one with the impression that this leadership is not at all clearly defined. For this reason the term *leadership* is better than the term *authority* to describe Peter's position. Yet this leadership was not the entirely unstructured leadership which rests on certain natural qualities asserted by a person and accepted by the group whose leadership he takes, either by seizing it or by general acclamation. The texts of the New Testament reduce Peter's leadership to a commission of Jesus himself, exactly as the New Testament reduces the apostolic office to a commission of Jesus himself. The historian and the theologian must take account of this attribution.

The language used to describe Peter's leadership is metaphorical, not legal, and of necessity somewhat imprecise. It cannot be ignored that both Matthew and Luke speak of Peter's leadership in connection with his faith. The words of Jesus to Peter follow Peter's confession that Jesus is Messiah; the confession is found also in Mark and Luke. The words are a response to Peter's faith, and without any other considerations the reader would conclude that it is Peter's faith, a faith not exhibited in this passage by the other disciples, which makes Peter a rock on which the "assembly" can be built and a trustworthy holder of the keys and of the power of binding and loosing. When Peter is commissioned to confirm in faith (Luke), he is commissioned because Jesus has effectively prayed that Peter's faith should not fail. In John, on the other hand, it is love rather than faith which is demanded in Peter as shepherd. This is not a discordant note, for faith and love are the basic qualities of discipleship. Peter must excel in these, because the group in some way depends upon him. He receives a great responsibility, but the terms of the responsibility are not specified in formally juridical terms. This should not obscure the magnitude of the responsibility.

How does leadership in love appear in action? The allusions to Peter's leadership in Acts are quite disappointing, if one wishes to convert his leadership into juridical terms.[3] At moments of uncertainty he suggests action. He speaks on behalf of the entire group.

Occasionally, as in the baptism of Cornelius, he makes decisions of a novel and important character, but his leadership must be described as informal and unstructured. It cannot be described as government, even in the loosest sense of the term. It is significant that his leadership is always exercised in and with the college of the apostles. Important decisions are always the decisions of the college, and in the baptism of Cornelius Peter's action is discussed and ratified by the Twelve.

Let us turn our attention to the other end of the development, the definitions of papal authority promulgated by the First Vatican Council in 1870. The Council explicitly defined the primacy of the Pope as a primacy of jurisdiction, not merely of honor.[4] The word *jurisdiction* was deliberately chosen to designate the authority to govern; informal and unstructured leadership is excluded. The Pope does not hold this power from the consent of the Church, but he possesses it as the successor of Peter, who received this authority as a permanent element of the church to be transmitted to his successors. This power is supreme and subject to the review of no one in the church; in particular it is not subject to the review of a general council. The historical echoes in this last statement will be discussed later.

How does Roman Catholicism bridge the gap between the New Testament and the First Vatican Council? Pontifical authority as defined in 1870 has a precision and an extension which are not found in the New Testament. Basically the Roman claim is that the pontifical office is a legitimate development of the powers granted to Peter. It is not a claim that one can find in the New Testament, a statement of the same powers in other words. It is not a claim that Peter thought of his own office in terms substantially identical with the definitions of 1870. As the church itself developed, so did the understanding of the primacy. The question is not whether development was necessary and inevitable; surely it was. The question is whether the modern definition remains within the terms of the New Testament in such a way that it has not turned into a completely different office. This is not the same as Cullmann's question whether there was any succession at all. Both questions can be answered only from the belief of the church as the development occurred.

The Roman claim to succession is based on the succession of the Pope as Bishop of Rome; it is not a claim to succession to the apostolic office and to headship of the apostolic college. Hence it is vital that Peter was "bishop" of Rome. The word must be placed in inverted commas because, as we shall see, everything indicates that the office of bishops as it appeared later did not yet exist during the life of Peter. Furthermore, it is difficult to see how an apostle could become a local bishop. The needs are satisfied if Peter was the chief officer of the Roman church, and this is an historical question.

It must be said that the question has no entirely convincing answer from strictly historical evidence. The New Testament does not place Peter in Rome. But the traditions which do place him there are quite early, less than two hundred years after his death.[5] Perhaps the most powerful support of the Roman tradition is the fact that no other place claimed Peter. It is not without interest that traditions concerning other members of the Twelve placed them in remote regions, in some instances outside the Mediterranean world. These traditions are of very doubtful historical value, but they show that no Mediterranean community had anything to justify a claim to the life or death of members of the Twelve; Peter is an exception. The tradition that Peter was "bishop" of Antioch is without historical value; but Antioch never claimed to be "the see of Peter." In any other historical problem of the same sort the evidence for the residence and death of a man in Rome would be ample, and it is no longer seriously contested.

This does not imply that the church of the city of Rome in the first two centuries consciously elected a successor of Peter; they elected a Bishop of Rome. It is precisely in these two to three hundred years that the problems of development are most complex. It is impossible within the scope of this work to review the history of the papacy even for this brief period, and the reader must consult standard works on church history for a full treatment.[6] We find instances of the Bishop of Rome acting in other jurisdictions both in teaching and in church discipline, but this is not of itself a demonstration of a consciously held primacy. The early centuries offer a satisfactory number of examples of bishops who refused communion with other bishops because they did not accept either their teaching or their discipline. Up to the time of Constantine, one has to say that one simply cannot measure the extent to which the Bishop of Rome exercised any real government outside of Rome.

The location of this influence may reveal something about both its quality and its development. The great bishoprics were found in the great cities. The three greatest bishoprics were in the three largest cities of the Roman Empire: Rome, Alexandria, and Antioch.

A type of jurisdiction exercised by Alexandria over other Egyptian sees is found at a date when no similar jurisdiction is yet attested for the Bishop of Rome in Italy; I say attested, for there is no reason to think that the Egyptian structure was unique.[7] Nevertheless, one must notice that Egypt, both under the Ptolemies and under the Caesars, had the most tightly centralized bureaucratic administration in the entire Mediterranean world.[8] It is altogether probable that the church in Egypt imitated the civil government in Egypt. Other important sees were also located in large political and commercial centers. Constantinople, the former Byzantium, became a great see only after the imperial residence was transferred there. Carthage was the administrative center of the province of Africa. Milan in northern Italy and Lyons in Gaul grew as bishoprics as these cities expanded as centers of civil administration. There is nothing remarkable about this. The church goes where the people are, and these cities presumably had the largest churches. They also made obvious efforts to obtain as bishops men of personal gifts and power. It would be remarkable if the city of Rome had nothing to do with the development of the power of the Bishop of Rome.

We mentioned Constantine as a turning point, with good reason. When Constantine himself became a Christian, the Bishop of Rome was Constantine's bishop. When the emperor dealt with the church, he dealt with it through that officer nearest to him. It was Constantine's desire that a council be held to settle the Arian disputes, and the Council of Nicaea (A.D. 325) was held under the presidency of the legates of the Bishop of Rome. They were appointed to the presidency by the emperor. It is, however, too simple to say that this appointment was all they had to support their authority. Not only was no question raised about the propriety of their nomination, but the precedent of Roman preeminence thus set was followed in later councils, despite the fact that bishops from other cities were able to obtain the favor of the emperor. No other bishop, not even the Bishop of Constantinople, attempted to say that the Roman See had no right to preside; and the dissident Eastern churches admit no ecumenical council since the last in which East and West met together. There seems to be here an acceptance of the primacy of the Roman See (without attempting to define the word exactly) which rests on more than the imperial good pleasure, but which cannot be traced with all clarity in the literary records.

It may seem that a connection between the growth of the Roman primacy and the historic reality of Rome as a city is not a legitimate *theological* development; and yet one should not consider theology too abstractly in detachment from the world in which the church exists. On the assumption that the church should have a primate, Rome was by far the best place for the primate to reside at the time when the need can first be seen clearly. The church is in the real world of men, and the shape of her growth is determined by factors in this world, not solely by her own inner dynamism. With the expansion of Christianity in the first three centuries, the question of unity became more urgent, so urgent that it needed a structural expression. There had to be a vehicle for the consensus of Christianity which was expressed by *communion*. For with the expansion of Christianity came the appearance of heresy; who was to say with finality that a man or a church was or was not Christian? Leadership occurred in those places where the needs of the church demanded it. In the Roman belief that the leadership of Peter was transmitted to his successors in Rome, in the centrality of Rome in the world, and in particular the association of the Bishop of Rome with the emperor lay the necessary conditions for the powers of that see to reach their full exercise.

There is no question that a primacy of Rome, even if not entirely understood in the fullness defined by the First Vatican Council, was accepted in Western Christianity after the fourth century; Western Christianity here means Italy and Africa and all that lay west and north of these regions. This primacy did not depend on the imperial residence, for Rome was no longer the imperial residence. It was due both to the assertion of a primacy by the Bishop of Rome and to the acceptance of the assertion by other Western bishops. In the West, there was no see which either contested the primacy of Rome or which asserted its own primacy. One does find the practice, by this time traditional, of the provincial or regional council of bishops of settling problems larger than the affairs of one diocese and also of expressing resentment when Rome appeared to interfere unduly in such provincial affairs.

There is still another factor which is of importance at least after the time of Gregory the Great († A.D. 604). Much of the expansion of the church in the West was originated and directed by the Bishop of Rome. The missions of Patrick to Ireland, of Austin to Britain, of Boniface to Germany, and of Cyril and Methodius to the Slavic lands were all papal missions. Such missions bypassed the nearest sees and were directly subordinated to the Roman See. It should be noticed that such subordination could hardly have been envisaged

if the Roman See had no peculiar position. Other missionary enterprises initiated from other sees manifest no such direct dependence
on the sees of their origin. Irish Christianity manifested a remarkably close connection with Rome from the time when historical
records begin to appear. Western monachism, which we shall treat
later, was also closely subordinated to Rome, so closely that it sometimes troubled bishops. One can see the threads which will ultimately tie the entire church to Rome and make it "Roman."

What one may call the mythology of Rome ought also to be considered, although it is difficult to discuss an idea of such vagueness
with any precision. When the barbarians destroyed the Roman
Empire, they destroyed something which they also venerated. Rome
had meant civilization for several hundred years, so much so that
earlier civilizations were hardly remembered. After the political
reality of the empire had disappeared, the cultural reality survived
as an ideal. There was no real survivor of ancient Rome except the
Bishop of Rome, the spiritual head of what had been the Christian
Roman Empire. When Charlemagne restored the Holy Roman Empire, it was natural that he should be crowned in Rome by the
Bishop of Rome. A thousand years later another conqueror would
feel the need for the support of the same church officer through the
same ritual action; but Napoleon could compel the Pope to crown
him in Paris, for he planned that Paris should be in his empire what
Rome had been in the Roman Empire.

The development of the primacy occurred in the Western church,
the church which finally became the Latin and Roman church. The
Eastern churches severed communion with Rome in A.D. 1054, but
the separation can be said to date effectively from the schism of
Photius in the ninth century. The reader must be referred to
standard works of church history for the complete story of the
Eastern schism,[9] as well as for the Protestant revolt of the sixteenth
century, the second massive rejection of Rome and its primacy.[10]
The formal cause alleged in both instances was that Rome had
fallen into heresy. Many other causes were operative which were
in fact more important. One can see a growing rift between Greek
and Roman Catholicism long before Photius. The rift was widened
when Constantinople became the imperial city; there was no emperor in Rome after 476. Constantinople obviously thought that
the primacy of Rome, which had been connected with Rome as
the imperial city, should not extend over the new capital. Furthermore, during most of the period from Justinian to Charlemagne the

Roman Church was frequently caught in the toils of the Caesaro-papism of the Byzantine emperors, and the Bishops of Rome were happy to accept the liberation of Charlemagne. That this exchanged one political domination for another did not become at once apparent.

There were other events which deeply affected the history of the Eastern churches: the shearing off of large portions of Eastern Catholicism by the heresies, which effectively wrecked the unity of the Eastern churches; the control of the Eastern churches by the emperors and the imperial use of the church as a political tool; the Muslim conquests of the seventh and eighth centuries, which took from Catholicism nearly all of western Asia and northern Africa (the latter was a part of the Western church). There was a cultural alienation as well as a theological alienation. Constantinople thought of the West as barbarized, while it alone carried the torch of Greek culture. The idea of Christian unity did not exist in a form which would have permitted peoples so alienated from each other to remain in one church. The strength of the Roman Church was precisely that it had in Rome a visible symbol and focus of unity which could exercise a real jurisdiction over churches which had become churches of the barbarians.

It should be added that in the tenth century, between Photius and Michael Caerularius, the Roman See experienced one of the several moral collapses of its history, and perhaps the longest and worst.[11] For the first but not the last time, the papacy, as a political instrument, became the object of contention between Roman aristocratic families. The corruption of the papal court under unworthy men approaches the incredible. The papacy was in no position to affirm a spiritual leadership of a dissident group; the adventurers and bandits who were elected to the papacy had no interest in affirming spiritual leadership of any kind. Survival itself was the miracle of the papacy in this period.

The second great rebellion, the secession of the Protestant churches, must also be considered as a political and cultural event, as well as a theological event. The power of the medieval papacy could not pass into modern times, and the Reformation was contemporaneous with the birth of modern times. Christendom was fragmented politically by the rise of the nation-states at the same time that it was fragmented ecclesiastically. One must note also that the papacy was morally weak when it met this crisis; or should it be said inversely that the moral weakness of the papacy created a

the abolition of the papal states, which were once the most powerful factor in the politics of the peninsula, have removed the danger as well.

The powers of the Pope are defined in canon law in words taken from the First Vatican Council as "the supreme and full power of jurisdiction over the universal church both in matters of faith and morals and in matters of discipline and government." This power is qualified as "genuinely episcopal, ordinary, and immediate over each and every church as well as over each and every pastor and believer, independent of any human authority" (Canon 218, Nos. 1–2). *Jurisdiction* means the power to make laws; it is not leadership by merely moral influence or persuasion. It is the power to compel obedience, not by police and courts as civil governments do, but by binding the conscience of the believer. Disobedience in modern times is punished by excommunication, which is expulsion from the Roman Church. Up to modern times, when the Roman Church was a political as well as a religious body, means of coercion like those used by civil society were employed. The Roman Church no longer claims the power to use such means, and without any explicit repudiation of its past has made it clear that in using physical punishment and the death penalty the Church exceeded the powers that it believes it has received from Jesus Christ. Excommunication is formally imposed by law for certain offenses; in flagrant violations of the Roman Catholic ethos which are not explicitly touched by the law, the Pope (or the bishop in his diocese) can deny communion by a particular law or by a process dealing with a particular case.

The phrase "genuinely episcopal" defines papal power in terms of something better known which, however, we must treat later; the Pope is in the whole church what the bishop is in his diocese. He is the bishop of the whole church. Thus his power is immediate; it touches each member of the church without passing through any intermediate officer. It is ordinary, which means that the power over the whole church is inherent in the office itself; it does not come from the appointment or delegation of the church or of any body within the church. The Vatican Council added expressly that the primacy of the Pope is a primacy of jurisdiction and not merely a primacy of honor. This was directed principally at the dissident Eastern churches, which at one time were willing to accept a merely ceremonial precedence of the Bishop of Rome. In fact history does not attest a period in which Rome was accorded a purely ceremonial primacy, and the question is not active at present.

The powers of the Pope are defined in very broad terms. His authority in matters of faith and morals will be treated under the heading of teaching. He also has ordinary and immediate power in matters of discipline and government, and this touches each church, each pastor (bishops), and each believer. There is no area of the Roman Church and no person who is not subject to a direct command of the Pope. The relations of pontifical authority to episcopal authority are not defined as clearly as they might be; this problem will be discussed in the chapter on the episcopacy. For the moment, we will examine matters of discipline and government. These will become clearer by studying the operations of the Roman Curia, the agency of pontifical government.

The Curia corresponds to the cabinet in a political government. In canon law, a certain number of permanent offices with definite functions are established. At the present writing the reform of the Curia has not removed any of these offices nor altered their functions. The establishment of these offices is entirely within the competence of the Pope, since the Curia theoretically is his personal assistant; it does the work which he assigns it, and it has no authority except that which the Pope gives its acts by accepting them as his own. In practice, different types of pontifical approval are employed; the Pope rarely signs any document personally, and he does not read most of them. A personal approbation of the Pope, when it is mentioned in the document, is taken to add to the significance of the document. Documents signed by the Pope himself, although they are prepared within the Curia, are in canon law personal utterances of the Pope. Types of these documents have grown up through the centuries of pontifical administration. The types are distinguished both by the kind of material which is handled and by the degree of finality which is traditionally attached to them. They are also distinguished by their scope; some are addressed to the entire Roman Church, others to particular regions or dioceses. The Pope may add temporary or extraordinary offices to the Curia, as he has done since the Second Vatican Council. These new offices include a commission on liturgy and a commission on ecumenical affairs.

Since the Curia is the personal staff of the Pope, the appointment to curial offices is also entirely within his competence. In fact, much as in civil governments, he personally appoints only the heads of curial offices. There has grown up a kind of Vatican "civil service." Any Roman Catholic priest may legitimately desire a post in the Curia, and certain Roman theological schools are recognized as the proper schools to attend to prepare for this career. Most of the curial offices are occupied by Italians. This is now a tradition of centuries, but dissatisfaction with it has always been expressed, sometimes rather loudly. One of the recommendations of the Second Vatican Council was internationalization of the Curia. This recommendation was directed principally at the higher administrative posts. There has been some resistance to this suggestion, which is hardly surprising; bureaucracies never vote themselves out of existence. The major motive for the recommendation was simply that the Curia tends to impose Italian cultural and religious patterns in its administration of the business of the Church.

The offices of the Roman Curia are enumerated and defined in Canons 242–264. It is of some interest that the possibility of over-lapping jurisdiction is envisaged in Canon 245; should the problem arise, the Pope appoints a committee of cardinals to settle the question. The most important of these offices are called *congregations*. The **Congregation of the Holy Office**, established in its present form by Paul III in 1542, is one of the three congregations of which the Pope himself is the *prefect*. This designation signifies the importance which is attached to the business of these congregations. In practice it means that the ordinary administration of these congregations is headed by a vice-prefect whose powers are no less in his own office than the powers of the prefects of other congregations. To the Holy Office is committed "the doctrine of faith and morals." It is thus the agency through which the Pope exercises his office as teacher and will be discussed in the chapter on the teaching office of the Church. It may conduct inquiries into teaching, whether in lectures or in publications, institute processes, and condemn works or authors for departing from established doctrine of faith and morals.

The Congregation of the Holy Office, formerly known as the Inquisition, has long enjoyed a bad name among Protestants; and this no doubt had something to do with the change of its name to the Congregation of the Faith, a change made by Paul VI in a *motu proprio* of December 6, 1965. The Pope made it clear that by changing the name he intended a change of character as well as of reputation. The Congregation was to do its work by promoting sound doctrine rather than by the detection and condemnation of error. In some degree the evil name of the Roman Inquisition throughout history was undeserved; most of the terror associated with the name belonged to regional and diocesan inquisitorial offices. The Spanish Inquisition was not the Roman Inquisition, in spite of the direct and immediate power of the Pope over the churches, pastors, and believers of Spain. In those days, this direct and immediate power was rather effectively filtered through the Spanish monarchy. Visitors to the Castel Sant' Angelo (now the property of the Italian government) are shown the dungeons and torture instruments of the medieval and Renaissance papacy; the visitor should not conclude that these facilities were made use of solely by the Roman Inquisition.

All these things lie in the past. The Congregation of the Holy Office, however, has been the object of vigorous criticism in recent years, criticism which reached its peak when a cardinal on the floor of the Second Vatican Council accused the Holy Office of injustice in its processes.[12] The criticisms have been directed mostly at the secrecy of the operations of the Congregation. The Holy Office is actually no more secretive than other congregations, but the nature of its business is ill adapted to secret processes. The Roman offices, which preserve many of the traditions and the practices of Roman law, admit secret denunciations. Instances are alleged of scholars who were forbidden to write or to teach without any specific charges of unsound doctrine. Still more hostility to the Congregation arose when it was commonly repeated in theological circles that men had not only been forbidden to teach or to write, but also forbidden to reveal the fact that they were forbidden. There grew a feeling that questions of sound doctrine deserved a hearing and a discussion and that no one should be condemned for unsound doctrine without an opportunity to defend his position. These conditions were included in the reorganization of the Congregation of the Faith under Paul VI. Whether these new conditions will touch the domination of the Congregation by what is called *Roman theology*, meaning the theology taught at certain Roman institutions, remains to be seen at this writing. Roman theology is not sympathetic to differences in theological opinion.

The celebrated Index of Prohibited Books falls within the competence of the Congregation of the Faith. The first such Index was issued by the Congregation of the Inquisition under Paul IV in 1557. In 1571, Pius V erected the Sacred Congregation of the Index, since merged with the Congregation of the Holy Office. The Index was abolished under Paul VI; the existing Index imposes no obligation on Roman Catholics, and no items are to be added to the Index in the future. The Congregation retains the power to issue a judgment concerning a book, but not to prohibit its reading. The prohibition of reading books is a comparatively modern practice in the Roman Church, although the condemnation of writings is much older. Related to this latter type of supervision is the censorship of manuscripts before publication, of which no instance is known before the mandate of Archbishop Berthold of Metz in 1486.[13] At this writing, no reform in this practice has been instituted, although demands for reform are heard more and more frequently. The opportunities for abuse are so many and so obvious that some action is thought to be in order.

The **Congregation of the Consistory**, established in its present form by Sixtus V in 1588, also has the Pope as its prefect. This highly important Congregation supervises dioceses; it erects and divides provinces (*see* The Episcopacy) and dioceses and appoints bishops. It supervises the administration of bishops and receives the reports and visits which each bishop must make regularly. By its power of appointment, it has its finger on the government of the Roman Church. Since bishops are less inclined to talk about their supervision than are scholars and teachers, little is known of the details of the "vigilance" which the Congregation exercises. Only the Congregation and the bishops are able to tell how detailed this vigilance is; the Congregation receives reports about bishops as well as from bishops. The power of episcopal appointment is a vital part of the centralization of the Roman Church and will be discussed in the chapter on the episcopacy.

The **Congregation of the Sacraments**, established by Pius X (1903–1914), has the power to legislate concerning the administration of the seven sacraments. These will be treated in Part II, Worship. Among the sacraments is marriage, but matrimonial cases come under the jurisdiction of the Roman courts. A few cases are reserved to the Congregation of the Sacraments. Outside of this area the Congregation does not deal with questions as sensitive as those which fall under the Congregation of the Faith and the Congregation of the Consistory, and sacramental ritual, which is of more interest to the public, comes under the jurisdiction of the Congregation of Rites.

The **Congregation of the Council**, established by Pius IV in 1564, administers those affairs of clergy and laity which do not fall to some other congregation. The most important of these are ecclesiastical property and revenues, one of the least known areas of Roman administration. This Congregation also supervises regional and national councils or episcopal conferences.

The **Congregation of Religious**, established by Sixtus V in 1588, supervises religious communities (*see* Religious Communities). The Holy See approves any community which wishes to serve in the church at large. This includes approval of the rule of the community, any changes which the community wishes to make in its rule, and abandonments of existing works. The Congregation may also recommend or impose changes in the constitutions and customs of a community and ask or require that the community undertake works designated by the Holy See. The Congregation is also empowered to suppress communities. This Congregation authorizes individual religious to abandon the religious life. Since religious, most of whom are not attached to dioceses, form a large mobile force, the Holy See exercises a rather close supervision over their operations.

The **Congregation of the Propagation of the Faith**, established by Gregory XV in 1622, does for missionary territory what the Congregation of the Consistory does for established dioceses. A mission territory by definition is a territory in which a hierarchy is not established; this will become clearer when we treat of the episcopacy and dioceses. A territory may remain missionary even after a hierarchy is established if, in the words of the law, it is still to some degree in an inchoate state. How loosely this term may be used can be seen from the fact that the United States was subject to the Congregation of Propaganda until 1918. The Congregation supplies clergy and funds to mission countries. It is expressly excluded from any cases which belong by their nature to the Congregation of the Faith, to the matrimonial tribunals, or to the Congregation of Rites. The history of the Congregation is, of course, a story of the passage of territories from its jurisdiction and the addition of new territories as the Roman Church moved with European civilization into new continents.

The **Congregation of Rites**, established by Sixtus V in 1588, supervises the rites and ceremonies of worship in the Latin Church; the significance of this restriction will appear in Part II. The Latin church has a long tradition of rigid uniformity in its rites and ceremonies, and it is the office of this Congregation to see that there is no deviation from established practice. Since the Second Vatican Council, this Congregation has come to the attention of the public, since all liturgical changes must be approved by the Congregation. The Congregation also handles processes of beatification and canonization of saints (*see* The Saints).

The **Congregation of Ceremonies**, established by Sixtus V in

1587, distinct from the Congregation of Rites, is not concerned with worship in the universal church, but directs ceremonies in the papal chapels and ceremonies conducted by cardinals outside the papal chapels. In addition, it is the office of ecclesiastical protocol, which determines questions of precedence in ecclesiastical functions at the papal court.

The **Congregation of Extraordinary Ecclesiastical Affairs**, established as a secretariate by Pius VIII in 1814 and made autonomous by Benedict XV in 1917, handles the erection and division of dioceses and the appointment of bishops in countries in which relations of the government with the Holy See are determined by a *concordat*. Italy is one such country. *Concordats* (Latin *concordat*, it is agreed), are treaties made by the Holy See with civil governments. Historically concordats have been used, not always successfully, to end disputes between the Holy See and national governments. It can be said generally that the Holy See, in order to secure those liberties which it deems essential for the work of the church, concedes to the civil government rather ample powers over church personnel and property. Several European governments, for instance, have by long custom the right to nominate candidates for the episcopacy or to veto candidates proposed. Such agreements are echoes of a time when the Roman Church was much more deeply and powerfully involved in European politics than it is now.

The **Congregation of Seminaries and Universities**, established by Benedict XV in 1915, supervises the discipline, course of studies, and administration of seminaries, with the exception of seminaries which exclusively prepare priests for work on foreign missions; these latter are governed by the Congregation of the Propagation of the Faith. "Universities" in the title of the Congregation does not include most Roman Catholic universities, but only those universities which are called pontifical. The Congregation approves the erection of pontifical universities, grants them the power to confer pontifical degrees, and exercises a supervision as close as its supervision of seminaries. Pontifical universities are almost all graduate faculties of ecclesiastical studies, and their teachers and students are almost entirely priests and seminarians. In the area of clerical education, a tradition of uniformity has arisen since the Council of Trent, and the Congregation directs this area closely. The Second Vatican Council recommended wider latitude for local and regional variations both in discipline and in courses of study.[14]

The Pope is prefect of the **Congregation of the Oriental Church**, established by Pius IX in 1862, and this indicates the delicacy of this area. Some Eastern churches have never seceded from the See of Rome, and a few others have been reunited. These churches are very jealous of their liturgical and disciplinary traditions, and Rome has made an effort to keep them from being Romanized or being absorbed into the Latin church. As they have existed, they are examples of what dissident churches could expect in reunion with Rome. Hence this Congregation handles all questions concerning the Eastern churches, even when persons adhering to the Latin rite are involved. The sole exception is questions which belong by their nature to the Congregation of the Faith.

Not infrequently some prelates of the Eastern Catholic churches have expressed dissatisfaction with the work of this Congregation. Eastern Catholics are a small minority in the Roman Church, and the prelates have asserted that the Romanizing process goes on in spite of professed intentions to the contrary. The very existence of the Eastern Catholic churches, it is believed, depends on the preservation of diversity in liturgy and church law and custom. The Eastern Catholics are not subject to the Roman canon law. They are therefore extremely sensitive to the Roman type of rigid uniformity which runs through much of the Latin church. Relations of these churches with the Roman See are not always harmonious, and this was brought out on the floor of the Second Vatican Council.[15]

In addition to the congregations there are pontifical courts and pontifical offices. The pontifical courts include the Sacred Penitentiary, the Rota, and the Signatura Apostolica. The **Sacred Penitentiary** is the ultimate court for cases which arise from sacramental confession, and naturally its processes are entirely secret. The **Rota** is best known for its matrimonial verdicts; it is the ultimate court of appeal in matrimonial cases. Matrimony, however, is only one area in which canon law provides judicial processes. While the Roman Church does not in modern times urge the ancient privilege of clerical immunity, it does insist that purely ecclesiastical cases involving ecclesiastical persons, property, or jurisdiction should be tried in ecclesiastical courts. The Roman courts are normally courts of appeal; each diocese has its judicial structure. The **Signatura Apostolica** is a kind of pontifical supreme court.

Church law, known as canon law, exists now in a code which was promulgated in 1918. Up to this date canon law was a vast and unclassified collection of decrees which had grown up through most of the two thousand years of church history. We frequently have occasion to refer to the code in describing the contemporary Roman Church, but it is no more a complete guide to the reality of the church than the laws of a country are a guide to that country. Thus when the *juridical* aspect of Romanism is mentioned, it should be understood that canon law is only one aspect of it. Catholics may ask whether certain areas of the life and work of the church should be juridically administered, but no one has yet questioned the need of satisfactory general rules for much of the business of the Church. A satisfactory general rule in a society is a law. The question is not whether the church must have law, but whether church law always exhibits those characteristics which should distinguish it from civil law. Church law follows the basic principles of Roman law, and thus it is in harmony with the civil law of most of continental Europe. These principles differ, however, from the principles of British and American common law, and people from common law countries are sometimes surprised at canon law procedures that do not startle Europeans. The major complaint which Catholics have against canon law and canonical courts is directed at the delays in canonical processes; this same complaint is urged against civil courts in most countries, and neither type of court seems to be notably slower than the other. In both types of court, the legal adage that justice delayed is justice denied is valid.

It may seem odd that the Roman Church has been uncertain concerning the characteristics which should distinguish church law. With the Second Vatican Council came a number of requests for changes in church law, not only in details but in the very conception of the law. The Holy See has put church lawyers to work on a new codification of canon law to replace the code of 1918. It is too early to speculate on the character of the new code. It is known that many canon lawyers ask not only whether the number of general laws within the Roman Church should be sharply reduced, but even whether the whole idea of church law should not be substantially revised. Church law, it is thought, should reflect the relations of persons whose primary bond of union with each other is love and confidence rather than a juridical structure. Law in the usual sense, many think, should have a very small place in the life and work of the Church.

Besides the congregations and the courts, there are *offices*. The **Apostolic Chancery** prepares certain pontifical documents. The **Apostolic Datary** handles appointments to certain benefices, ecclesiastical posts which are supported by founded revenues. The **Apostolic Camera** administers the temporal affairs of the Roman Church during the interregnum which follows the death of a Pope. The purely "spiritual" business of the Congregations is arrested until a new Pope is elected. In the curial reform instituted by Paul VI, the prefects of the congregations lose all powers at the death of the Pope.[16]

The **Secretariate of State** is an office, not a congregation; but in some recent pontificates the Cardinal Secretary of State has been the most powerful man in the papal administration. The Holy See maintains formal diplomatic relations with most countries of the world and informal relations with the others. Pius XII caused something of a curial sensation when, after the appointment of Cardinal Montini to the see of Milan, he did not appoint a successor but acted as his own Secretary of State. The Holy See is no longer an active power factor in the political world; but it has been accustomed to make statements which touch critical political issues, and these are framed according to the information acquired by the Secretariate of State. Most of the operations of this office are highly confidential, as such operations are in other departments of state or foreign affairs. While the Pope is sovereign of the State of Vatican City, the Secretariate is little concerned with the usual type of diplomatic business. Heads of states deal with the Pope not as sovereign of Vatican City but as the head of the Roman Catholic Church with a half billion members. In a number of countries, what Roman Catholics as a group think of their government—on the rare occasions when they think as a group—determines whether that government stands or falls. In modern times the Roman Church regards it as highly important for its work that the relations of the church with the civil government be at least polite.

A final office should be mentioned even if only as a curiosity for those who are unaware of its existence. This is the **Secretariate for Latin**. Latin is still the official language of pontifical documents, and this office is entrusted with their composition. Since pontifical documents are identified by the first two or three words of the text (such as *Rerum Novarum* or *Casti Connubii*), this office also sees that by chance the same words are not used twice to begin a document. Latin as the official language is now under some criticism. It is true that it is an international language with the advantage that it belongs to no living nation, but facility in Latin is no longer as common, even in the Roman Church, as it once was, and it is urged with some reason that Latin is not an adequate vehicle for the discussion of modern problems, particularly when they involve technology.

The mission of the diplomatic officers of the papacy go far beyond foreign affairs, which are the concern of the Secretariate of State. The general designation of representatives of the Holy See abroad is *legates*. The rare title of legate *a latere* is given to the representative who, in the words of canon law, represents the Pope as an *alter ego*. The powers of this legate are not determined by canon law; they are defined by the personal wishes of the Pope and may be as broad as he wishes to make them. Countries which have an ambassador at the papal court receive a legate called a *nuncio*. Such a legate is an ambassador and belongs to the diplomatic corps of the capital where he represents the Holy See. Hence the canon law gives him the duty of promoting good relations between the Roman Church and the civil government. Countries which do not maintain diplomatic relations with the Holy See and have no ambassador at the papal court receive an *Apostolic Delegate*. The United States is the most notable example of this situation. The law does not give the Apostolic Delegate any power to deal with the civil government, but both the nuncio and the delegate are empowered to exercise "vigilance" over the condition of the Roman Church in the country of their mission and to convey information concerning it to the Holy See. The legates are the normal channel through which communications from the Holy See pass to the church of the country. The law provides for the delegation of other powers to the legates, but these are not specified. The legates are forbidden to interfere with any bishop in the exercise of his jurisdiction.

This system of representation has been submitted to some questioning in recent years. There are doubts that the papal representative need be Italian, since he represents the Pope as head of the universal Roman Church. Many feel that the difference of nationality can make it difficult for the legates to understand the church of the country of their mission. Information, it is believed, may become misinformation when it is presented with misunderstanding. While no charges of interference by a legate have ever become public, it is a known fact that a papal representative may have as much influence as he chooses to wield. He is in a position both to promise and to threaten. Unlike the bishops of the country, he need take no public responsibility for any action of the church. This area of the papal administration is very likely to come under a searching examination.

It will be noticed that no office of the treasury is included in the above enumeration. This part of the pontifical administrative structure is well concealed. It is known that the Roman See disposes of enormous sums both in liquid cash and in investments and real property, but no public statement is made of the administration. This has permitted rumors to arise concerning large corporations, not only in Italy but also in other countries, in which the Roman See is said to have a large or a controlling interest. In recent times desires have been expressed for some public accounting of the pontifical funds. Until this is done, the rumors may be expected to continue. Neither the source of the funds nor their disbursements are known. It is known that the Holy See has a large number of charities, but nothing is known of the details. It will be noticed that the administration of pontifical funds follows quite logically from the type of monarchical power which the Roman Catholic Church believes the Pope has. The canon law (1518) defines the Pope as the supreme administrator and steward of all the temporal goods of the Roman Church; this is the same kind of ordinary and immediate power which he has over faith and morals and over government and discipline. In temporal affairs, as in spiritual affairs, the Pope is responsible to no human authority.

The problem of ecclesiastical pomp is not unrelated to the above topic, since pomp is obviously rather expensive to maintain. A full pontifical ceremony is an impressive pageant; the color scheme—the white of the Pope, the scarlet of the cardinals, the purple of the bishops, the black of the lower clergy—glitters like few displays in the world. The papal court still maintains the splendor which was once attached to the royal courts of France, England, Spain, Austria, and the lesser monarchies. Now all these monarchies are gone except England, and a papal ceremony impresses the viewer as much by its archaism as by its splendor. It is one of the few survivals of the pageantry of the Renaissance. On a lesser scale, pageantry is seen in cathedrals and even in parish churches. The legends of the saints are full of anecdotes of holy bishops and priests who sold off the apparatus of pomp in order to give the proceeds to the poor. The modern Roman Church is able to unite organized charity with the retention of pomp. There has always been in the Roman Church some hostile reaction to ecclesiastical pomp, and perhaps as much now as at any previous period. It is perhaps less concern with the expenses of pomp and more concern with the evident contrast between the pomp of the modern church and its humble origins. In the days of Christendom, a pope or bishop could match himself with kings, and it seemed easier to do this if the prelate could make as formidable an appearance as the king. Roman Catholics have often felt, as many still do, that the church in which they believe should stand before its members and the world in the full panoply of power. Pomp is the exterior symbol of power and of the respect paid to power.

In modern terms, we would call this a question of the image. The question is whether the Roman Church should project the image of power, or whether the power it has should employ the same symbolism as that which is associated with secular power. Since the Second Vatican Council, a few steps have been taken away from pomp toward simplicity. It is very likely that the steps will become more numerous and firmer. The Roman Church is encumbered with a heavy incrustation of tradition and custom; uncomfortable as the incrustation may be, it is not a simple matter to abandon procedures which have been in use so long that no one has alternatives to them. Nor should one discount the normal human desire for solemn trappings of things which men believe are important; the Roman Church is not the only society in which pomp is cherished.

This skeleton outline of papal administration is not intended to be a picture of the actual working of papal administration. Such a picture would be too large for this book, and it has been attempted, with indifferent success, by a number of journalists. What the skeleton does show is the business with which the papacy is concerned. One sees at once that the concerns of *institutional* religion have become quite numerous and complex. A description of the institutional religion does not give the complete picture of Roman Catholicism, but it is very difficult to describe anything else. One can see also the degree to which the Roman administration is centralized and what is meant when some decentralization is requested by Roman Catholics. Certainly this centralization is one of the most important features of Romanism. No major decision is made in the institutional church which is not Roman or Roman approved, and a countless number of minor decisions are also Roman.

Romanism, however, is as much an ethos as it is centralization. Any administrative body of such antiquity and continuity is bound to develop a style. This style is beyond description in a neat formula, and yet any Catholic who is more than superficially concerned with church administration is heard to say at times, "That is the Roman way." Both he and his listeners understand what is meant, although they would be hard put to define it. One feature of Romanism is heard in the adage, "Rome moves slowly." The delays in Roman processes are sometimes maddening, but nothing else is expected from the Roman Curia. No bureaucracy is rapid, and it is doubtful that the Roman red tape is more complicated than any other system. Another feature of the Roman way is—or at least used to be—a desire for smoothness. Rome does not admit that anything is wrong, and it is difficult to disturb its serenity or to drive it to actions which seem to show feeling. It has a self-assurance, if one can attribute this to an organization rather than to a person; but self-assurance is manifested in its personnel.

Rome does not believe that its actions are open to inspection or that it owes any one an explanation of what it does. Hence its operations are generally secret; one does not expect Rome to foreshadow its decisions or to announce reasons for them. This sometimes gives the Roman processes a slightly comic cloak-and-dagger atmosphere, and one is conscious of the archaic flavor of a Renaissance court. Yet Rome is probably the greatest city for journalistic leaks of all the world capitals. It is the Roman way that things should be revealed in the press from "a Vatican source" or "a Vatican spokesman" who refuses to be identified. In the United States, "the White House spokesman" of the press is usually the President when he refuses to be quoted, but one should not erroneously transfer this way of speaking to Rome, Journalists have said that the Vatican staff contains enough members who are willing to sell their information or misinformation. When secrecy is normal, the irresponsible journalistic leak also becomes normal.

All of this fails to present the entire reality of the papacy, and it is really impossible to present it. One must attend a papal audience in order to appreciate the symbolic value of the Pope. He is venerated with that veneration which is due to the Vicar of Christ—to use a common but theologically slightly inaccurate title of the Pope. One must not think that this veneration is due to the press relations of the Vatican; Vatican press relations are as a rule abominably bad. The Pope is the one visible symbol of the Roman Catholic Church, and he is viewed as such both by believers and by nonbelievers. He represents to believers a continuous chain that originated with Jesus Christ, and to nonbelievers he represents a half billion people to whom he can speak with authority.

A papal audience is really a religious act in the proper sense of the word; Catholics here profess their faith in their church and, through their church, in its founder. They experience in the Pope the present activity of the Risen Christ. One must also understand that many of the same Catholics who seek a papal audience as the high point of their European tour are quite ready to say, if the Pope should speak on social questions, that he should limit himself to religion and not meddle in politics. They do not think that this takes away from their Romanism. They venerate the Pope as a religious symbol rather than as a religious leader. Romanism has developed to the point where in the minds of many Roman Catholics the one basis of their religious profession is submission to the Pope. Many of them do not think of their submission in the terms in which the papacy has spoken of it nor even in the terms which are set forth in this brief sketch. One who views Roman Catholicism from the outside must be aware of this ambivalence in the minds of many Roman Catholics and recognize that it ultimately defies rational analysis. The real "power" of the papacy, in the sense of power to bring men to do something which they would not otherwise do, is unknown, even to the Pope himself.

## 4. The College of Cardinals

The title of *cardinal* is purely a title of honor and of itself carries no ordinary ecclesiastical jurisdiction in the sense explained above. The word cardinal is derived from the Latin *cardo*, hinge, and it signifies the importance of this body in the Roman Church. The College of Cardinals is the most powerful group within the church, and this does not contravene anything said above about the Roman Curia. Every congregation, court, and office of the Curia has a cardinal as its presiding officer. The College has two classes. One class includes cardinals who are residential bishops and who remain in the sees which they govern. Cardinals who are not residential bishops are expected to live in Rome and to take posts in the papal administration. Journalists have noticed a kind of interlocking directorate in the Roman Curia; cardinals who are members of important congregations are likely to be members of other congregations as well. Prefects of congregations are certain to have seats in other congregations. An examination of the listings in the *Annuario*

*Pontificio* shows that the administrative decisions lie with a small group of cardinals. All of this may be less meaningful than the fact that the College of Cardinals elects the Pope—always from its own membership, as we have noticed.

Cardinals are appointed personally by the Pope with the advice of the Congregation of the Consistory, and announcements are made in Consistory. The cardinalate is normally the term of long and distinguished service in the papal administration. The cardinalate outside of Rome has come to be associated with certain large archdioceses throughout the world; it is only rarely in modern times that the title is conferred for any other kind of service to the church. Certain religious orders traditionally have representatives in the College. The number of cardinals has grown constantly over the years, in spite of efforts to limit it. The College is described in canon law as a senate of the church, and the expansion of the church has made it necessary to expand the college in order that all major Roman Catholic areas may be represented. There is still some discontent with the fact that over half the College is Italian. This concentration is due not only to the Italian cardinals of the Curia, but also to the fact that Italy has a disproportionately large number of sees whose bishops are traditionally cardinals.

The Roman Catholic Church, we have noticed, does not really elect a Pope; it elects a Bishop of Rome. The possibility of transferring the papal residence elsewhere causes a few theological problems; but the Bishop of Rome could remain Bishop of Rome even if the see were transferred, or even if it became purely titular, like the nonexistent sees of titular archbishops and bishops. The cardinals elect the Pope because they are the clergy of the diocese of Rome, and the Bishop of Rome is the only bishop who is elected by his clergy. The cardinals are, of course, a kind of shadow diocese of Rome. There is a real diocese of Rome, which is administered by a cardinal vicar; naturally he cannot have the title of Bishop of Rome, although he does for the diocese what any bishop does. The cardinals are divided into cardinal bishops, cardinal priests, and cardinal deacons. The cardinal bishops have the titles of Rome's six ancient suburban suffragan sees. Each of the cardinal priests has a church in Rome of which he is the nominal pastor. These are the ancient parish churches of Rome, and not infrequently the new cardinal priest has found that his first task was to renovate his titular church. The cardinal deacons are likewise attached to some ancient Roman parish church. These titles have nothing to do with the holy orders which the cardinal has. Most cardinals are bishops, and at the beginning of the Second Vatican Council John XXIII thought it wise to ordain fourteen curial cardinals to the episcopal order so that they might enjoy precedence. These titles empower the cardinals to elect the Bishop of Rome. As we remarked above, it is quite in harmony with the ancient traditions of election that they should elect one of their own—that is, a member of the Roman clergy.

It is evident that the College of Cardinals has a twofold function: it is an electoral body and a senate of the Roman Church. These two functions are not of necessity related, and the union of the two functions in a single body has led to certain questions in recent times. The most important of these questions can be summed up as a question of selection and a question of representation. Viewed from both aspects the selection of cardinals by the personal choice of the Pope is thought to be of doubtful value. If the College were the personal advisers of the Pope and no more, one could hardly deny to the Pope the right granted to all heads of state and of business corporations to select his own staff. But the College can be viewed as the personal staff of the Pope only if one thinks exclusively of the cardinals who reside in Curia. The anomaly of allowing the personal staff to select the head of the organization from among its own members is as evident in Roman Catholicism as it would be elsewhere. Effectively it means that the Pope, while he does not actually determine his successor, determines the small group of persons from whom his successor will be chosen. Personal choice by the Pope creates a kind of personal loyalty among the chosen which can be an obstacle even to good performance as advisers. In other organizations, there are features which prevent staff loyalty, necessary as it is, from working to the harm of the organization. To the outside world, the College of Cardinals presents the image of a small self-perpetuating power group. This is not the whole reality, but the Roman Church cannot afford to be unconcerned about the image. The College is not a representative electoral body. Nothing in the constitutional traditions of the Roman Church seems to say that it should be. Yet when the Bishop of Rome or of any other diocese was elected by his clergy, the election was representative to a degree which has been lost.

The history of the College shows that it has been open to political influences of the most pernicious kind. The historic veto exercised by the great Catholic European monarchies through their cardinals in the conclave has disappeared with those monarchies, and it is now expressly prohibited by church law. The student who will take the trouble to read the rather dreary and detailed laws governing papal elections can easily visualize the scandals which these laws are designed to remove. The cardinals are locked up both to keep them in and to keep any one else out; there is no opportunity to communicate with any one. The subsistence diet which is given them is intended not only to get them to do their work quickly, but also to make long drawn out negotiations within the conclave extremely uncomfortable. The ballots are so designed as to give each voter absolute secrecy; no reprisals are possible, theoretically, against a man who votes the "wrong" way. For the same reason the most severe penalties are laid on any one who reveals any of the processes of the conclave. Nothing is revealed except the number of ballots taken, announced by the traditional smoke signals. These penalties have never been enough to keep some of the information from becoming public. Each cardinal takes an oath to vote according to his best judgment and to admit no other influence; one can only say, assuming that the cardinals are faithful to the oath, that in some elections cardinals have made a judgment which cannot be explained. Electioneering is absolutely prohibited, and an election which is secured by any antecedent promises is null and void. So also is an election in which it is proved that the electors were intimidated. This provision has not been invoked since 1378, when most of the College voided their own election of Urban VI on the grounds of undue pressure exerted upon them and elected Clement VII, thus initiating the Western schism.[1] None of the safeguards of the papal election is unrealistic; every one of them is the result of experience. Yet the fact remains that a body so small can be frightened or bought, not in its totality but enough to influence the election. Scandalous procedures have not succeeded in actually electing a Pope since the eleventh century, as far as historians can determine, but they have kept men from being elected, which is not a trivial matter.

When the College is spoken of as a senate of the Roman Church, the reader should remember that the term *senate* is not used in the same sense in which it is used of the ancient Roman Senate, which was the real governing body of the Roman Republic, nor of modern parliamentary bodies like the United States Senate, which is a law-making body. The College of Cardinals is actually a body of senior advisers. It overlaps, as we have seen, the Roman Curia, but not randomly; the cardinals head the offices of the Curia. The cardinals who live in their own dioceses are advisers of the Pope on matters which concern their own nations and regions. Here there is an over-lapping with the papal diplomatic staff of nuncios and delegates, and this has been painful at times. There is a manifest structural defect at this point which needs correction. Too much is left to the chance of the personal ability of individuals, and the Holy See has not successfully overcome the difficulty inherent in two concurrent functions.

In modern times, the term *senate* suggests a representative body, and the College is not regarded as a representative advisory body any more than it is a representative electoral body. For one thing, over half its membership is Italian, and Italy is not half the Roman Church. The reader must understand that, in the Roman conception of monarchical pontifical power, the Pope need not form a repre-sentative body of advisers; but it is precisely this Roman view which is now under question. The important thing is not that the consti-tution of the Roman Church does not require the Pope to form a representative body, but that the church needs such a body so badly that he can ill afford not to form one. As we shall see, the represen-tative body which has emerged after the Second Vatican Council is a different body from the College of Cardinals. At this writing it seems possible that another ambiguity of concurrent functions may emerge with it. Should this problem be solved, the question of representation in the advisory body will also be solved; but unless Rome moves with more speed than the usual Roman pace, it will not be possible for another generation to see how the new structure works.

The nonrepresentative quality of the electoral body will remain, but calls are being heard for a new electoral structure as well. We have noticed that the politico-legal theory behind the College is that it is the only body competent to elect a Bishop of Rome. As long as this is the prevailing theory, the College will continue to elect. There is no doctrinal reason, however, which would forbid a wider electoral base, since the pontifical power defined in canon law is ordinary and immediate in the entire church. In other words, the Pope is no more a bishop in Rome than he is elsewhere. He can therefore be elected by the whole church of which he is the pastor. He could be elected by the bishops of the whole church. This procedure, which would imply the convocation of an ecumenical council each time a Pope is elected, is somewhat terrifying, and many would judge it impractical. Candidly, it could not have been thought of before modern communications appeared. These make such an election possible, and it would not be inconsistent for the Roman Church to change its procedures with the development of technology. The same modern means of communication also make it possible for the Holy See to supervise distant countries more closely and to summon prelates to Rome more frequently; the technology has already affected the procedures. But even if a universal suffrage of the bishops should be judged impractical in contemporary times, an election by an episcopal electoral college is not at all impractical. Such a body would be as representative as the Roman Church could expect in the foreseeable future. Very probably such an electoral body would elect from its own membership, not restricting its choice to the College of Cardinals. This would give the church a broader basis of choice, as well as a broader electorate.

It has been noted that the College is the most powerful group within the Roman Church. Even after the functions of its members have been reviewed, it is difficult to analyze their power. The curial cardinals obviously have the power which comes from their posts in administration, but the power of cardinals who are residential bishops is more intangible. Normally the appointment signifies that the cardinal has personal friends and influence in high places in Rome. More often than not it signifies personal friendship with the Pope. When a cardinal deals with his fellow bishops, they are quite aware of these realities. The reception of the honor places him in the group of men whom the Pope consults, and among the things he is consulted about is the appointment and promotion of bishops. Theoretically a cardinal can always obtain a personal audience with the Pope.

The influence of the cardinals is not limited to ecclesiastical circles. Cardinals outside the Curia are most frequently bishops of sees in large, important cities. These sees are usually wealthier than the smaller sees. Furthermore, they are usually proud of the fact that their archbishop is a cardinal; it is a witness to the magnitude and importance of the cities. Having a cardinal is like having a large sports arena; it symbolizes that the city has become "big league." The joy with which Los Angeles, California, greeted its first cardinal was both amusing and pathetic. It had nothing to do with his religious significance; it was exactly the same response which the city gave when it received its first major league baseball team. It meant that Los Angeles was finally reckoned among the U.S. giants with New York, Chicago, Philadelphia, and Boston. That the cardinal is a civic symbol has other effects which are neither amusing nor pathetic. The late Cardinal O'Connell was known in the Massachusetts State House and the Boston City Hall as "Number One." This designation attested the crude political fact that the candidate of whom O'Connell disapproved could not have been appointed garbage collector. Since the late Cardinal Mundelein of Chicago, the State of Illinois has given the Archbishop of Chicago the license plate Illinois 1 for his automobile. Since the governor of Illinois must also have this number, there are two such plates in the state. In these and in some other large cities of the United States, the cardinal is the head of the local church in cities where the voters are one half or more Roman Catholic. Politicians know this and act accordingly. The cardinal does not need to engage in politics; he knows that no politician wants to offend him. The political power of a cardinal can be seen even in Poland, where Cardinal Wyczynski has successfully defied a government which is formally and openly totalitarian.

The description of the College as a senate has recently raised another question. Since cardinals are rarely chosen until they have had a long career, the College becomes a gerontocracy. Most of the cardinals are still bishops or heads of Roman congregations at ages long beyond the ages at which men are retired from business and government. No satisfactory reason can be given for the statistical fact that cardinals have a life expectancy much in excess of the average. A cardinal rarely dies at an age less than eighty years, and it does not seem possible for the Holy See to predict this. One need not elaborate on the reasons why this causes concern. Some feeble efforts for a retirement program have been made during and since the Second Vatican Council; the efforts have been feeble because most of the votes had to come from the men who would be retired. This has come to mean that the Roman Church rarely enjoys the best and most vigorous years of the human span of life in its most important and sensitive posts. It has more than a little to do with the conservative, even reactionary, character of both thinking and acting on the upper levels.

Several points advanced here may suggest that the College of Cardinals is an archaism which will disappear with the movement of history. To take the point just made, a college of elders did not create the same problems in times, only a few generations behind us, in which life expectancy was notably less. If the government of the Roman Church should be really decentralized, if the election of the Pope were committed to the bishops, and if the reduction of ecclesiastical pomp made the cardinal less a symbol of the Church Triumphant, there would appear to be little reason for the survival of the College. Cardinals could come to mean no more among bishops than monsignori mean among priests. The cardinalate could become what we said it is at the beginning of this topic, a purely honorific title. Perhaps most of the problems of the cardinalate arise from the fact that a purely honorific title is so much more than purely honorific. When this occurs in other organizations, it is regarded as a defect in structure.

## 5. *The Episcopacy*

We have seen, in treating apostolic succession, that the Roman Church considers the college of bishops as the successor body to the college of the apostles but does not consider the individual bishop as the successor of an apostle. A bishop is not an apostle in the strict sense of the term. It is the entire college of bishops which carries on the apostolic office; that is, the entire college succeeds to the mandate of Jesus Christ to preach the gospel throughout the world, to administer the sacraments, and to govern the church. The bishops, according to the common theological teaching of Roman Catholicism, hold their offices "by divine right" or "by divine institution" (Canon 329, No. 1). This means that the episcopal office exists through the constitution of the church; there cannot be a church without bishops. In such a church, apostolic authority would have ceased to exist.

As we have seen, bishops, as the church has historically known them, do not appear in the New Testament. We find in the New Testament officers of local churches called *episkopoi* (Greek *episkopos*, "overseer," from which the English word *bishop* is derived) and *presbyteroi* (Greek *presbyteros*, "elder," from which the English word *priest* is derived). These officers are not mentioned frequently, and everything indicates that they were members of a college or board. The New Testament churches do not appear with the supreme local authority vested in a single person, but no historian doubts that such an authoritative person existed by the end of the first century A.D. The letters of Ignatius of Antioch make it clear not only that he was the supreme officer of the church of Antioch, but also that he did not think that his position was in any way unusual.[1] The church acquired the episcopal structure in the formative years of its history, and it has not abandoned it since. Some Protestant churches have rejected the episcopal structure in favor of a congregational type of government, which they believe reflects more faithfully the churches of the New Testament. It may be said that these churches reached this structure not only on biblical grounds but were also moved by certain abuses of episcopal power which led them to treat the office as an illegitimate intrusion of the postapostolic period. The technical name which Roman theology gives to bishops is *monarchical bishops*; this means that the bishop alone possesses jurisdictional power in his diocese.

The jurisdiction of the Roman Catholic Church is organized territorially in such a way that there is no place on earth which is not subject to some episcopal authority; there are some interesting and complex rules that govern ecclesiastical actions on shipboard, which have been adapted to aircraft. A Roman Catholic always has a bishop. The normal territory is called a *diocese*; the name is borrowed from the reorganization of the Roman Empire under Diocletian, who divided the empire into regions to which the name of diocese was given.[2] Therefore each bishop has a place; and a residential bishop is given in church law the somewhat quaint designation of *Ordinarius loci*, "the ordinary of the place." The word *ordinary*, as we have noted, means that he has jurisdiction by virtue of his office. In existing practice, however, not all episcopal jurisdictions are dioceses, and not all bishops have territories. Missionary territories, which are subject to the Congregation of the Propagation of the Faith, are territorially divided, but their offices are called vicars apostolic or prefects apostolic; the difference signifies nothing but the size and population of the territories. These territories are by definition inchoative, and a vicariate or a prefecture is organized with the intention that it should grow to diocesan stature. One important difference between the mission territory and the diocese is that the Pope can limit the powers of the vicar or prefect, who is in all other respects the effective bishop of his territory. The Pope cannot limit the jurisdiction of a diocesan bishop because his jurisdiction is, as we have seen, ordinary. When a bishop is appointed to a diocese, he receives the fullness of episcopal power; the Roman Church does not conceive that he could receive anything else, since the office is defined by divine institution.

Not all bishops have territories, by which we mean territories which they govern by ordinary jurisdiction. Every one is acquainted with the *titular* bishop who has no territorial jurisdiction. Yet since a bishop without a place is inconceivable, the titular bishop or arch-bishop is given the title of an ancient see which no longer exists. These sees are said to lie *in partibus infidelium*, in the territory of unbelievers; the designation echoes the Moslem conquest of the Near East in which these sees were destroyed. Thus the titular bishop does have ordinary jurisdiction, but in a territory where it cannot be exercised. Vicars and prefects apostolic are titular bishops, and therefore they do not have ordinary jurisdiction in the territories which they actually govern. They are what diocesan bishops are not, delegates of the Pope in their territories. Titular bishoprics are given to other men whose office in the church is of sufficient scope to demand a dignity greater than that of the simple priest but which is not ordinary jurisdiction over a place. They are frequently held by higher officers of the Curia who are not cardinals, normally by apostolic nuncios and delegates, and by coadjutor and auxiliary hishops, whom we will discuss in connection with diocesan bishops. This multiplication of the title makes it advisable for the sake of clarity to employ the language of canon law here; therefore when-ever the residential bishop of a diocese, the only officer who is a bishop in the full sense of word, is meant, the term *ordinary* will be used. When titular or auxiliary bishop is meant, the term *titular* or *auxiliary* will be added as the context demands.

The institution of the titular bishopric is now hundreds of years old, but it may possibly have become archaic. As we hope to show, the office of bishop is of such a character in the Roman Church that the title cannot be merely a title of honor. Should honor and prece-dence be so important that distinctions must be externally sym-bolized, then some other title should be devised. The multiplication of the title cheapens the office; and the Roman Catholic Church can-not afford to allow this office to be cheapened. What the bishop does can be done by no other officer, and the title should be reserved for those who have this unique power and responsibility. It is not without some advertence to the cheapening of the title that in church law it is necessary to use the word *ordinary* of those who have genuine episcopal jurisdiction.

A bishop is a bishop; this remark, almost couched in the language of Gertrude Stein, means that no ordinary is any more or less of a bishop in his diocese than any other ordinary. He is not subject to any other ordinary. The territorial division of jurisdiction has cer-tain regional groupings; a group of contiguous dioceses are formed into a *province*. Within a province one episcopal see, usually the oldest or the largest, is called the *metropolitan see*; the others are called *suffragan sees*. The ordinary of the metropolitan see is by definition an archbishop. He has no jurisdiction over the suffragans nor any jurisdiction within the suffragan dioceses. He is empowered to conduct official inspections, called visitations; and he is expected to inform the Holy See of abuses which he observes. He also presides over councils of the ordinaries of the province.

Some sees of great antiquity have the title of *patriarch*; in the Latin Church this is purely a recognition of antiquity and conveys no jurisdiction. In ecclesiastical processions, ordinaries, other things being equal, rank according to the antiquity of their sees. The title *primate* signifies the oldest diocese in a country. No one pretends to understand why Ireland has a Primate of Ireland in Dublin and a Primate of All Ireland in Armagh. In England, the ancient primatial see of Canterbury is held by the Anglican Church; the Roman Catholic primate is the Archbishop of Westminster, a see established in 1850. For obvious prudential reasons, the Roman Catholic Church, when it restored the English hierarchy in 1850, took the title of no see held by an Anglican bishop. It should be added that the indirect influence of archbishops, apart from jurisdiction, can be considerable. Their appointment attests the fact that they are known in Rome, their sees are usually found in larger and wealthier cities, and they are generally older and more experienced than their suffragans. They are always consulted, or ought to be, about appointments to their suffragan sees or about the promotion of their suffragan bishops.

The diocese has developed from the original idea of the bishop as the pastor of his church; we shall see better what this means when we consider the parochial structure of Roman Catholicism. Originally the "church" of Antioch, for instance, meant the one community of Christians in the city of Antioch. In this church, the supreme officer was the bishop, assisted by his deacons. With the growth of local churches to the point where the assembly could no longer meet in a single "church" (the name of the assembly was transferred to the building), it became necessary to divide the city into regions. Yet this did not bring with it the multiplication of bishops, which of itself shows something of the ancient idea of the unity of the local church. The priesthood, as we shall see, was a communication of the power of the bishop, or rather of the power of the bishop to do some things. It still remains true that the Roman Church conceives of episcopal power only in its fullness. The priests were agents of the bishop, who remained the pastor of the church of the community.

In the ancient church, however, there seems to have been nothing to correspond to the vast modern dioceses. One can say generally, it seems, that if a place had a name and a church it had a bishop. One can see the effects of this in the multiplication of dioceses in the older countries of Europe. The city of Perugia in Italy, with a population of 41,500, has an episcopal see. It is only a few years since the city of Oakland, California, with a population of 367,000, was established as an episcopal see, and the diocese of Oakland includes among other places the city of Berkeley, with a population three times that of Perugia. The policy of the Roman Church in recent years has been to divide dioceses into smaller areas, although it has been able to do little with such clotted urban centers as New York and Chicago. Metropolitan London has two dioceses within its corporation limits, as does New York City; but the diocese of Brooklyn is older than the creation of metropolitan New York in 1898.

Generally speaking, one can say that there should be more dioceses rather than fewer. The idea of the ordinary as the pastor of his church loses much of its meaning when his "church" includes over a million people. It is true that the modern world manages enterprises of a vastness unknown to the ancient world, although one should not think of the Roman Empire as a small enterprise. The tradition of the diocese was that any one of the members of a church should have ready access to his ordinary. Indeed the very idea of episcopal power, as will be seen, supposes such easy communications in order that it may realize itself. Beyond a limit of magnitude which cannot be measured exactly, the bishop cannot be a pastor. This is certainly one of the more urgent problems of contemporary Roman Catholicism, and one could wish to see more ordinaries and fewer titular bishops.

The selection of ordinaries is one of the most secret processes in Roman Catholicism. The alleged reason for the secrecy is that no one will have his feelings hurt by knowing that he was considered for appointment but not accepted. Even this secret is not very well kept, but the processes are still withheld from the public. The appointment of ordinaries, as we have seen, is done by the Pope through the Congregation of the Consistory. The qualifications for the office as set down in Canon 331 are quite general and would suffice for almost any office of any responsibility in the church.

Plainly the appointing body looks for other qualifications which are not mentioned in the law. The qualification of legitimate birth (not satisfied by a subsequent marriage) may surprise some; it marks the end of an era in which royalty and nobility could provide for their bastard sons by giving them a bishopric. There is a long history of such things as lay investiture and interference by kings and noblemen and even by modern "democratic" governments in the appointment of bishops to explain the reservation of episcopal appointment to the Roman See. It was noticed earlier that the great Catholic monarchies of Europe had by custom and tradition certain rights of presentation and veto. It is slightly paradoxical that the anticlerical lay governments which succeeded the monarchies insisted that they should retain these ancient privileges.

In the early centuries of the church, the bishop was elected by the whole local church; this was gradually restricted to the clergy. The election was announced to the bishops of the region, who signified their acceptance by granting the new bishop *communion*. In some difficult cases, we read of bishops of powerful sees who supervised elections in other dioceses.[3] Any defender of the system of Roman appointment will urge that the Roman Church abandoned elections because of the politics they involved. They were open to ambitious clergy and to laymen who desired to have a bishop appointed whom they could control. In the centuries between the collapse of the Roman Empire and the rise of the monarchical nation-states of Europe, the bishop was often the sole power of any kind, secular or religious, in his region. These prince-bishops, some of whom led their own troops into battle, were often indistinguishable in their attire and manner of life from other noblemen. Their dioceses were their personal fortune, just as another lord owned his estates, and as feudal lords they owed allegiance to an overlord. The diocese could not in the Roman discipline be entailed, but it could be held by the same family. Who should occupy such sees was of great interest to others besides churchmen. The lay investiture controversy, of which Pope Gregory VII (1073–1085) was the hero, removed the worst of the abuses but did not entirely remove lay and political interference.[4] Nothing, it seems, has ever removed it entirely. An ordinary never ceases to be a leading figure in the country in which he has his see. As such, he is potentially an object of great interest to the government of the nation. That popular or clerical election produced some great prelates is undeniable; but the Roman apologist will say that these great prelates were obtained in a system open to abuses from which exclusively Roman appointment is safe.

The system of Roman appointment is the object of criticism in the contemporary church, however. It is evident that a Roman bureau cannot know the candidates for sees throughout the world, and, while the methods are secret, it is known that the Roman office acts on local recommendations. These recommendations come from the ordinaries of the country involved; special weight is attached to the recommendations of the papal representative, of the cardinals of the country, and of metropolitan ordinaries for their suffragan sees. One does not know what these recommendations contain, but a few things can be observed in the results. Most bishops come from a career of church administration, and one can deduce that administrative experience has a high priority in the qualifications. It is also evident that administrators are better known to bishops than are priests in other employments. One notices regarding appointments for the United States that the North American College in Rome is not called the mother of bishops without reason. Appointment rarely comes to a man who has not spent some time in Rome. Whether this is connected with Roman acquaintances or with some unspoken belief that residence in Rome is a qualification is uncertain, but the association is there. So rarely is a theologian of distinction appointed to a see that one is safe in concluding that learning has a low quotient of value in the qualifications.

The apologist for Roman appointment must face two criticisms: one, that Rome may have excluded one type of politics but not another; secondly, that the system does not produce great prelates. The reservation of appointment to Rome has not met the problem of the ambitious clergyman; and it should be said candidly that clerical ambition has long been and is one of the major problems of Roman Catholicism. Ambition simply moves in different channels. Granted enough of the general qualifications to begin with, the ambitious cleric does not have to solicit votes in a diocese. He needs only an administrative appointment and the cultivation of influential men both in his own country and in Rome. A pattern of behavior and a degree of competence are set for him with sufficient clarity. All he has to do is cooperate; and one may say that cooperation is the major qualification. Roman Catholic priests have applied to their own church the lines of Gilbert and Sullivan concerning the man who polished up the handle of the big front door, and it should not be thought that influential (which here means wealthy) laymen are entirely without influence in the recommendation of bishops.

The second criticism involves something of a profile of the Roman Catholic bishop, since it is only normal that ordinaries in their recommendations should tend to reproduce their own kind. A genuine profile of the episcopacy cannot be drawn, not even for a particular country; the system is not so rigorous that it produces total uniformity. The world was given an excellent and so far a unique opportunity to see over two thousand bishops in action at the Second Vatican Council. What became at once apparent was that most of them were not very active. A few leading figures emerged rather early, and these figures dominated the proceedings. The Council stunned the world by some of its actions; but what has happened in the Roman Church since the Council has made many observers wonder whether the bishops voted entirely in accord with their accustomed habits of thought and action. The leading figures of the Council were not typical of the episcopacy as a whole, but a profile should be such that it admits them, for the bishops accepted their leadership.

Let it be said that bishops as a group are men of above average intelligence. A seminarian who does not rank high in his class will not be recommended for graduate studies, and very few bishops have not had some graduate studies in theological learning. The late Cardinal O'Connell of Boston boasted that he led his class in the seminary; the close second to O'Connell had a long and distinguished career as a priest-scholar. This does not attest that bishops are learned or that they are broad-minded, but it is dangerous to deal with a bishop on the assumption that he is stupid. Let it be said also that bishops as a group are highly disciplined men, a trait they share with all men who survive in government and management. They do not show their feelings, and they have learned to conceal their thoughts. Like business men and politicians, they are or could be great poker players. Let it be said also that as a group they do not like to throw their weight around openly, although there are more exceptions to this rule than to the preceding two. They prefer to have their power operate without being obvious; it makes for smoothness and does much to prevent hard feelings. As a group, bishops are able to carry a great deal in their heads; any ordinary will show a surprising knowledge of his diocese in detail, which means that he does his homework. Bishops as a group are loners in the good sense of the word, if it has a good sense; they have a very small group of close friends, and they do not lean on people. They are independent because they are accustomed to have their way. They show the mark of men who rarely deal with anyone who has not come to ask them for something. They are the men who call others but are not called by them. In at least one of the United States (one of the ten largest), the ordinary of the capital city was accustomed to summon the governor to talk to him, and the governor came. Bishops are also men of sturdy health, who rarely miss appointments or working days because of illness. They run to above average rather than below average height. And—in spite of all that is said above—I know no professional group which is capable of exhibiting more personal charm.

The above attempt at a profile may seem to be flattering, and it is intended to be. One may ask what basis it leaves for the second criticism against the Roman system; for a managerial group which can be described in these terms would seem to be the fruit of excellent selection, a selection which the United States government and General Motors would do well to equal. This second criticism is that the system fails to produce great prelates; it fails because the one qualification which the Roman Curia seeks above all others in a candidate is that he be safe. And what does "safe" in this context mean? We must remember, as we noticed above, that a national hierarchy tends to reproduce its own kind. It is a well-known fact that the German, Dutch, and French hierarchies are not regarded in Rome as safe. The Italian and Spanish hierarchies are regarded as safe. In both classifications we speak generally, for there are exceptions. A man may appear safe when he is appointed, but turn unsafe in his discharge of the office. The late Cardinals Meyer of Chicago and Ritter of St. Louis were certainly regarded as safe when they were appointed; both became unsafe. The hierarchy of the United States is probably regarded as safe with an undesirable number of soft spots.

Safe in this context may be defined as the refusal to venture toward new points of view and the habitual determination to retain positions which are authenticated by long experience and general acceptance. Another word for this would seem to be conservatism, but "safety" is really more conservative than conservatism. Most people begin from fixed positions. The weakness of safety is that it does not admit that circumstances have changed and that what was once a good fixed position is no longer tenable. Safety shows itself in a lack of sympathy to novelty; *novelty* is an ugly word in theological and canonical language. Safety is suspicious of the discoveries of scholarship and positively hostile to new theories formed on these discoveries. It is not receptive to new social theories or new types of social action. It is not receptive to new liturgical practices. It is slow to entertain revision of the existing structures of management and operation. Paradoxically it is quick to adopt new gadgets; this writer was once struck by this paradox in a Catholic press which used the most advanced (and expensive) presses to print eighteenth-century theological thought. Now in popular thinking this type of safety has come to be identified, justly or unjustly, with the Roman See, and the critic says that the Roman See looks for bishops on whom it can depend to maintain the Roman theory and practice.

What validity does this criticism have? In the simplified form in which I have summarized it, it is certainly exaggerated. One can see the results of such attitudes, however, and one result is that bishops generally seem to think that it is their primary duty to protect the Establishment. A "radical" ordinary is one who permits closely controlled experimentation in his diocese. The safe man is slow to act—although some bishops have been jarred from a safe position by civil disturbances in their dioceses. The Holy See never appoints a "controversial" figure as bishop. The late John Courtney Murray had, it seems, all that could be desired in a bishop, and other controversial figures of similar stature could be mentioned. A system which cannot find room for such men in what the Roman Church regards as its most vital positions suffers from some weakness.

One cannot at the moment go beyond speculation in this area of criticism, and this is unfortunate, because the matter is of some importance. What can be said is that Roman appointment and the usual Roman background tie the bishops to Rome more closely than they ought to be tied or were tied in the early church. As we shall see when we discuss episcopal power, a bishop's relations with the Pope are quite complex and difficult to define, but the ordinary is not the agent of the Pope nor his delegate. The Roman Church believes in genuine episcopal power that is not given to the bishop by the Roman Pontiff. Pontifical power must not be conceived in a way which destroys episcopal power.

Not unrelated to this problem is the question of episcopal promotion. It is sixteen hundred years since it was said in an official church document that a bishop who moves to another church commits spiritual adultery.[5] No such stigma is attached to transfer now. It is normal that large sees should be given to men who have had experience in smaller sees. Thus the Roman system continues after the first appointment. I have already alluded to the unpleasant subject of clerical ambition. One need know no more about bishops than that they are human to know that most of them, if they believe that they have proved ability, respond positively to a greater challenge to that ability. It is difficult to imagine a bishop accepting gracefully his nonpromotion on the grounds that he is not a big enough man for a bigger see. Whether he will be promoted to a bigger see depends on how he stands at Rome. Possibly it should depend on something else. The man who hesitates to offend Rome, when it is not entirely clear what does óffend Rome, has rather effectively hampered his own freedom of action, the freedom which a bishop ought to have and must have.

For reasons such as this, the practice of election has been mentioned more frequently since the Second Vatican Council. The Roman Church has had experience both with elections and with centralized appointment; both have produced good results and both have had some remarkable failures. If one judges by the results, there may not be much to choose between one way and the other. Election is urged because it does meet certain problems inherent in centralized appointment, because the things which compelled its abandonment do not seem to be clear and present dangers now, and because election is more in harmony with the democratic government which modern Western man, at least in theory, still professes to be the best for him. If it is urged that elections in modern democratic countries sometimes furnish an excellent argument for retaining centralized appointment, the democratic citizen will respond that there is no real danger that ecclesiastical elections will exhibit all the unsavory features of secular politics. He will urge that a man who is approved by a large number has at least as good a chance of being a successful bishop as one who is appointed by a very select group who do not make public either their names or the motives of their choice. He will say that what is desired in a bishop can be recognized by both clergy and laity, and most certainly that what is desired in a particular diocese can be recognized better by the people of that diocese than by any one else in the world. He will say this in spite of the fact that in some American dioceses at this writing a racist would stand an excellent chance of being elected bishop; after all, Rome has already produced some bishops whose record of interracial relations is less than glorious. He will add, furthermore, that a bishop who is elected by his people will have two things in his favor: one, that he will feel a responsibility toward the electorate which an appointed bishop need not feel; another, that the electorate will feel something of a compulsion to support their own man as long as he makes it possible.

At this writing it does not seem that popular election of bishops can be discussed as a real possibility. Election of bishops by the clergy is more likely. The problem can be put in very simple language. Can the clergy of a diocese be trusted to recognize the qualities desired in a bishop? And if they cannot be trusted, is not the Roman Catholic Church so deeply in trouble that centralized appointment will not cure it? Election should not be proposed as if it were free of problems; it is a calculated risk. All its defenders can really say is that election could promote to the episcopacy excellent men who do not now reach it. This is a great deal to say in favor of election. One should not think of excluding the advice of bishops from the electoral process; it should have an important place, particularly in filling a metropolitan see. In the early church, a bishop was not legitimately elected until his brother bishops granted him communion; under Roman appointment they no longer have this voice in the acceptance of their colleagues. A candidate elected by the clergy whom he would govern and by the bishops of the province, and approved by the bishops of the region or the country, would seem to be as fully qualified as human diligence could judge, including the diligence of the Congregation of the Consistory.

Ordinaries are "ordinary and immediate pastors" of their dioceses (Canon 334, No. 1). These terms, as already explained, mean that the ordinary has his power in virtue of his office and that it is not received by delegation. They have the right and the duty to govern the diocese in spiritual and temporal matters, and they are possessed of legislative, judicial, and coactive power (Canon 335, No. 1). The distinction between the power to make laws, which are general and permanent, and the power to command, which is of itself particular and temporary, is important in church law. Without this power, called jurisdiction, the bishop could in theory govern only by issuing commands to individual persons and particular groups. The power to judge means the power to issue decisions which are in the proper sense of the term legal and not merely arbitrations. The power to compel is the power to bind the conscience of the subjects, sanctioned by the power to inflict ecclesiastical penalties. This is the same power which the Pope has over the whole Roman Church.

Episcopal power, like pontifical power, is defined in church law in purely juridical language; as we shall see, it goes beyond this conception. In theological language, episcopal power is understood as the threefold supremacy in teaching, in administering the sacraments, and in governing the diocese. We reserve the teaching office and the strictly sacerdotal office for discussion elsewhere, and limit ourselves here to the structures and practices of episcopal government.

The ordinary is called a monarchical bishop. He alone possesses all ecclesiastical power in his diocese. Pastors of parishes are said to have certain "ordinary" powers; but these are sacerdotal, not powers of government. No one does anything as a Catholic in the diocese which is not ultimately, if not immediately and directly, authorized by the ordinary. We have said that the Roman Church regards the episcopacy as its most vital and sensitive post. The ordinaries stand at the head of the action of the Roman Catholic Church on the local level, and they have no ecclesiastical superior other than the Pope. They are the backbone of the ecclesiastical structure, and what an ordinary does can be done by no one else. What the ordinary fails to do cannot be supplied by another agent. The whole church exists for the believers in the microcosm of the diocese; this is where they experience its reality. It is as strong as the local ordinary. One can understand the deep concern of the Roman See with the appointment of men to this responsibility. Criticism of the Roman appointment does not touch the Roman concern, but simply asks whether centralized appointment is the best way for Rome to meet the concern which it must have.

Obviously even a small diocese is too much for the personal administration of one man, and the ordinary has a staff, called a *curia* just as the staff of the Pope. At the top of the staff are auxiliary bishops, if the ordinary has them, and they are becoming more and more common. One must distinguish between those bishops called auxiliaries, whose work we describe below, and those bishops called coadjutors. A coadjutor is appointed with the right of succession to the see of whose bishop he becomes the "helper." Certain effects of such an appointment are obvious, others are provided for in church law. The appointment of a coadjutor generally means that the ordinary is no longer capable of administering his office; and since up to the moment of this writing ordinaries rarely resign, the Roman See delicately sends his successor. The coadjutor can also be appointed by the Pope apostolic administrator of the diocese;

this deprives the ordinary of his jurisdiction. Even without such an appointment, it is normal that the coadjutor becomes the effective ruler of the diocese, since it is he who will carry out the policy which is formed after his appointment. In any hypothesis, Canon 351, No. 3 provides that the ordinary may not delegate to any one else responsibilities which the coadjutor is able and willing to undertake.

The system has obvious defects, and one suggestion raised but not voted through in the Second Vatican Council was a compulsory retirement age for ordinaries. It should be understood that Rome never deposes an ordinary for anything less than heresy or formal schism, but it does have ways of persuading him to resign. In theological language, the bishop is in "a state of perfection," and it is not admitted that he is imperfect. The appointment of a coadjutor may signify no more than the manifest feebleness of the ordinary, whether from old age or chronic ill health. Church law provides procedures if the ordinary loses his mind. Ordinaries have often asked for coadjutors; the appointment makes it easier for the ordinary to transfer the management of the diocese while he is still able to dispose of it. The appointment may also cover profound incompetence or scandal, but the image of the hierarchy is protected. The Roman Church is not the only organization to use such devices to protect its image.

The appointment of auxiliary bishops comes from the fact that only the bishop, who alone has the fullness of the priesthood, can administer the sacraments of confirmation and holy orders. This sacerdotal responsibility can demand much time for travel and liturgical functions. The Archdiocese of Chicago, to take an extreme example, can present 40,000 candidates for confirmation and 200 candidates for orders in a single year. Dioceses with a smaller population compensate for these numbers by the distance which the ordinary must travel, which in some instances can be 500 miles from his see city. An auxiliary bishop is ordained to episcopal orders and can relieve the ordinary of some or nearly all of his liturgical obligations. Earlier the cheapening of the episcopacy by the multiplication of titles was spoken of, but no one questions that the sacerdotal functions of a bishop can be killing. The Roman Church now accepts it as theologically proved that a simple priest can be authorized to confer the sacrament of confirmation; and there really seems to be little reason to ordain a man a bishop for this purpose. Theologians are not ready to admit that any one with less than episcopal orders can confer the priesthood; but this is less of a burden on the ordinary.

Since auxiliary bishops are selected with the same care with which ordinaries are selected, and normally with a view to their promotion to a residential see, they are usually men of such a character that the ordinary commits to them the most important posts in his administration. It must be said in favor of the promotional system that an apprenticeship in a diocesan curial post of the top rank familiarizes a man completely with diocesan administration. This should not be thought unimportant. The Roman Catholic Church is the oldest continuous administrative body in the world, and it has developed its own form and style—encrusted with what many think are completely unnecessary complexities of procedure. In Roman Catholic administration, great store is set on the formalities, and learning all of them is not something one does overnight. Rome, according to clerical gossip, has been known to return documents without action because the proper formulae of introduction or conclusion were not followed. Very probably in such cases there were other factors at work also. In this instance, we have a clumsy way to do things, but it is important that those who do them should know the way.

The diocesan office, usually known as the *chancery*, bears a resemblance to the Roman Curia; it deals with the same type of business. The vicar general, as the name suggests, can act for the ordinary in any business which the ordinary has not reserved to himself or which by church law he must reserve to himself. What is referred to the vicar general need not be referred to the ordinary; church law gives him "ordinary" power to act for the ordinary, but with reservations. He is appointed personally by the ordinary and can be personally removed. His power is to be employed "according to the mind and will" of the ordinary (Canon 369, No. 2), which in more conventional language means that the ordinary sets policy. Within these guidelines, the ordinary is expected to give and does give the vicar general ample powers of action and decision. In very large dioceses, the ordinary may have several vicars, each with "ordinary" jurisdiction over certain areas of diocesan business.

The chancellor, according to church law, is in charge of documents and records. In actual practice, the chancellor has responsibilities far beyond this. A great deal of routine business falls to the chancellor's office; because of the multiplication of documents (to the point of red tape) a great number of questions and problems

have predetermined answers and solutions, and no more is required to handle them than the ability to find and process the proper
document. It has been true since the Old Kingdom of Egypt, which
had professional scribes, that those whose office is to compose the
documents usually have a great deal to say about their contents.
One who wishes to see "the bishop" will usually see the vicar general or the chancellor first. It is a part of their duties, to some
extent, to protect the ordinary from unwarranted intrusions, and
to recognize and handle the business which they are capable of
handling. Practice differs here from diocese to diocese; some officials
are certainly overzealous in protecting their principals. Some ordinaries are nearly inaccessible, either through the zeal of their
subordinates or through their own wishes. Others are more accessible
than many men of lesser responsibilities, and this has nothing to
do with the size of the diocese, much to do with the size of the
ordinary. In one of the largest archdioceses of the world, a personal
conversation with one of the late ordinaries could be obtained,
usually within a day or two, by a telephone call to his secretary.

The officer who usually goes by his Latin title of *officialis* is in
charge of the diocesan courts, which handle processes instituted in
canon law. The average Catholic will not meet the officials unless
he is a party or a witness to a marriage case, although the jurisdiction of the courts is not limited to marriage.

These and a few other offices of less interest to the general public
are canonical; that is, canon law provides that they be instituted.
In modern dioceses, a great number of other offices have come into
existence for various areas of diocesan business for which canon law
does not directly provide. The first of these in importance is probably the office of secretary to the bishop, although its importance
is extremely hard to define. The ordinary has a personal secretary
(in large dioceses he may have several), always a priest, who usually
lives in the episcopal residence and accompanies the ordinary on
business journeys. The secretary has no "power" in the juridical
sense of the term; his influence rests on the fact that he knows more
about the business which comes to the ordinary than anyone else.
He is usually both a source of information and a confidential adviser, and it is not unusual that those who wish to present a delicate
petition somewhat out of the routine to the ordinary will first sound
out the secretary. Since the post has no canonical standing, however,
it is simply up to the ordinary how much influence he allows his
secretary to have; and one must be rather close to the operation to

know how much this is. As far as other clergy and laity can see, the dominant virtue of the secretary is discretion. The ideal secretary remains nearly anonymous, pleasant in personal relations (for hostility which he incurs will rub off on the ordinary), able to converse on a large number of topics of general interest which have nothing to do with the business of the diocese.

Where the diocese operates schools, the office of school superintendent has become extremely important. The superintendent of schools of the Archdiocese of Chicago directs the fourth largest school system in the United States, exceeded in size only by the public school systems of New York City, his own city of Chicago, and Los Angeles. He has the same control over several million dollars' worth of plant and thousands of teachers and students which a public school superintendent has. Since this is a full-time occupation, the ordinary is accustomed to leave this operation entirely to the superintendent. The office does not differ much in its scope and procedure from any school management.

The office of Catholic charities in large dioceses can be another multimillion-dollar operation. It is a tribute to the clergy who direct these offices that their work is so rarely subject to criticism. Like the superintendent of schools, the director of Catholic charities does not enjoy much of that secrecy which we have seen is so prized in the Roman way. This office, unlike most others, has its antecedents in the New Testament; the first subordinate officers mentioned in the New Testament had as part of their responsibility the distribution of food to the poor.

The office of superintendent of cemeteries is often greeted with patronizing chuckles, but he deserves better. Not only does he handle large portions of diocesan property, but he works in an area in which feelings are very sensitive.

Beyond these offices the ordinary is free to appoint diocesan directors of any organized Roman Catholic activity. In some dioceses, the size of the population and the number of activities demand a large number of clergy for these positions. One finds organizations for youth, for students, for families, for workers, for professional groups, even for athletics. In the United States for a generation there have been offices for the evaluation of motion pictures. All these offices illustrate our statement above that there is no organized Roman Catholic activity which is not ultimately submitted to the ordinary.

In the Roman Catholic experience, the most "successful" bishops, success meaning that the diocesan business is conducted smoothly with a minimum of dissatisfied people, are the bishops who make best use of their staff. Best use means that the bishops are careful to select men who are both competent and personable, give them ample delegation of power and responsibility, and treat them with confidence which the officers reciprocate. Bishops with such a staff are completely informed about their diocese but rarely have to intervene with direct action. They are thus released to be accessible to those who seek them and to do some positive thinking and planning about the diocese. Such bishops verify Machiavelli's claim that he could tell the quality of a prince after fifteen minutes' conversation with the subordinates of the prince. Such dioceses exhibit the Roman system at its best, and may make one wonder whether the need for renewal and reform is as acute as many claim that it is.

The ordinary is provided by church law with certain advisory bodies. In full canonically erected dioceses, the major body is the *cathedral chapter*. In any diocese the cathedral church should be the church in which divine worship is conducted with greatest solemnity and care. This is the responsibility of the chapter, and the full performance of the solemn worship of the Roman Church does not leave much time for other activities. The members of the chapter have the title of *canon*, and they outrank simple priests. In addition, according to Canon 391, No. 1, they serve as a senate and council of the ordinary, and the government of the diocese falls to them in the interval between the death of the ordinary and the installation of his successor. They elect a vicar capitular to head the administration of the interregnum.

Cathedral chapters have always been one of the more evident manifestations of ecclesiastical pomp, more suited to the era of royalty and nobility than to the era of democracy. Furthermore, the maintenance of solemn worship according to the standards of the cathedral chapter becomes in modern times a serious financial burden. Many chapters disappeared in the period of European revolution and were never restored. Yet this is probably not the only reason why not many survive, and why the dioceses of the United States, one of the most populous and wealthy regions of Roman Catholicism, have never been fully canonically erected. By church law, the chapter has what is called a deliberative vote; that is, the ordinary needs the vote of the chapter to act in a few situations. Where there is no chapter no one has a deliberative vote, and the action of the ordinary can be impeded by no one, according to church law.

Where there is no chapter, the ordinary must have a board of consultors, which he names himself. The law specifies no business which must be submitted to them and no business which is withheld from them. It is left to the ordinary what he shall submit to them, and their power is purely advisory. At the death of the ordinary, the administration of the diocese does not fall to them; in customary practice it devolves upon the vicar general. This board is distinct from the council for the administration of temporal affairs which the ordinary should have; this council may include laymen. It will be observed that the ordinary is amply provided by law with advisory bodies, and ordinaries, being intelligent and able men, make use of these bodies. It will also be observed that the ordinary is entirely independent of juridical restraint, except where there is a cathedral chapter.

The diocesan synod, which canon law (Canon 356, No. 1) prescribes every ten years, is the full assembly of the ordinary and the clergy. It is not a legislative nor even a deliberative body in practice; the law states that the ordinary is the only synodal legislator, and free discussion is limited to the preparatory committees. In practice, the synod is an occasion on which the ordinary promulgates synodal laws. These have a more permanent character than particular decrees which the ordinary may issue at any time concerning any matter.

The senate of priests which was recommended by the Second Vatican Council could be something quite new in episcopal administration, at least in recent centuries.[6] There are obvious weaknesses in a system in which the presiding officer chooses his own advisers, especially when his authority is absolute. An advisory body is not the same thing as a staff; the staff is expected to act according to the policy of the person or the body who makes the decisions. An advisory body is supposed to have some share in the formation of decisions. A staff advises rather on how decision are to be executed. One who forms a staff generally looks for people "with whom he can work." The advisers of the ordinary in the existing organization are staff officers. The senate of priests is not a staff. It may be partly, mostly, or entirely elected by the clergy; and this will certainly confront the ordinary with some men "with whom he cannot work." The senate will present points of view which the ordinary is not likely to hear from his staff, or if he does hear them, he will hear them with prepared criticisms and no real defense. The senate, as most ordinaries who have instituted it have provided, must represent different age groups in the clergy and different types of clerical employment. We shall see when we come to the priesthood that there are few organizations in the world where seniority means as much as it does in the Roman Catholic Church. No particular material is defined by the Council as proper to the interest of the senate; but senates have expressed great interest in appointments and promotion, retirement, and processes for grievances. The Council encouraged the ordinaries to consult with as many of their priests as often as possible, and to do this through structures and not merely by unplanned encounters.[7] The senate of priests will certainly become an important part of the diocesan structure, perhaps the most important part. It still has no deliberative vote, but it will have an influence as the voice of consensus which no other body within the diocese has at present.

The rural deans (or *vicars forane*) have a territory, usually outside the see city, over which they have certain duties of inspection and reporting. Normally the clergy of each deanery assemble twice annually for conferences on theological topics and to hear the communications of the ordinary. The rural deans usually have certain powers in urgent cases of conscience which make it unnecessary to recur to the ordinary. The rural deans are pastors of parishes; it is not a distinct office in the sense that its holder has no other office.

Church law, as we have seen, calls the power of the Roman Pontiff over the whole church episcopal power; and the relations of pontifical and episcopal power must be classified as unfinished theological business. The First Vatican Council was concerned with asserting pontifical power clearly and without ambiguity. The Council was a belated response to several politico-ecclesiastical movements in the European monarchies which attempted to limit pontifical power in particular countries. Febronianism and Josephism claimed that pontifical decrees had no validity in a Catholic country unless they were ratified by the monarch.[8] Joseph II of Austria, after whom Josephism was named, attempted to establish a headship over the Austrian Church which in its effects did not differ notably from the supremacy asserted by Henry VIII of England. In England, royal supremacy issued in the final separation of English Catholicism from Rome. Gallicanism, which derived its name from the medieval Latin *Gallicanus*, "French," claimed that pontifical acts needed the approval of the bishops of the country acting as a body in order to have the force of church law within the country.[9] Behind this theory of episcopal control was the French monarchy, which had long sought in various ways to submit church government to the crown and, during the fourteenth century, had actually gained control of the papacy. The rejection of these opinions in the First Vatican Council was of great importance because it was not simply a pontifical utterance, but a document signed by the entire body of Roman Catholic bishops.

Gallicanism and Josephism were extreme forms of a suspicious fear of Roman authoritarianism; the fear was not extinguished by the First Vatican Council. Expressions of this fear were repeated during the sessions of the Second Vatican Council. They are heard in suggestions for the decentralization of church government and for more freedom of ordinaries from Roman supervision and Roman directives and from the necessity of appealing to Rome. In order to balance its presentation, the First Vatican Council needed a statement of the episcopal office and episcopal power that corresponded to its statement of the papal office and papal power. The interruption of the Council when Rome was seized by the troops of Victor Emmanuel II in 1870 made it impossible for the Council to finish its business, which had been planned to go on in the manner described. For the following ninety years, the Roman Church had a very clear statement of papal power and no statement at all of episcopal power. It is not surprising that the movement toward centralization continued. As we have already observed, it was just in these ninety years that modern communications were developed. European culture itself seemed to support centralization.

The Second Vatican Council did speak at length of the episcopal office, but it did not resolve the theological problem of the relations of the papacy and the episcopacy. The problem can be put briefly in these terms: how can there be two ordinary and immediate jurisdictions over the same people in the same affairs? It will help us to grasp the problem if we recall that the college of bishops is conceived as the successor body to the college of the apostles. The college of apostles received apostolic authority from Jesus Christ; this is what the Roman Church means when it says that the college of bishops and the episcopal office exist by divine right and by divine institution. The bishop has his authority by his office and not by the delegation of the Pope. The definition of the power of the bishop is not within the competence of the Pope, except in so far as the Pope is the spokesman of the church. That is, once we suppose that there is a definition of episcopal power, it is within the competence of the Pope to discover it but not to modify it. In spite of this, the Pope is supreme bishop of the entire Roman Church.

The bishops, however, are not the subjects of the Pope in the same sense in which other Roman Catholics are his subjects. The bishop is a member of a college of which the Pope also is a member and the primate. It is to this college with its primate that, in Roman Catholic belief, Jesus Christ committed the authority to govern his church. The Pope can deal with the bishop only as a colleague, which is not the same thing as a subject. The question can be put in these rather crude terms: is it within the competence of the Pope to perform in a diocese acts which are regarded as acts proper to an ordinary? Most canonists, hesitant about offering a flat affirmative, might well say that since the Pope has immediate, universal ordinary jurisdiction, he could perform such acts, but would prudently refrain from doing so, unless the most extreme needs demanded it. The power of the Pope to depose bishops is at least at this writing not doubted. That a bishop should fall into heresy or schism is not an unreal hypothesis; church history furnishes a sufficient number of examples. Yet canon law has no explicit provision for deposition, but affirms the power of the Roman See to act in each situation according to the needs of the situation. One sees here a certain hesitation to be too explicit about the power of deposition; and one can say that the Roman See has not acted and would not act in such an extreme situation without consultation with other members of the episcopal college.

The power of the Pope, as it appears in actual practice, is employed in expressly general directions for the whole church, which each ordinary adapts to his diocese. Rome does not like to reverse an episcopal action openly. Yet the Roman network of congregations has created a large number of cases which cannot be finally resolved except by Rome. There are numerous instances in which an ordinary is able to evade responsibility because Rome does not permit something. Yet on examination one finds that one is not dealing with commands of the Holy See but with the "wishes" or the "mind" of the Holy See; earlier we translated these words by *policy*. How particular can policy become, or when does it become so particular that it ceases to be policy? In any case, it can be said that Rome avoids language or action which appears to be a command to a particular ordinary, at least in public. To this extent Rome respects the structure. It is not clear that Rome always knows and respects the local situation. We have observed above that Rome has its own means of exerting pressure, and crude exhibitions of power are not necessary to achieve ends.

Episcopal and pontifical authority can be conceived, it seems, only in terms of the college, which is the ultimate subject of apostolic authority. The Pope cannot be the primate except as the primate in the college; it is not an admissible hypothesis that the primate and the colleagues are really separable. This would mean that the church had perished—certainly an inadmissible hypothesis in Roman Catholic theology. But no single bishop is the college, and no single bishop is the fullness of apostolic authority. One can think of the Pope as the primate through whom the authority of the whole college touches each of its members. Each bishop must govern in harmony with his colleagues; of this harmony the Roman Pontiff is the bond and expression. He and he alone can speak for the whole college to any single colleague, and it is only as the spokesman of the college that he can speak with any authority. The First Vatican Council specified against Gallicanism that the Pope does not need "the consent of the Church" for his utterances to be valid, but this definition was formulated against Gallicanism, which effectively denied that the Pope was the spokesman of the college. As the primate, he symbolizes and incorporates the consensus of the college. There is no doubt that the consensus is more apparent and more meaningful when the Pope is actually in close communication with his colleagues, but the history of the Roman administration does not show an unbroken effort to sustain close communication. The nature of power is one thing, its use is another.

Up to this point we have discussed the theory and the law of episcopal power. As we have said of the papacy, a theoretical consideration does not disclose the whole reality. A more concrete description of episcopal power is much more difficult to present than a concrete description of the power of the papacy, since the conditions in which the power is exercised vary so much from country to country. Nevertheless, some attempt must be made if we are to have more than an abstract treatment. There are certain common features that can be set forth, with the caution that even these may not appear in the same way everywhere.

It was noted previously that a Roman Catholic experiences the total reality of his religion in the local church. This means the diocese, and this in turn means the ordinary. One of the problems of the parochial structure is that the parish does not give the Roman Catholic the whole experience. The whole experience demands the presence and activity of the ordinary, and in modern large dioceses this presence and activity are more often mediate than immediate. The need for the experience is the theological basis for the absolute power which the ordinary has in Roman Catholicism.

Episcopal power will be considered first as it is exercised in the management of church property. This does not indicate that it is of primary importance, but it is of more importance than most people realize, because it furnishes an economic basis of power. The ordinary is the supreme administrator of all property held by the Roman Church in the diocese, with the exception of property held by religious orders (*see* Religious Communities). The extent of the power of the ordinary varies from one country to another and can be seen at one extreme in some dioceses of the United States. Here the ordinary is a *corporation sole*, which means that the corporation is vested in a single person. He has no board of directors to whom he is responsible. He owns the property of the diocese as the ordinary citizen owns his house. When he dies, it is willed to his successor, designated as "the Roman Catholic bishop of X." This system was devised in the nineteenth century to meet the problem known as *trusteeism*. In the early nineteenth century, many Roman Catholic immigrants from Europe brought with them the practice of ownership of churches by lay trustees. Numerous quarrels between lay trustees and bishops and clergy led to the institution of the corporation sole. Not even the pastor of the parish has independent administration of parish property. More frequently the diocese, the parishes, and other organizations are separate corporations. In these corporations the bishop may be chairman of the board, or he may have the power of appointing the members of the board. At the other extreme are those European countries in which much church property passed into the hands of the state in the nineteenth century. Here the state not only maintains the property but, in several instances, pays the salaries of the clergy. In such countries, the ordinary has less property to administer, but the principle of episcopal administration remains.

It is obvious that in such countries as the United States, ownership and administration impose a tremendous burden on the ordinary, but it is also obvious that he has a solid economic basis of power. Ordinaries have been known to threaten recalcitrant congregations with the demolition of their church; this is fully within their power, and the action could be vindicated, if necessary, in a civil court. He may control the administration of the parish or school property and funds as closely as he desires. In some countries, the ordinary assesses parishes for expenses that belong to the diocese. He has the power to approve budgets, to set salaries, and to select investments. In a large diocese, the ordinary may be the sole owner of multimillion-dollar properties. He has the same economic power in the community which is possessed by any one who owns this kind of property. Even where the ordinary is not the sole owner of diocesan property, church law prescribes that no major decision may be made in its administration without his approval.

Episcopal power is exercised most directly and most completely over the clergy of the diocese, and this topic will be treated more fully in the chapter on the priesthood. Each diocesan priest at his ordination makes a promise of obedience to his ordinary. The promise is couched in quite general terms and is not comparable in theory to the vow of obedience made by religious (*see* Religious Communities). It is not the generality of the terms but the power of the ordinary which gives the ordinary a control over his clergy that can be surprising. The ordinary decides, not necessarily without consulting the person involved, but in theory with no obligation to consult him, in what type of priestly work he shall be employed and what preparation he shall receive for it. The ordinary, as we have seen, sets salaries for his clergy, but he does not have control over their personal funds. The ordinary has complete powers of appointment and promotion; here again he may consult, but only if he wishes. Through personal commands and through synodal laws, the ordinary may dictate in some detail, if he so desires, such things as proper clerical attire, proper places where clerics may seek recreation, and the hours the clergy should keep. The power of promotion and transfer is the hinge on which episcopal control of the clergy moves, but this is not the ultimate basis of power. This basis is that the Roman Catholic priesthood is perhaps the one human profession and occupation from which no honorable resignation is now possible. The priest who resigns simply loses all standing in the Roman Catholic community, even if his resignation is processed through due canonical channels. This attitude toward the "ex-priest" is changing in the contemporary Roman Church.

Church law provides some small limitation on episcopal power by the institution of *irremovable rectors* of parishes, which means that these clergy may not be removed without canonical process, but in practice there are very few pastorates which are designated as irremovable rectorships, and the number does not increase. The ordinary may not deprive a priest of his *faculties*, which means his license from the ordinary to perform his priestly functions, without due cause, but unless the priest wishes to sue the ordinary in an ecclesiastical court, the ordinary is the judge of what constitutes due cause. The powers of appointment and promotion make it unnecessary to resort to *suspension* from faculties except in extreme cases. And it should be noticed that transfer to another diocese, while not impossible, is quite difficult, and such a priest becomes a marked man in the place to which he transfers.

No explanation is necessary to show that in such a system everything depends on the humanity of the ordinary, and the administration of dioceses shows that the normal attitude of most ordinaries is one of benevolence. It is not a universal trait, however, and this has been enough to cause some questioning, both during and after the Second Vatican Council, as to whether some modification in the structure of absolute power is not desirable. At this writing, no real modification has been achieved, although the senate of priests already mentioned (p. 57) can be such a modification. The experience of priests, as most of them attest it, is that processes of appeal for priests are largely ineffective. Currently the public, both Roman Catholics and others, have become much more keenly aware of movements beneath the hitherto smooth surface of the Catholic clergy.[10] The number of withdrawals, many with public explanations, has risen sharply in a short time. The response has been mixed, for the Roman Catholic public generally does not easily accept the hypothesis of withdrawal for a valid reason, but the problem has suggested to many observers that modification in the structure of episcopal power may be absolutely necessary if the Roman Church is to maintain its staff of priests.

The power of the ordinary over the laity is much less and, in fact, depends more on his moral stature and personal influence than it does on his jurisdiction. It is here that the question of what the Ordinary can do becomes important, both for clergy and laity. Almost nineteen hundred years of episcopal history show that the ordinary who employs nothing but his jurisdictional power is extremely unimportant as a churchman. This may help others than Roman Catholics to understand why Catholics seem to live in contentment with absolute episcopal power. The ordinary is the spokesman of the Roman Church and its primary actor in the diocese. It is not entirely true to say that no one else can show leadership, but it is true to say that no one can show leadership unless the ordinary permits it. He and he alone can mobilize the strength of a diocese, and only a regional or a national group of bishops can mobilize the strength of a region or a nation. Without episcopal support, or at least episcopal tolerance, no form of Catholic action moves very far. If the ordinary himself does not speak articulately to issues of common concern or permit others to speak, the Roman Catholic Church remains mute on the issues, for the Roman Church speaks officially only through the bishops. As was said of the Roman Pontiff, the extent of the power of the ordinary to move men is really unknown. One can read of bishops who exhibited this power and of bishops who did not exhibit it. It certainly is not conferred by appointment.

The ordinary is much more *immediately* the pastor of his diocese than the Roman Pontiff is pastor of the universal church. This brings up again both the personal qualifications of the ordinary and his communications with the clergy and laity of his diocese. Proved capacity for leadership was not mentioned among the qualifications for episcopal appointment because there is no evidence that this quality is sought, and admittedly it is difficult to identify with certainty. The Roman Church has been rich throughout her history in men with proved leadership who did not become bishops. One may say that most of them achieved more in some other state than they would have achieved as bishops. This can be granted, because in the hypothetical order anything could have happened; the point is simply that these men did not become bishops, while others with a proved lack of capacity of leadership did. The achievement of the priest or lay leader can be assessed, but the loss inflicted by a timorous and wavering ordinary, who is unable to bring his clergy and laity to any more than submission to routine directives, cannot be. It would be difficult to compare the importance of Ignatius Loyola, whose influence was very wide, with the importance of Charles Borromeo, who was an ordinary, or to say that one of them would have been missed more than the other in his position. Nevertheless, Roman Catholics seem ready to admit that only a leader of men could have filled the spot of Ignatius Loyola, but that we would not need a similar leader in the post of Charles Borromeo. This passes comprehension.

The question of the communications of the ordinary with his clergy and laity is closely connected with episcopal leadership, for no man can lead others who does not communicate with them. This also touches the problem of the maximum size of dioceses. What does the much abused word *communicate* mean when it is applied to bishops? It should mean at least that the primary concern of an ordinary is persons, not property, and that persons will get more of his time. It means knowledge and understanding of people to the degree possible, a knowledge which is not gained through ceremonial appearances. It is not so much that the ordinary knows most of the people in his diocese as that he is known by them, that he emerges as a person and not as a corporation. It means the accessibility mentioned above, with full awareness of the fact that the accessible ordinary may be devoured by his diocesans. At this point, as at some others, one is reminded of the old American adage quoted by President Truman concerning the Presidency: if you cannot stand the heat, stay out of the kitchen. It means that the ordinary shows respect as well as demands it, that he deals with every person as a responsible human being, that he does not patronize or—regrettably it must be added—bully. It means that in every decision which involves other persons nothing is done until a full meeting of minds and wills is achieved. It could be suspected that such an ordinary might bring more people to his mind and will than one who depended simply on power and pressure. One of the most engaging bishops in all literature was created by Victor Hugo in *Les Misérables*. What the unbeliever thought a bishop should be is for Roman Catholics a fairly truthful portrait.

The Second Vatican Council has moved toward these things in its document on the episcopacy.[11] While the document retains the idea of juridical power and does not modify the absolute quality of that power, it is not here that the emphasis falls. It is not the document which the First Vatican Council would have produced. The primary theme of the statement is the pastoral nature of the episcopal office, and the pastoral nature of the means by which the bishop is to fulfill his responsibility. There emerges an idea of episcopal leadership which transcends mere juridical power and mere administration. The bishops here produced their own idea of their office in the second half of the twentieth century. By doing this they assured that further modifications will come, and the modifications can mean only that the episcopacy will be conceived less in terms of power and more in terms of leadership.

## 6. *The Priesthood*

In the Roman ecclesiastical structure, one descends from the Roman Pontiff, the bishop of the entire Roman Church, to the ordinaries, the bishops of local dioceses, to the priests, the immediate point of contact between the sacred personnel and the laity. Like the episcopacy, the priesthood as we know it does not appear in the New Testament; it is an early but apparently postapostolic development of the ministry. The development came when the single "church" community became too numerous for the single bishop to serve. The difference between episcopacy and priesthood will be discussed in the chapter on the sacrament of Orders, for the difference ultimately is one not of jurisdiction but of sacred power communicated by ordination. This sacred power, as we have seen, consists of the power to preach, to administer the sacraments, and to govern. The Roman priest does all of these as the delegate of the ordinary, who appoints or licenses him to act as minister. The priest has no ordinary jurisdiction in virtue of his orders; he needs the explicit commission of the ordinary to act. Hence the ordinary can define the limits of the use of his power and may restrain him from using it at all. The license to use sacred power is called *faculties*, and the withdrawal of faculties is called *suspension*. Suspension is one of the more severe canonical penalties which can be imposed on priests, and it may not be inflicted without due cause, as has been noted. This absolute dependence of priests on the ordinary in their ministry is the other side of the total responsibility for the diocese which in Roman belief and practice rests upon the ordinary.

Many who are not Catholics find the institution of *monsignors* puzzling. This is purely a title of honor granted to priests and conveys no office or jurisdiction. Monsignor, my lord, is an Anglicized form of the Italian style of polite address. Priests who are called monsignor are honorary members of the papal household. Some, with the title of *protonotary apostolic* or *domestic prelate*, are called *right reverend* and hold the title permanently. Others, with the lesser title of *Papal Chamberlain* are called *very reverend*; their honor expires at the death of the Pope. The monsignor is entitled to wear a purple gown or a gown with purple trimmings. The gown of the protonotary apostolic looks much like the gown of a bishop to the uninitiated. The honor is obtained for his priests by the ordinary. It generally attests either a high ranking post in the episcopal chancery or long and distinguished service in the pastoral ministry.

The primary type of priest is the parish priest or pastor. The Roman Church divides its dioceses territorially, and the parish has a distinctly defined geographical area within a diocese. Certain exceptions to this arise, most frequently in countries such as the United States of the nineteenth century where large foreign groups moved into the country at the same time. Parishes in cities where such groups settled were often determined not by territory but by language, which effectively meant by ethnic extraction. A person was allowed to attend the parish of his language, which had no boundaries, rather than the parish in whose territory he resided. The Roman Church has always regarded this situation as temporary and less desirable than regularly constituted parishes; but foreign-language parishes have sometimes persisted far beyond the time in which they were genuinely needed. Many have felt that such parishes pose a threat to the unity of the Church.

The pastor has *the care of souls* within his parish, which means all Roman Catholics residing within its limits. It was mentioned that the ordinary ought to know as many of his people as possible and be known by them, but the pastor ideally should know every member of his parish personally, and it is the rare pastor who does not seriously attempt to do this. When the parish grows to such numbers that this becomes unrealistic, it is the common practice to divide the parish and erect a new parish. Large parishes are operated by a team of priests rather than by a single man, and it is the team which knows the whole parish. The care of souls means that the parish church is the place where the Catholics of the territory worship, receive the sacraments, hear sermons, and seek direction and instruction when they wish it. Where the Roman Church engages in education, it is normal that children attend the parish school.

A parish that is too large for a single priest but not large enough to justify the erection of a new parish will be served by a pastor and one or more assistant priests; in some places these are called by the title of *curate*. Normally the priests of the parish reside in a *rectory* adjacent to the church which serves both as residence and as offices. This apparently unhealthy arrangement reflects the conviction of Roman Catholics that there should never be a minute in the twenty-four hours when a priest is not available. Priests sometimes compare a busy rectory to a fire station, but even if the tension of nearly constant demands on the priests' time is not equally great everywhere, it is obvious that such close living can be extremely difficult if personal relations are less than perfect.

The relations of pastor and assistant are perhaps the most poorly structured in the entire ecclesiastical administration. Priests tell an anecdote about the candidate for a degree in canon law who was asked in an examination to enumerate the rights of assistant priests. After some thought he said, "the right of Christian burial." One need not and should not exaggerate the problem, but it would be unrealistic to pretend that the problem does not exist or that it has nothing to do with the effectiveness of the priestly ministry. The weakness of the law leaves room for a domineering pastor to keep his assistants practically in a state of perpetual adolescence. It permits him to overwork them or, by one of the paradoxes of the ecclesiastical world, to underwork them, to keep them from responsible participation in the ministry of the parish. Pastors are normally permanent, while assistants are usually transferred after a few years in a parish. The pastor is not only head of the parish but also the head of the household; details of housekeeping such as the cuisine, the furniture, and the use of heat and electricity can as often be the cause of disagreement as the administration of the parish. The built-in difficulties of the life of the rectory are enough to assure one that the humanity of both pastors and assistants must be remarkable to make it succeed as well as it does.

The pastor is the responsible administrator of the parish property under the ordinary. In a large parish, it can easily become his major occupation. This is regrettable, and no one regrets it more than priests. The modern urban parish may serve five thousand people, have over a thousand children in the parish school, and employ twenty to thirty teachers and a secretarial and maintenance staff of a dozen. Besides the church, the buildings include the rectory, the school, a residence for religious who teach in the school, and possibly a hall for meetings. Even with assistance, this is not a trivial burden. Many Roman Catholics now wonder whether such plants are not already archaic and whether the parish of the future will not be small in numbers and with very little plant, leaving the pastor free to be a pastor. This problem will arise again in Part IV, the Works of the Church; our concern now is with how these works affect the priests.

In the dioceses, salaries are fixed for pastors and for assistants. This effort to equalize the ministry simply does not succeed. Some parishes are wealthy and some are not, and some pastors receive more income than others. This affects the stability of the pastor, for parishes are ranked according to their income. The promotion to which a priest may look is appointment to a parish with more secure revenue and with a larger staff. No organization sets more importance on seniority than the Roman Catholic Church. An assistant becomes a pastor not on his competence but simply because of his age; the oldest man gets the first opening. When a desirable parish is opened by the death, retirement, or promotion of its incumbent, custom requires the ordinary to offer it to the senior pastor of those who may wish it. The undesirable features of promotion by pure seniority are evident and need no elaboration, and perhaps the worst feature of such promotion is that it affirms implicitly that competence is not important. The older practice of holding a *concursus* for vacant posts has given way to seniority. A *concursus* is a competitive examination in theology and preaching. As was noticed for episcopal appointments, these qualifications have a low value quotient. It should be said that not all priests seek the more affluent positions. There is no diocese in which pastors have not declined promotion because they preferred to stay with the people whom they had come to know and love. A priest will never give this as the reason why he refuses to move uptown, however; he will allege that he does not care for the administrative burdens of a large parish.

It is impossible to describe the typical life of the parish priest, for the life varies from country to country, but the typical day in a large parish in the United States will illustrate at least some of its basic features. There are scheduled ceremonies of public worship each day in the church. Both the doorbell and the telephone will ring at frequent intervals, not only all day long but into the evening, the hours when lay people are more likely to be free from their employment. Some of the calls are purely business, concerned with such domestic details as purchasing, maintenance, and repair, and conversation with employees. Other calls will come from parishioners who seek counseling. Such ritual services as weddings and funerals must be arranged. Officers of parish organizations will call to discuss their programs and problems. Many priests have regular classes of instruction in schools; other groups meet for instruction in the rectory. The parish is often an unofficial center of Roman Catholic information for the press, for local merchants and business men, for ministers and members of other Christian churches, and for those who are simply curious. A priest is sometimes called to the telephone to settle a bet made at a cocktail party. He may be summoned to a hospital, and in any case the wise pastor visits his sick daily. Sunday is not the typical day. The entire morning and some of the afternoon or evening are spent in conducting public worship in the church, but Sunday afternoon and evening are usually the only periods of the week when the rectory will be reasonably free of the telephone and the doorbell.

What does not appear in this sketch is a regular period for reading, and this is often one of the lamentable effects of the parish routine. All too often the priest cannot count on as much as an hour without interruption during the day to keep abreast of theological learning and cultural affairs. It should be added that most of his time is spent in personal encounters, and these are more fatiguing than work with things or with papers. In modern Roman Catholicism, it may not be simply true that the clergy are overworked, but many of them are; and it is always true that the parish priest is not permitted to organize his work so that he gets the most out of his time. This is one aspect of the parochial ministry which has not received sufficient attention from ordinaries and Roman congregations, and it is more urgent than they seem to think.

The parish priest is the primary type of priest, meaning that he is most fully the *priest* as the ministry is traditionally understood in Roman Catholicism. In the large and complex modern Roman Church, however, there are an increasing number of priests who are otherwise engaged, the specialized priests or the "hyphenated" priests: priest-administrators, priest-teachers, priest-scholars, and for a brief period even worker-priests. Apart from the Roman and diocesan curias, the Roman Catholic Church sponsors a large number of church-related organizations. If these are large, they always have at least one priest-director or -adviser who may have no other employment. Priests are often full-time teachers in Roman Catholic high schools, colleges, and universities, and a large number engage in scholarship in the sense that they write technical books and articles for technical journals. Not all priest-teachers and priest-scholars are engaged in theology, the properly ecclesiastical branch of learning; it is difficult to think of any learned discipline in which one will not find Roman Catholic priests. The development of the specialist priest has been spontaneous rather than planned, although the tradition of the priest-scholar goes back at least as far as Jerome (347–420); but Jerome himself was a priest-administrator (secretary to Pope Damasus 382–385) before he was a scholar. In the early centuries of the Roman Church, the deacons corresponded to the modern priest-administrators, for they had the care of the temporal goods of the church. As the administration of church business expanded, it was only natural that it should be committed to "church men." It is not so much that the hierarchy never trusted the laity, although this is more or less the truth of the matter; it is rather that, as we have seen, the priest is totally subject to the bishop. Now hyphenated priests have come to realize that they are professionally engaged in work in which their priestly orders are not at all involved, work which could be done just as well by laymen. The problem that arises is not unlike the problem of the multiplication of bishops; the order of the priesthood seems to be cheapened. There is no reason to ordain a man a priest or a bishop except to enable him to act as a priest or a bishop.

It is not exaggerated to say that there is an identity crisis in the contemporary Roman Catholic priesthood which at this writing seems likely to grow more serious.[1] It is not only the hyphenated priests who feel the crisis; it reaches the parochial clergy also. There are other factors at work which will be treated later, but one of these is certainly the question what the priest *is* in the modern world and what he can *do*. The parish priest finds himself more and more involved in what appear to be trivia or at least not the things for which his priestly training and his priestly orders qualify him. Often he is not sure of his priestly training; seminary education has been submitted to searching criticism.[2] He becomes uneasy about his role and his influence; he fears that he may become meaningless. He knows that priest-administrators do necessary work, that priest-teachers and priest-scholars have served the church with distinction, that the parochial clergy are the living ministry of the church, but he also recognizes that he lives in a rapidly changing world and that the forms of his ministry may become outmoded before any one realizes it.

A major part of the identity crisis is the isolation the priest often feels. What Paul says of himself was very probably true of other officers of the apostolic church; he supported himself by working at a trade, and thus he shared the life of the people he addressed. Gradually and without plan, the isolation of the clergy from the laity has grown over the centuries. It is impossible to generalize about this, for conditions differ from one country to another. The isolation is marked by such things as clerical garb, which sets off the priest more than the uniform sets off the military man. There is a long series of prohibitions of things which are regarded as innocent for the laity but unbecoming for the clergy. If all these things were enforced in any one place—and they nearly are in some dioceses—the list would be quite comprehensive. It would include the theatre; the opera; moving pictures; sports events, especially racing; restaurants and bars; riding in an automobile with a woman of any age, even an infant or the priest's own mother; public beaches; going anywhere after sunset except for an urgent summons for priestly ministry, which means death actual or impending. The list reminds one of the prohibitions associated with British or American Puritanism rather than with the proverbial freedom of the Latin Catholic countries, yet it is precisely in the Latin countries that most of the prohibitions are effective. In these countries, the proverbial freedom is distinctly for laymen. Yet an English priest friend once observed that although in his country he was free to write a play, produce a play, direct a play, or manage the stage and properties, the one thing he could not do with a play was sit in the auditorium and watch it. None of these things can be regarded as really serious losses of human values; but they contribute to the isolation of the priest, who is sometimes forbidden first-hand experience of things which are regarded as a normal part of civilized, educated living. While it is true that many of the prohibitions are widely ignored, a structure which clings to laws of alleged importance that have become meaningless is not in the best of shape. Where many of these prohibitions are in force, the clergy are not even known to the laity, and they are therefore distrusted.

The worker-priest movement in France after the Second World War was a serious and imaginative effort to break out of isolation.[3] It was estimated by the French hierarchy that France had become to all intents and purposes a non-Christian, missionary territory and that a new approach was necessary to reach the French people. The worker-priests left both the clerical garb and the clerical dwelling, took employment in factories and apartments in workers' residential areas, attempted to make friends as person to person, and, once the friendships were formed, to make their apartments the centers of social gatherings which would become discussion clubs. The movement was suppressed by the Holy See after a very short time (March 1, 1954), altogether too short to show whether this approach would succeed. Such methods were not really novel, however; they were more or less the same ones which Paul of Tarsus used when he moved into a new city. The reasons alleged for the suppressions were that some of the worker-priests, far from bringing workers to the Roman Church, themselves became communists, and that some others took women. With the secrecy characteristic of Roman operations, no full report of the success or failure of the movement was ever made public. Most Roman Catholics who were concerned or interested at all felt that Rome had acted hastily and without consideration. The movement is not really dead, although its continuance was hedged with so many restrictions that the original idea was nearly lost. The conclusion drawn by many was that Rome believed the isolation of the clergy was a value in itself, not to be risked even for the possible gain of a mass return to Roman Catholicism in France.

Certainly the major factor in maintaining the isolation of the Roman clergy is celibacy. The Roman Catholic Church is the only Christian Church which has a universal law of celibacy, and the universal law can be traced no earlier than the First Council of the Lateran, 1123. The law estabished as universal a customary law which had by that time come to prevail in the majority of later dioceses. Celibacy came into the clergy from monasticism; and the monks, as will be seen, were not instituted to perform the sacerdotal ministry. The question has been agitated recently and promises to be agitated still more. It is by no means a simple question. Protestant ministers have said—out of the hearing of their wives—that the Roman discipline of celibacy has something to be said in its favor. It does free the priest for the service of others. There are no family claims on his time, nor has he demands on his income; to put it rather crudely, a celibate priest can be supported at a very low rate. An unspoken advantage is that a single man is much more easily kept in total subjection than a man with family responsibilities that must be recognized; there certainly could be no rectory if the priests were married. These advantages—leaving open whether total subjection is an advantage to any one besides the bishop—must not be denied. The question is whether they can realistically be exacted through a discipline of universal celibacy.

It has to be recognized that celibacy is not recommended as anything but an option in the New Testament and that even Paul does not associate it with the ministry.[4] In the Roman Church, it is the priesthood, not celibacy, that is an option. Whatever the reasons of convenience, as suggested above, or of long tradition that may be adduced in its defense, the connection between the two does not represent the New Testament understanding of either the ministry or celibacy. The Catholic Church does not pretend to adhere literally to the biblical text; celibacy is proposed and defended as justified by the historical experience of the living church. It is a law which the church made and which the church can unmake. The discussion can proceed only on whether it is prudent to retain the law, not on whether the law represents New Testament teaching or whether it has been a good law in the past. We are forced to consider some of its disadvantages.

Some of the defenders of celibacy have urged that no such consideration is possible until a complete social-psychological study has been made of the life of married clergy in Orthodox and Protestant churches. With all respect to these gentlemen and to the learning which they prize, this would postpone the discussion to a future in which very few men now living would have any part. Some disadvantages need no survey to be presented, nor would all the data of a survey be relevant. It is a statistical fact that half of the marriages in the State of California end in divorce. Arguing on the principle that I see implied in this position, the statistical fact would furnish ample justification to the Federal Government for imposing celibacy on all Californians, who would have to be judged as a group incapable of marriage. Whether marriage succeeds most of the time where the clergy are married or whether it is more or less helpful to the ministry is interesting but not to the point. It is no more significant than a similar survey would be for the laity. I have no opposition to such a survey as long as it is accompanied by an equally full survey of the celibate clergy. It is not without interest that all attempts at such surveys have been met with deep, even rancorous hostility by those who want a survey of married clergy. It is an evident fact that celibacy too has its failures and that it is sometimes an obstacle to the ministry, and to suppose the problem will be solved by calculating the ratio of failures per thousand for celibate and married clergy is to put more weight on statistics than they can carry.

The discussion should not proceed on the assumption that marriage will solve all the problems of the Roman Catholic clergy. It will no more solve all their problems than it solves the problems of all who marry. The institution of married Roman clergy would certainly create new problems, and some of them will be serious. The question ultimately is one of which set of problems the Roman Church judges it can best live with. Since we deal with action, not with theory, and with church law, not with immutable dogma, it is possible to weigh quite pragmatically the projected advantages and disadvantages of different courses.

One must begin with the undeniable fact that marriage is the normal state of man and woman and that one who remains single deviates from the normal pattern. This does not imply that all marriages are happy and successful or that the single person is by definition unhappy. It does not mean that the celibate is necessarily abnormal, nor does it mean that he risks psychological difficulties which are less of a hazard in marriage. It means that he must, to preserve a balanced personality, find compensation for a relationship that most men need for completeness. Man achieves fulfillment by *doing* something, not by *not doing* something. The liability for a celibate person is that he risks becoming narrow and self-centered, less sensitive to the needs and wishes of others, less capable of genuine, outgoing love. To point out that many married persons are narrow, self-centered, and unloving is not to the point. What is to the point is that people who achieve successful, happy marriages have been compelled to rid themselves of these defects, and the daily facts of their marriage have everything to do with it; if they meet the demands of the discipline of marriage, they achieve a level of personal fulfillment which the celibate must find in another way. No one will deny that the discipline of the priesthood offers compensations for the absence of the discipline of marriage. The priest learns that he must think of himself as carrying on the ministry of Jesus, that he belongs to all and must love all, that he really has no life of his own but must find his fulfillment in the lives of those to whom he ministers. These are valid considerations, and the priest who has integrated his life does so by means of these principles. The question is whether these abstractions can be equally forceful for such a large number of men. Our desired survey might show how many celibate clergy fail to find such compensation and so to that degree are not fully successful as priests nor as happy in their lives as one might hope.

That the priest does not find compensation does not depend entirely on himself any more than happiness in marriage is the work of only one of the partners. I have tried to set the priest in the ecclesiastical system in which he literally occupies the lowest place. To find the necessary compensation for his solitary state, he needs the understanding and love of every one in the system, from the Roman Pontiff and his Curia, through the bishop, down to his fellow priests. In fact, as has been suggested above, he does not always find personal concern and compassion. To rise above this may impose, as a matter of routine, a personal heroism that can never become routine. Priests who do not find compensation should not have to bear all the blame for their failure. Like the married man, the priest cannot live alone, and he fails when he is forced to live alone.

Celibacy without compensation is evidently an obstacle to the fullness of the ministry, and no one, not even priests themselves, can measure how much of an obstacle it is. One need not appeal to certain general conclusions of modern psychology on the place of sex in the development of the person; were these conclusions valid, celibacy would be intolerable and would never have been tolerable. The reality of the obstacle is amply attested by experience. In perhaps no other profession is the person so closely identified with the profession as in the Roman Catholic priesthood. At this writing, no rethinking of the priestly mission has been done which would make the identity less close. As long as this remains true, the integration of the priestly life is vital to the health of Roman Catholicism. Simple insistence on the values of celibacy and on the strength of a long tradition contributes nothing to the personality compensation which is missing. The hierarchy, if it wishes to retain compulsory celibacy, must do its part to see that the life of priests is not almost impossible.

There is still another difficulty, more obvious and more scandalous, but possibly less damaging than the slow erosion of the character of the priest. No figures are available on the number of priests who fail to meet the obligation of celibacy, now or in the past. Kindness forbids the mention of names, but reliable reports are that in some regions concubinage becomes, if not normal, at least so common as to arouse no comment. In other regions, the open scandal of the desertion of the priest remains relatively rare, but it should be remembered that Roman Catholic administration has learned to conceal such events. Here also one could ask for a survey. No one can now say that the number of failures of this type is so large that celibacy has been proved unworkable, and it is doubtful that figures would prove this. We simply have no way of knowing how many failures can be considered tolerable. If the number were made public, I suspect that both Catholics and others would be truly astonished that it is so small; and it is for this reason that this aspect of the problem seems less important than the first point. That most priests can live a celibate life does not prove that they do it *well*, unless one wishes to apply the dictum of Dr. Johnson concerning women preaching to this situation: "Sir, it is like a dog walking on its hind legs. You do not wonder at how well it is done; you wonder that it is done at all." In regions where many do not live a celibate life, the institution of celibacy may seem to be nothing but sheer, vast hypocrisy. It is hard to think of anything of value that is preserved by such an institution.

Many observers believe that the discipline will be changed much sooner than one might expect. The change would be a return to celibacy as an option for priests as for laymen. As a purely philosophical question, it can be asked whether a man can renounce not only marriage, but also his right to marriage. The question cannot be answered here, but it ought to be discussed. The practical problems which a married clergy would introduce into Roman Catholic discipline should not be underestimated, but they are problems with which the Orthodox and Protestant churches have learned to live. Some find the possibility of great scandal in clerical adultery and divorce; for reasons not easy to ascertain, they do not see the same scandal in clerical concubinage.

Another feature of the identity crisis of priests is the problem of their freedom. We have attempted to give some idea of how much the personal freedom of the priest is restrained. One must understand that in practice the discipline is more tolerable than the description; but the theory of absolute power remains unchanged. The problem here is the clash of an antiquated structure with contemporary culture. The relations of the priest with his ecclesiastical superiors made quite good sense in the days of feudal power and absolute monarchy, because they were not dissimilar to the relations of the layman with his secular rulers. In modern times, outside of the totalitarian countries, they are wholly at variance with the patterns of the society from which the priest emerged and in which he lives. It is not meaningful to say that the priest freely chose this obedience. Because of his cultural background, he could not really know what he was choosing, for he had had no experience of it. No elaborate explanation should be necessary to show that an adolescent boy will accept limitations of his freedom which are too much for a mature man. The priest, even when he is a mature man, is often like the schoolboy looking forward to the freedom of vacation or of graduation. He looks to release from the seminary and then, in the phrase current among the clergy, to the day when he can put his feet under his own table. In the nineteenth century, this did not create an identity crisis. In the twentieth century it does, and the Roman Church has been slow to recognize the change.

Recognition at this writing seems certain to come; it will be forced not by an identity crisis but by a vocation crisis. Here again exact figures cannot be obtained; the Roman Church conceals its troubles as well as its administration. Few will deny, however, that the Roman Catholic clergy are suffering substantial losses; the number of priests who have departed from the priesthood is growing at the same time that the number of candidates who enter seminaries is shrinking. Here those who love surveys can well ask those who depart, as well as those who do not enter, why they choose as they do. Until such a survey is made, one can only speculate. Celibacy is assigned as the most common cause; this may be a deceptive oversimplification. The life of the priest, as one can deduce from what has ben described above, can be very lonely. A priest may have found the loneliness and the lack of liberty intolerable before he found the celibacy intolerable. He may, as has been indicated, have begun to wonder whether his priestly ministry is meaningful to the church, the world, and the people whom he serves. Facile explanations here explain nothing, and, unless the Roman Church investigates seriously the causes of this condition, it will have no one else to blame for the troubles which it will certainly face. It has no structure to take up what would be lost by a sharp diminution in the number of its clergy.

Against this should be set something which is altogether real but difficult to describe, something that has been called the freemasonry of the Roman Catholic clergy. No other group in the world is known to me in which perfect strangers can achieve understanding and community after merely learning each other's names. They will almost surely find mutual acquaintances, they have had the same experiences, they have encountered the same problems, and they have many tastes in common. They will very probably think much alike and speak a common professional language. But the freemasonry goes deeper than this. Priests depend on each other, trust each other, and protect each other. The friendships they form with a few are close without being sentimental; the priest by his training is likely to abhor sentimentality. Even one who abandons the priesthood is not abandoned by his friends in the priesthood. Toward each other priests are remarkably tolerant and forgiving. The freemasonry includes pastors, assistants, priest specialists, diocesan and religious clergy; but priests who are promoted to the episcopacy leave it. Very probably most bishops wish this were not so, and it should not be so. The "system," as many call it, into which the bishop is admitted makes it impossible for priests to trust him as they trust each other. They believe he has obligations toward something to which they feel no obligation. As a rule priests are perfectly at ease only in the company of priests; when they are with laymen or with bishops, they fear that they are observed.

There is no doubt that this freemasonry is one of the strengths of the Roman Catholic priesthood, that it contributes to the compensation of which we have spoken, and that more than anything else it enables priests to perform their duties and remain in their profession. There is likewise no doubt that such a freemasonry would be largely destroyed in a married clergy. Defenders of celibacy can afford to reflect on this loss; one does not easily think of something to replace the freemasonry. It should cause some concern that the freemasonry seems to be weakening at the present moment. One can also call this morale or *esprit de corps* or other noble names; whatever one calls it, it is created by the body of priests, not by ecclesiastical superiors or by the laity. If it is weakening, these others can neither strengthen it nor replace it. One may hazard a guess that the isolation and the unfreedom of the priestly life have reached such a point in our changing world that even the traditional freemasonry is unable to assist enough priests to bear it. On the other hand, the freemasonry now has an organ and a voice in the senate of priests. Where these organs have begun to act, one can sense a resurgence of morale in the local clergy.

As with the papacy and the episcopacy, we must now consider the reality of the power of the priesthood in Roman Catholicism. It was common in nineteenth-century Protestant polemics to call Roman Catholics priest-ridden. Protestants now know enough about Catholics not to use the term, but the situation is not simple. In some of the older, traditionally Roman Catholic countries, anticlericalism has become so deeply imbedded that the priesthood is almost totally without power or influence. In some other countries priests have more of both than even Catholics desire. The novels of Honor Tracy describe a country in which the priest is usually the most powerful man in the village and one of the most powerful men in the city, and the proper word here is power, not influence. I believe that it was D. W. Brogan (in a passage which I am unfortunately unable to trace) who wrote some years ago that Protestants are often frightened at the size of the crowds at the Roman Catholic church on Sunday. They are frightened because this would be an infallible sign of the personal power and prestige of the minister at a Protestant church. He assures Protestants that the Catholic crowds signify nothing of the sort. The church is the only place where Roman Catholics can obtain spiritual services which they believe essential, and a crowd at the church says no more about the personal power of the priest than a crowd at the post office says about the personal power of the postmaster. This observation shows an insight into the reality of Catholicism which is surprising. Not even all priests understand why crowds assemble at the church, and they sometimes think they have power which they do not have.

It is precisely at the level of the priestly ministry, however, that the spiritual power of the Roman Church touches the laity; and once one goes beyond the essentials Brogan described, the power of the priesthood is simply the power of personal influence. The personal influence of Vincent de Paul during the regency of Anne of Austria was so great that it was real power. Some years ago in the United States, Father Coughlin was heard with attention and almost fanatic loyalty by millions on the radio every Sunday, and he drew enormous crowds at personal appearances. When he attempted to turn this power in a political direction, it suddenly disappeared. Bishop Fulton Sheen, when he was still a priest, attracted audiences as large or larger, but he never attempted to lead them in any particular direction. One should say of both men that they were quite influential but without real power. On a smaller scale, this is true of every priest, parochial or specialist. He must persuade, he cannot coerce. The power of persuasion can be very great, but it remains persuasion. Even a large following of the persuaded is subject to other pressures that may be more powerful than persuasion.

That a priest can lead a small group is no assurance that he can lead a large one; he is usually well aware of the limits of his leadership, perhaps too well aware. In the United States, many pastors who think of themselves as powerful rather than as influential have hesitated to attempt to lead their parishes away from racial prejudice and segregation. They have been the led rather than the leaders. A priest can preserve his leadership by not going beyond what he thinks acceptable; if he does this, he has a low idea of leadership. It is at this point that the power of the ordinary becomes important. The priest, instead of depending on his personal influence, becomes the spokesman of the ordinary and of his brother priests. When this leadership is mobilized, as happens too rarely, it gets things done, but it is a part of "safety," which we mentioned earlier, that one does not risk losing all of one's influence by attempting to extend it beyond the expected.

Earlier it was noted that the person and the mission of the priest are closely identified. In their training, Roman Catholic priests have it dinned into them that what they are is more important than what they say or do. One of the most "powerful" priests of modern times was a nineteenth-century pastor in France named Jean-Baptiste Marie Vianney. M. Vianney was so poorly endowed with native intelligence that he nearly missed ordination because of failure in studies. He had no gifts of eloquent speech. His charge was the parish of an obscure village. His power rested simply and entirely on authentic, transparent personal holiness. Every Roman Catholic priest knows him. The Catholic experiences Catholicism in the priests he knows; the ordinary is a remote figure, and the Pope is practically superhuman. The priest is taught that when the Catholic experiences the church, he should experience Jesus Christ. It is his responsibility to see that the experience is authentic. Where this conviction is genuine and deep, it gives the priest a personal power which can be neither described nor measured.

## 7. The Laity

When one compares the laity in the Roman Catholic Church with the laity in the New Testament church, or even with the laity in Protestant churches, especially those churches which are called *congregational*, some striking differences are apparent.[1] The New Testament does not exhibit that kind of clergy-laity polarity which is seen in Roman Catholicism. Except for the pastoral epistles (attributed to Paul but really the work of his disciples), the New Testament writings contain little which is addressed to the "clergy"; neither the word nor the idea as it has developed is found in the New Testament. The Christian message and the Christian way of life are presented to all members of the church equally. By contrast, in Roman Catholicism the laity are passive members of the church. If the work of the church is conceived in the usual threefold division of government, the sacramental system, and preaching, the laity are the governed, the recipients of the sacraments, and the listeners. Of course, the laity are not simply inactive, but the long tradition of church office and functions leaves no place in the structure for lay activity. Lay activity will be discussed in Part IV under the heading of the works of the church, and it will be evident that the laity are deeply involved in these "works." But it will also appear that in Romanism *ecclesiastical* has become synonymous with *clerical*.

The one activity which is steadily and seriously urged on the laity is the activity of supporting the economic structure of the Roman Church. This is not said cynically. The Church engages in a vast operation that demands proportionately vast resources of personnel and plant. Except in those countries where the state pays the salaries of priests and maintains the churches, the Church has no source of revenue other than its members and its investments. It is normal that the expenses of a parish are borne by the voluntary contributions of the parishioners. Other activities, such as educational and welfare work, must be supported by voluntary contributions. These services should in theory be offered without charge. The realities of modern economics usually make this impossible, but in no case can a welfare activity charge its beneficiaries enough to cover its costs. Hence the Catholic layman is solicited for contributions wherever the Church carries on such activities.

In spite of his passive role in the church structure, the layman is ultimately the one for whom the activities of the church are conducted. To a certain extent, he directs the activities simply by his presence and his character, even though he has no active voice in the operations. The Roman Church has known enough of mass apostasy and rebellion, even violent rebellion, to keep it from taking its members too casually. It can remember, if it wishes, such gross misreadings of the lay mind as it committed in France before 1789 and in Spain before 1931. In Europe the real or alleged alliance between the Roman Church and the propertied classes during the rise of industrialism in the nineteenth century led to a massive loss of membership among the working classes. Yet many observers believe that the Roman and the local hierarchies have learned very little from these defections.

The Roman Church is subject to pressure from lay forces. It should not be thought that this pressure is always wholesome. The problems of the Church with European states concerning the election of popes and bishops have already been mentioned, and the church emerged from these struggles with a clear determination to remain free from this type of lay domination.[2] There can be no doubt that it was the pressure of the propertied classes that retarded the development of social consciousness in the Roman Church.[3] In the United States, lay pressure kept Catholicism from any deep involvement in the problems of segregation and interracial justice. The same lay pressure has kept the Roman Church from any clear utterance either about war and peace in general or about any particular conflict. Gordon Zahn, in a study of Catholic support of German National Socialism, has made the point that while the Hitler government was of a very rare type, nothing in the principles and practices of other countries exists which would prevent Roman Catholics from supporting the same type of government should it arise in their own countries.[4] This topic will be discussed in the chapter on Church and State, evidently an area of lay influence.

Lay influence and pressure are at their strongest where the church touches the secular areas of politics and economics. In most of modern Europe, the Roman Church encounters anticlericalism when it ventures into these areas. Strictly speaking, anticlericalism is not a position; it is a rejection of clericalism, which is a position. Clericalism claims a decisive voice for the clergy in secular affairs. It is not proposed in these terms; what is claimed is not a voice for the clergy but a voice for the church. Here is uncovered one of the weaknesses of Romanism; the church is identified with the clergy. Anticlerical laymen respond because they fear that when the clergy speak for the rights of the church and the good of the church, they mean the rights of the clergy and the good of the clergy. One does not know whether to be surprised that anticlericalism is strongest and deepest in those countries which are traditionally Roman Catholic. It is scarcely found in Germany, England, Scotland, the United States, and the English-speaking provinces of Canada. The obvious explanation, although not necessarily the correct one, is that these countries have no tradition of clericalism.

If we limit ourselves to church activity proper, apart from the sensitive areas where the ecclesiastical and the secular touch each other, we find a growing number of laymen in the Roman Church complaining that the clergy treat them as children.[5] The layman accepts his passive role in the administration of the sacraments; he recognizes the sacred power of orders, and he knows he does not possess it. He does not understand why he should be a passive spectator at liturgical functions; the Roman Church is changing in this respect (see The Eucharist). He does not see why he should be a mere subject of the government of the church, especially if he enjoys some special competence. If he is an educated man, he does not know why he should have his thinking about his belief directed by clergy. This dissatisfaction is not the same thing as the old-style anticlericalism; it is new, and to some churchmen it is more threatening. The church was formerly threatened with exclusion from politics, law, and economics; it now appears to be threatened by a lay invasion of its own structure of doctrine and discipline. Going on the assumption that the layman is a passive member of the church, this is indeed a serious threat.

These complaints vary in intensity from place to place, but they are heard most frequently in those countries where the major strength of the Roman Church lies: in the countries of Western Europe, in the British Isles, and in North America. The strength is greater here rather than in countries which have a larger nominally Catholic population because they have a larger proportion of active communicants and because the leading thought of the contemporary church comes from them. It is important that the source of the complaints is very largely the educated Catholics, and in particular the Catholics who engage in intellectual work such as teaching, writing, and journalism—in a word, just those Catholics who are in the best position to make their complaints heard. They manifest a restlessness among the laity that is difficult to measure. Many doubt that they are representative spokesmen, but there is no doubt that they are influential both in the Roman Catholic community and outside it.

The Second Vatican Council recognized this restlessness without explicitly referring to it. The Council presented, in a form so general that many found it unsatisfactory, a new idea of the role of the laity in the Roman Church, or rather a sketch of a new idea.[6] The new idea arises from the Council's treatment of the church in the world and its recognition that the church exists in a world which is mostly non-Catholic and nonecclesiastical.[7] All nonecclesiastical activity is grouped by the Council under the designation *secular*, and the Council declares that the secular is the proper area of the layman.[8] This may seem to imply an exclusion of the clergy from the secular, the very exclusion which was so long demanded by the anticlerical governments of Europe, but this could hardly have been the implication of the Council. It must have meant that the secular is the proper area of lay decision, not necessarily the exclusive area of the layman.

The Council thus raised an interesting question that it did not really answer. Can the traditionally docile and submissive layman continue to exist if the secular is his proper area? How much and what kind of clerical direction can be admitted in this area? If the Council meant anything different from customary practice, it must mean that the direction of the hierarchy and the clergy in the area of the secular must be no more than general, with no specific and particular instructions for action. It is the work of the layman to specify and particularize in action the principles which it is the office of the clergy to proclaim. If this is the true intention of the Council, then a great deal of hierarchical and clerical direction ought to come to an end. The layman must have a freedom of decision and of interpretation which traditionally he has neither had nor claimed. One may ask, for instance, whether education belongs to the area of the secular; hardly any one in this generation would deny that it does. One may ask whether literature and journalism belong to the secular, and again no one would deny this, even when the writer and the journalist touch upon religious questions. Both of these activities are instances of areas where a more or less rigorous hierarchical and clerical direction has been exercised. Yet the Council produced a surprising declaration of the principles of academic freedom which would meet the demands of thoroughly secular education.[9] A problem has been created in Romanism since the Council because so many bishops and clergy have as yet failed to manifest in practice the principles which the bishops in council voted to accept.

How does the Roman Church think it is involved in the area of the secular? The Catholic Church, with other Christian churches, would not hold that its doctrine and its disciplines should have no effect on life in the secular world. From the New Testament onward, the Christian church has proclaimed that there is a Christian way of life which must be lived in the world, and it has never recommended the kind of withdrawal practiced by such groups as the Amish. Realistically the modern church does not expect many outside Christianity to listen to the proclamation of the gospel; a post-Christian world is a new and peculiar kind of missionary field. The church does recognize that Christianity is best proclaimed in the lives of people who profess a faith which is meaningful to them. In Catholicism, these are the laity, since the clergy are concerned almost entirely with church members. The Council treats the laity as adults who can and must work out the form and style of Christian life which they must live. The clergy may and must render judgment on how authentically Christian this life is, but the Council denies that they are able to describe it in more than general principles.

While the Council clings to the traditional language of submission and obedience to hierarchical and clerical control, the fulfillment of its directives will destroy the traditional language and the things which it signifies. If the secular is the proper area of lay decision, then clergy who engage in activities touching the secular, such as social welfare work, education, and journalism, should be submitted to lay decision. In fact, this is neither a strange nor a new situation, yet in traditional Romanism there is a repugnance to the exercise of authority over a priest by a layman. This is a relic of clerical privilege, mentioned earlier. In the future there will be, it seems, no room even for this relic of clerical privilege, and it is difficult to foresee the changes in the relations of clergy and laity which will occur. One can be reasonably sure that they will be profound.

If the secular is the proper but not the exclusive area of the laity, so likewise the ecclesiastical is the proper but not the exclusive area of the clergy. The Council did not intend a complete division between the two states and the two areas. The new and original suggestions of the Council will institutionalize the participation of the laity in the life and work of the church, and even in decisions. The Council proposes councils of laymen both in the dioceses and in the parishes.[10] Like the senates of priests, these are merely advisory bodies. The areas of their activities are left vague and undefined, but it is clearly suggested that the advice of laymen is desirable in the administration of the economic goods of the church. The Council did not limit the competence of the lay councils to economic affairs, however, and the laity have been quick to see the absence of this limit. With or without invitation, the laity in some numbers have taken the opportunity to express themselves on such problems as the reform of the liturgy, the necessity and the propriety as well as the management of some Roman Catholic operations in welfare and education, on Catholic literature and journalism, and even on such properly theological problems as the morality of war and the morality of the family. In October, 1967, the world synod of lay delegates convened at Rome at the invitation of the Pope surprised the world and frightened the Pope by calling for an early declaration relaxing the rigid teaching of the Roman

Church on contraception.[11] This was an instance of how lay councils can be vehicles of a lay consensus, and it happened a remarkably short time after the Second Vatican Council.

That lay speech and lay activity have been a disturbing element in Romanism since the Second Vatican Council ended its sessions is known to all the world which reads the newspapers. To some the signs are alarming, threatening either a schism or a mass revolt against pontifical and episcopal authority. Others see not a revolt, but simply a loss of power and prestige by the papacy and the episcopacy; Catholics will not so much reject them as pay little attention to them. Others see no more than an unrest which the Roman Church must suffer until it stabilizes itself in a new position which in some respects will differ radically from its old position and may ultimately differ more radically than any one now alive realizes.

Many of the laity have heard the declaration of the Council as a call to a fuller and more active share in the life and work of the church. The enthusiasm of the response has sometimes been embarrassing to hierarchical and clerical officers. At this point, the generality of the documents of the Council appears to be a weakness. The structures for a new type of lay activity do not exist, and it seems that considerable effort is wasted in scattered and unstructured efforts. Many of the clergy are slow to accept the fact that anything has changed. Lay councils have not been rapidly established, and many clergy fear election of lay councils by the laity. The laity usually interpret this as a desire to have laymen whom the clergy can dominate. It should not be thought, however, that all laymen respond in the same way to the Council. More than a few exhibit a repugnance to a new idea of the laity, even a horror of it. They seem to wish no more action, no more freedom, no more responsibility than they are accustomed to. Thus at a crucial moment in its history, the Roman Catholic Church seems to have less of that unity of which it has boasted and which Protestants fear than it has ever had. The fable of "monolithic Romanism" has been shattered in this generation and for generations to come.

Yet a more astute observer might note tokens of a dynamism which the Roman Church has not manifested for many years. A student of the history of Romanism knows that in its past crises it has often been the laity as much as the clergy, or even more than the clergy, which has recued Romanism from what appeared to be an inescapable decline. As was said of the papacy, the episcopacy, and clergy, the true extent of the power of the laity in the church has never been measured.

The brevity of this treatment compared with the preceding treatments of clerical office should not be taken to indicate the comparative importance of the lay state in the Roman Church, but it must be recognized that the laity have not been an active part of the Roman ecclesiastical structure. The scope of lay activity will be seen further in the section on the works of the Roman Church. In the strictly ecclesiastical functions of preaching, worship, and government the laity are inactive.

## 8. Religious Communities

Roman Catholic religious communities have parallels in other non-Christian religions. Groups united by a common dedication to their religion can be found in ancient Israel (the sons of the prophets), in certain male and female priestly societies in ancient Egypt and Mesopotamia, in some of the mystery cults of Hellenistic and Roman times, in the Vestal virgins of Rome, in the Qumran group in Judaism, and in Buddhism.[1] These groups live totally or at intervals in community and have a manner of life distinguished from others by obvious external signs. The parallelism should not be pressed too closely; Roman Catholic religious communities have drawn no evident traits from these other groups. The Protestant churches abandoned religious life in community at the Reformation; in quite recent times religious communities have arisen which are deliberately formed after the model of Roman Catholic communities.[2] All such groups in all religions have in common that they are professional religious persons; religion is their occupation.

The tradition of religious life in Roman Catholicism is venerable. Its origins are usually found in "the fathers of the desert" in Roman Egypt.[3] These were men who literally withdrew from the world to live in solitude. In Egypt, the lonely desert is very close to the thickly populated valley of the Nile. The flight from the world was religiously motivated; it was an effort to achieve a closer communion with God by abandoning human society and human comforts, even the meager comforts of the impoverished Egyptian peasant. The solitary lived alone on a subsistence diet, depended on begging, and occupied himself entirely with religious contemplation. The name *anchorite* given to these men has interesting sociological implications. In late Roman Egypt, it was not uncommon that peasants, impatient with oppressive bureaucracy and grinding poverty, simply walked off their jobs in the field. The need of their produce usually brought the bureaucrats to grant their modest demands without delay. This strike was a withdrawal (Greek *anachoresis*), and the name given to the striker was *anachoretes*, "withdrawer," the Greek word from which the English *anchorite* is derived.[4] The name suggests either that the withdrawal of "the fathers of the desert" had mixed motives or more probably that no distinction was made between them and the striking peasants.

Even before the conversion of Constantine, the number of anchorites had increased to a point where many solitaries living in close proximity to each other elected one of their members as their "father" (*abbas*, "abbot," a word derived from Aramaic). The need, we may be sure, arose from the fact that the humanity of the solitaries sometimes broke through their Christian renunciation. In the fourth century, similar communities arose in other desert areas, notably in Syria near Antioch and in Palestine in "the desert of Judah," the arid declivity which falls from the plateau of Judah to the valley of the Jordan and the Dead Sea. When the peace of Constantine came to the church, many Christians desired to live out their life in contemplation near the holy places. Jerome, with the contributions of some wealthy Roman friends, founded a monastery for men and a monastery for women near Bethlehem. The members of communities were no longer anchorites but monks (Greek *monachos*, "solitary"); and for their support some simple employment was included in the life, such as the traditional weaving of baskets. The work was supposed to be of such a type that it would permit contemplation to continue uninterrupted.

The traditions of early monasticism indicate that the monks were a rugged unruly group, and the need for rules was seen quickly. The most important monastic rule in the Eastern church is associated with the name of St. Basil.[5] The rule of St. Augustine in the West was not really a monastic rule but rather a domestic discipline for priests living in community with their bishop. With or without rules, the monks of the East appear throughout the centuries from Constantine to the Moslem conquest as a turbulent group, deeply involved in ecclesiastical and civil disputes, and often vigorous supporters of heresy. Whatever the original monastic dedication may have meant, it does not seem to have endured in much of Eastern monasticism. Even before the schism with the Greek churches, Eastern monasticism had no enduring influence in the Roman

Church. Western monasticism became and remained Benedictine, so named after St. Benedict of Nursia in Italy, who founded his communities in the fifth century.

The Rule of St. Benedict is one of the works of genius which have arisen in the Roman Catholic Church.[6] Its vitality and flexibility can be judged from the fact that Benedictine monachism endures in the modern Roman Church in a vigorous condition. It is very difficult to assess the importance of monachism in preserving Roman Catholicism through the Dark Ages which followed the collapse of Rome; it may have been more important than any other single factor. This does not imply that monachism had no unfavorable aspects—a few of these must be mentioned—nor does it imply that monachism endured for all these centuries with no ups and downs and no reforms; Philip Hughes has shown that the decay of monasticism in England was one of the important causes of the internal decay of the English Church before the revolt of Henry VIII.[7] The overall positive strength of monachism, however, has made it proof against the corruption which destroys.

The power of the Benedictine Rule lies in its simplicity. It achieves order in the community without a deadly regulation in details. The Benedictine government is loose and paternal, and the Benedictine spirit of community is fraternal. The abbot is elected for life, just as the father of a family does not serve for a term of office. His government is more the work of his personal charisma than it is the execution of a master plan. Benedictine monks can be rather vain about the variety of spirit which can be found in different monasteries, all accepting the same rule. In theory and fairly well in practice, in spite of the centralized administration of modern Romanism, each Benedictine monastery is an independent religious community.

The Rule of St. Benedict leaves no room for the solitary. The life is lived in common, including common meals and dormitories; in modern times the dormitory has been abandoned for individual rooms. The monks take recreation in common daily. In fact, the ancient Benedictine tradition left the monk little privacy, and the type of intellectual work in which many modern Benedictines engage has forced some revision of this tradition. The Rule of St. Benedict is wise and articulate on the problems created by a large number of men living in such close association and presents an ideal of fraternal life in community which has often been achieved.

The Benedictine motto from the beginning has been *Ora et labora*,

"Pray and work"; and some observers have said that it is the addition of the second imperative which protected Benedictine monachism from the failures of Eastern monachism. What is called the Divine Office in Roman Catholicism is a set form of prayer employing the book of Psalms, hymns, formal prayers, and readings from the Bible and the writings of the Fathers of the Church. This Office, properly and solemnly performed, is mostly chanted, and its performance demands several hours of each day. The hours of the Divine Office are distributed throughout the monastic day; the prayer traditionally began before dawn, was continued at early morning, noon, mid-afternoon, and evening. The monastic day began before dawn and ended at sunset. This solemn common prayer was the community monastic prayer, and private personal prayer was not introduced until quite recent times. The performance of the Divine Office became one of the legacies of monachism to the Roman clergy, all of whom have been obliged to its recitation for hundreds of years. Except in some of the older European cathedrals, however, the Office is not performed in choir; each priest recites it privately. In the economy of the Roman priesthood, it is fortunate that private recitation takes much less time than choral recitation, but monastic tradition supposed that prayer should be conducted in a spacious and leisurely manner.

The work of the early Benedictines was manual. Each monastery, especially in the years of the barbarian invasions, had to be self-sufficient. Benedictine monasteries traditionally were located in remote places, no doubt from a desire to flee the world but also from motives of security. The monastery had its own farms and its own domestic operations, and each monk was assigned a task. Historians have often pointed out that the monasteries became islands of peace and security in the disorders of the Dark Ages, and that villages and towns sprung up around them. The abbot sometimes governed a secular community as the prince-bishop did. The industry of the monks created a problem which St. Benedict himself did not foresee; the monasteries became great landlords and quite wealthy. It was rarely, however, that the monastery did not dispense its wealth generously to its neighbors.

Thus the flight from the world ended in another involvement with the world, but an involvement which was authentically Christian. If this presentation seems sympathetic, it does no more than reflect the judgment of historians, whether Roman Catholic or not.[8] It was an accident of history that the monasteries assumed the role of conservers of literary tradition. The occupation of scribe was accepted early as a legitimate monastic task. Practically all the surviving literature of the ancient world is preserved in copies made in monasteries. Thus the monasteries served as schools in centuries when there were no other schools. The monastic scribes left no legacy of creative thinking, but they preserved the materials for the revival of learning in the Middle Ages.

The monasteries produced bishops and popes, and this was not the least important element in the influence of monasticism. From the sixth to the thirteenth century, the Roman Church suffered from serious weaknesses in its clergy, and monks were often the only available candidates for church offices. This also was a danger to the monastic life which St. Benedict did not foresee, and later monastic writers included warnings against ambition in their writings for monks.[9] Every reform movement in the Roman Church during these centuries originated in monasteries or was carried on mainly with the support of the monasteries. The legacies of the monasteries to the clergy have been mentioned; some monastic reformers concluded too easily that the way to reform the clergy was to monasticize it. Thus clerical celibacy and monastic obedience were introduced into the life of the clergy.

In the thirteenth century, a revolution occurred in Roman Catholic religious life. The contributions of monasticism to the church were restricted by the rule of cloister or enclosure, which limited the conversation of monks with *externs* and prohibited the entrance of externs into the monastery. The orders of friars, such as the Franciscans, the Dominicans, the Servites, the Carmelites, and the Augustinians, were instituted to combine monastic practices with freedom of movement. When the friar was in the friary, he lived in an institution that was organized and regulated like a monastery, including common life, enclosure, and the choral chanting of the Divine Office. The friar, however, was permitted and encouraged to make excursions from the friary to engage in the ministry. The proper name of the Dominicans, the Friars Preachers, indicates the purpose for which the order was instituted. Other orders of friars also engaged in preaching with a less formal dedication to the work, and during the Middle Ages almost all preaching in the Roman Church was done by the friars. They are associated with the practice of the parish mission, which is a sustained campaign of daily preaching for a prolonged period, ideally a month but sometimes less, and a program of search and restoration of Catholics who have lapsed in their morality or the practice of their religion. The rise of the friars coincided with the rise of the medieval universities, and the names of friars are numerous in the list of great medieval scholars. The list includes the Franciscans Alexander of Hales, Bonaventure, Roger Bacon, and John Duns Scotus, and the Dominicans Albert the Great and Thomas Aquinas. The monks could not engage in these works, and the success of the friars indicates the low esteem in which the secular clergy was held and their lack of influence. Like the monks, the friars also produced bishops and popes in large numbers.

The sixteenth century saw another revolution in the religious life, contemporary with the Protestant revolt but not a direct response to it. The friars were still limited in their mobility by the monastic character of the friary. They were not restricted to a diocese, as the secular clergy were, nor to the monastery, but the chanting of the Office and traditional restrictions in association with externs consumed time and kept them from realizing the full opportunities of the ministry. Hence a new form of religious community arose called *clerks regular*; the largest and best known example of this type is the Society of Jesus, popularly known as the Jesuits. The clerks regular abandoned the monastic type of residence entirely, and originally made no attempt to maintain residences at all. Each member theoretically could be an independent worker, detached from any direct contact with his religious superior. The choral recitation of the Divine Office was not imposed, and the rule of enclosure was much relaxed. No distinctive clothing (the religious habit) was worn, as it had been by monks and friars. The clerks regular lived like secular clergy, distinguished by the peculiar religious obligations of poverty, chastity, and obedience, which will be discussed below. To many officers of the sixteenth century church, such communities seemed to be an abandonment of the religious life altogether, and there was considerable opposition to the foundations of clerks regular, but the new form of the religious life proved so well adapted to the needs of the Roman Church that all communities founded since have either been clerks regular or imitated their style.

One feature of religious life that has existed from the establishment of the first Benedictine monasteries is what is called *clerical exemption*. Monastic and preaching orders were not subject to the bishop of their place of residence, and by reason of their origins needed no authorization of the bishop to engage in the ministry.

The papacy extended its patronage to the religious orders, which were factors of renewal and reform. This religious privilege was and is still jealously guarded, although religious orders no longer have the freedom of earlier years. In a certain sense, they were and are regarded by many bishops as irregulars, even though one of their canonical designations is *regulars*. Ignatius Loyola seems to have been the first to think of religious exemptions in terms that were in one way wider, in another way narrower. Living as he did in the age of geographical discovery and the age of the Reformation, he made his own order available for the needs of the universal church as defined by the Pope and offered his community to the Pope for assignment. The Popes have been and are grateful for this resource, and all orders now have similar commitments without the specific stipulation which Ignatius Loyola wrote into his rule. Heads of larger religious orders reside in Rome and belong to the entourage of the Vatican, although they are not members of the Vatican staff. The Pope thus has at his disposal a large number of men, many of whom are highly trained specialists, from whom he can draw for service in any part of the world. Any entirely new undertaking is usually committed to religious orders, at least in its beginning; for example, the foreign missions in which the Roman Church has engaged since the sixteenth century were all begun and in many regions are still carried on by religious orders.

Religious orders of women have a briefer history, but even in the early centuries women withdrew from life in the world and remained virgins. Sometimes this meant that they remained in the house of their father. Communities of women, like communities of men, appear in the fourth century. Until the seventeenth century, communities of women were strictly contemplative; that is, they engaged in prayer and domestic work. Unlike the monks and friars, they did nothing which would support them. In fact, the friars originally were mendicant friars, that is, beggars; it was a sacred principle that they refused any fee for their services and depended on gifts which they begged. In practice, the work in which the friars engaged made it necessary for the begging to be committed to specialized officers. Religious women, on the other hand, were rigorously cloistered, neither receiving visitors nor going abroad and conversing with the rare visitors admitted through a grill; a community of women could not exist except on founded revenues. As readers of Chaucer know, they could go on pilgrimages; and the same genial writer reveals that cloister did not keep religious women from all contact with the world.[10] Up to the Reformation the number of religious women was notably smaller than the number of religious men. Like the monks, the nuns chanted the Divine Office in choir. Occasionally the exceptional woman like Catherine of Siena exerted an influence as great as the influence of any man in the church, but generally the religious woman of the Middle Ages, like her sister in the world, was a depressed member of society.[11] The government of the communities of women was really in the hands of the clergy.

A revolution in the life of religious women was initiated by Vincent de Paul, a priest of seventeenth-century France. Vincent became concerned with the poverty and ignorance of the peasants and took practical measures to do something about it. One measure was the enlisting of unmarried young women to nurse the sick and to teach small children. Because of the prevailing conviction that religious women must be cloistered contemplatives, Vincent refused to organize his groups of women as religious and insisted that they were laywomen united in a voluntary association.[12] They did not wear a distinctive habit and went to any place where their work took them. He gave them the name of Daughters of Charity. The Sisters of Charity are the model after which several hundred communities of women have been organized since the seventeenth century. Since the time of Vincent de Paul, Rome has recognized such groups as genuine religious; this has given them full standing in the Roman Church, but it has impeded some of the original freedom of the Daughters of Charity.

Modern Roman Catholic religious communities combine a diversity of origins, but since they are now regulated by canon law, they have come to resemble each other more than they did in their foundations. From earliest times there has been within the Catholic Church a movement toward the total dedication of individual persons to religion; this is not peculiar to Roman Catholicism, as we have seen, but the Roman idea of this dedication has its own character. The religious profession in Romanism is made by pronouncing vows, which canon lawyers define as the promise of something which is possible and better than its opposite. Religious vows are distinguished as solemn (pronounced in groups which are called *orders*) and simple (pronounced in groups which are called *congregations*). Theologians have difficulty distinguishing between the two types of vow. Theoretically a solemn vow should admit no dispensation, but in practice it does. It is considered a dedication which approaches in permanence marriage or the reception of priestly orders. Simple vows may be taken for a period of years, and such temporary vows are a common practice in congregations. When they expire the person is by that fact no longer a member of the community and is free to leave. Final profession, whether simple or solemn, means that the vows are pronounced for life.

All religious communities pronounce the three vows of poverty, chastity, and obedience. The Benedictines by exception retain their ancient formula of poverty and stability, meaning that the monk vows to remain in the monastery in which he makes his profession. Stability is considered to include the other two vows. These vows are based on what are called in Romanism the three evangelical counsels, called *evangelical* because they are found in the Gospels and *counsels* because they are not of obligation on all Christians. The importance of poverty in the life and teaching of Jesus is immediately evident to any one who reads the Gospels; in fact, he may not so easily see how it can be treated as a counsel. The recommendation of chastity is found both in the Gospels and in Paul; it is clearly a counsel, and it is illustrated both in the life of Jesus and in the life of Paul.[13] Obedience to a religious superior is not found in the New Testament in any terms, and the vow has traditionally been explained as a means of fulfilling the New Testament teaching on humility and self-abasement.[14] It will be observed that these vows are directed to the votant rather than to the church, and the original religious foundations existed for the spiritual good of the members rather than for any service to the church or to one's fellow man. The life of the evangelical counsels is supposed to imitate more closely than the secular life the manner of living which Jesus himself followed.

In fact the imitation of Jesus is a very subtle and elusive thing, and religious orders have had their problems. The vow of poverty makes it impossible for the religious to own property, if it is a solemn vow, and unlawful for the religious to use property without permission of the superior whether the vow be solemn or simple. For those with simple vows, this is understood even of property of which they retain or acquire ownership. But throughout their history most communities have rarely lived in real poverty; the communities are able to support their members in what may be called frugal comfort. The accumulation of corporate wealth has sometimes become embarrassing, and most European countries since the eighteenth century have occasionally relieved the communities of their goods. In practice poverty means permission to use things, but this cannot be extended to the point where the religious must consume too much time in simple requests for permission. Most communities have accepted the custom of the *peculium*, which allows the individual religious to accumulate sums which come to him personally and spend the savings as he desires; it may be spent on such things as the purchase of books or a vacation, which the community does not always provide. All communities have the rule of common life stated in canon law; this means that housing, food, clothing, and the necessities of life are to be provided by the community and not by the individual religious. The rule is an effort, not always successful, to preserve at least a semblance of equality among the religious. Poverty also means a constant war against what religious call "creature comforts," an ambiguous term which has never been defined. In modern times, this has sometimes approached the ridiculous. Communities were slow to adopt such things as inside plumbing, gas and electricity, the telephone, carriages and then automobiles, typewriters and even office chairs. All of these things are eventually adopted and rationalized; but the rationalization is painful. The traditional attitude is that anything which is more comfortable or easier than its opposite is very probably a little bit sinful. The poverty of religious communities is often a bizarre combination of niggardliness in some areas and extravagance in others. One community in recent times constructed a new building to house religious at a cost which averaged $16,000 per person, not a modest figure for any type of housing. Yet the building is not luxurious, nor has it been filled to capacity since its erection.

By the vow of chastity the religious renounces not only the use of sex, which Christian morality forbids to all celibates, but also marriage. The ancient rules of cloister were principally intended to protect this commitment by limiting the conversations of religious with the opposite sex to the bare minimum of necessity. When communities engage in some form of work or ministry, this minimum must be enlarged. There is nothing in rumors, ancient and modern, to the effect that religious communities are massively unfaithful to this vow. Even when conditions were at their worst, the scandal was rare. Nor is there anything to the more modern rumor that religious become unbalanced because of their enforced celibacy. It is doubtful that the number of religious who need psychiatric assistance is notably larger in proportion than the numbers of seculars. With this premised, it must be said that enforced life in communities composed entirely of one sex does create problems, even if they do not reach the proportions of mass psychoneurosis. Even more than the clergy, religious are excluded from the normal world in which men and women live and work together. They are often ill at ease or unduly familiar. Religious men prefer to work with men, and religious women prefer to work with women. This preference is not peculiar to religious, but it is more obvious and emphatic in them. Most communities have in their background a rule which discourages or forbids work with members of the opposite sex. In the modern world these rules have fallen into abeyance, but the tradition from which they arose is still living. The wearing of religious garb sets the religious apart in a way which almost makes of them a third sex, and it affects the religious themselves as well as those who see them. In those few countries where the wearing of religious habits has been effectively prohibited by law, it is observed that religious are much more at ease in their dealings with seculars.

It was noted in the chapter on the clergy that the control of the bishop over his priests is nearly absolute. In communities of religious, the obedience is absolute in theory as well as in practice. No religious rule omits the admonition that the commands of the superior are not open to review by the subject. Thought about the commands is explicitly discouraged, and the term *blind obedience* is a commonplace in the literature of religious communities. The same literature contains anecdotes in which docile obedience to a command is praised as the supreme ideal, such as the monk who walked into a lake at the command of his superior but by a miracle did not sink, and the monk who was commanded to capture a lioness with his bare hands and bring it to his superior.[15] One who is not within the religious life and tradition can easily misunderstand such anecdotes. In no religious community is the irrational use of authority praised and admired, but it must be said that irrational obedience frequently *is*. The model of religious obedience is the obedience which Jesus paid to his father. Here if anywhere the imitation of Jesus becomes subtle and elusive. Religious communities depend altogether too much on the quality of the persons who become superiors. The structure has no channels for the resources which the community has in its subjects. The peculiar strength of religious communities lies in their ability to mobilize and direct mediocre talent within an organized structure which assures that the talent will be fully realized and will thus accomplish more than it would if it were self-directed. This peculiar strength has its corresponding weakness, which is that better than mediocre talent achieves less than it would if it were self-directed. John Henry Newman after his submission to Rome considered entering a religious community.[16] He gave up the idea because he felt that the community he had in mind was so rigorously organized that he could not be sure of freedom to do the work to which he felt called. No one, including members of this community, now thinks that his decision was wrong, yet a community which cannot make room for men of the caliber of John Henry Newman suffers from some weakness.

It must be said that religious obedience in practice is not as horrible as it might appear in the documents or in some lurid anecdotes. In the Middle Ages, recalcitrant monks and friars may have been incarcerated, but this practice has long disappeared. In 1318 some rebellious Franciscans were condemned and executed as heretics; disobedience was construed as heresy.[17] Other types of pressure are now employed. A venerable witticism found in most communities describes religious government as despotism tempered by rebellion. Most religious superiors really fear the absolute power which is committed to them and may sin from failure to use their power more than from abusing it. Religious communities draw their members from the world in which they live, and the quality of religious obedience in modern times is certainly more relaxed than it was when absolute authority was normal in civil as well as in religious society. The most important factor in determining the quality of obedience, however, is the discovery and appointment of men and women who are able to bear responsibility. No community has yet found a way to make sure that this will happen. In older orders, the *chapter* of professed religious shared the authority of the abbot or superior, and his decisions were reached after discussion by the chapter. The chapter also elected the abbot or superior. More recent communities have imitated the absolutely centralized government instituted by Ignatius Loyola in the Society of Jesus, with no chapter and no election of any superior except the supreme officer and his council, and it should be added that the franchise in this election is held by a very small number. Centralization has also affected the older orders with their chapters, which are probably less democratic now than they were originally.

Very few of the original monks were priests. Most of them were *lay brothers*. Clergy, whether religious or secular, are distinguished from laity, whether religious or secular; religious, whether clergy or laity, are distinguished from seculars, whether clergy or laity.[18] The number of priest-monks gradually increased, and the orders of friars and clerks regular had an even larger number of priests. Thus the religious orders reflected the social levels of medieval and early modern Europe. The lay brothers were domestics, drawn from the lower social classes. A member of the nobility or gentry who became a lay brother became a saint almost by that single action. This did not mean that members of the lower classes could not become priests, religious or secular. The Roman Church in the days of monarchy and nobility was the only organization in which a gifted young man from the lower classes could acquire an education and enter a career leading to a bishopric. But the lower classes generally were illiterate, and few of them could aspire to be religious priests. A similar distinction between *choir sisters* and *lay sisters* existed in communities of women. In the early modern period there arose communities of men who did not wish to take holy orders but who did wish to make the religious profession and engage in religious work. These formed the communities of brothers, usually teaching brothers. These groups were not and did not wish to be identified with the domestics of the clerical orders, and they were not in sympathy with the rule found in some older orders which prohibited the lay brother from acquiring any more learning than he possessed when he entered, and in fact nearly prohibited him from reading anything.

Catholics as well as others are sometimes bewildered at the number and variety of religious communities, and they ask why there are so many which seem to be so much alike doing the same things. It is a fairly crude rule of thumb to say that religious orders were founded to engage in some work which an earlier community was founded to do but had ceased to do; some, like the friars and clerks regular, were founded to do something in a different way. Others arose to do something in a region where no one was doing it and became international simply by their success. A large number of communities, both of brothers and of sisters, was formed to educate the children of the poor. It is not widely known that the interest and activity of the Roman Church in this area is much earlier than modern systems of public education. It is true that the primary interest of the communities was in religious education, but this could hardly be done without some minimal instruction in reading and writing. No religious community of this type was ever founded which did not in its beginnings furnish instruction with no charge.

But the multiplication and diversity of religious communities have deeper roots than diversity of ministries and needs. It is difficult to explain to the extern how religious communities each feel that they have a peculiar spirit and a peculiar style which differentiates them from any other group. Not only do they feel this, but they can usually explain it if they are asked. They are quite jealous of their identity, and their preservation of some remarkable archaisms in costume and domestic customs has much to do with their sense of identity. The celebrated cornettes, the wide white-winged head-dress of the Sisters of Charity seen on the battlefield of Gettysburg after the combat, were dreadful nuisances in crowded streets and public conveyances and quite difficult for the wearers to maintain. But they gave a rare sense of identity, and others besides the Sisters of Charity felt a tinge of regret when the cornettes were abandoned for a more practical and entirely undistinguished headdress. The Dominican friar cuts a striking figure in his white tunic and black mantle, while the crude brown heavy serge of the Friars Minor suggests Francis of Assisi with no explanation needed. Other communities with less striking externals—the Society of Jesus is distinguished by no distinctive habit—depend more upon their traditions, on their achievements, on the great men and women who have been among their members. Religious communities themselves are convinced that each of them has its corporate personality, and one who does not see it is kindly forgiven as not being very perceptive.

The number of religious men and women in 1965 was listed as 330,107 men and 1,209,159 women in 201 communities of men and 1,116 communities of women.[19] Most of these are *active*, engaged in some work or ministry, rather than *contemplative*, cloistered and engaged in prayer and domestic employments. Without this pool, most operations of the Roman Catholic Church would be impossible. As was said, foreign missions since the sixteenth century have normally been committed to religious. Their engagement in Catholic education at all levels from elementary to university is so deep that the number of schools operated by seculars is insignificant. Many communities were founded to help the sick poor, and in modern times this has grown into the operation of hospitals. In foreign missions the gospel has usually been followed closely by medicine. Religious conduct other types of institution for the assistance of the sick and needy far too numerous for complete listing. They care for orphans and conduct schools for delinquent children. They have homes for the aged. There is no type of eleemosynary work and social assistance in which religious are not engaged, and in many types of work they were the pioneers, now imitated by government agencies. Most communities of men still carry on the original preaching mission of the friars. Religious feel that they are the agents through whom the church fulfills the gospel mandate of almsgiving. The support of their operations demands enormous sums, which they obtain, as the mendicant friars supported themselves, by begging from the laity.

Unfortunately it is impossible in the modern world for the religious to carry on these works free of charge, as they did originally. Civil government rather than ecclesiastical organizations is now the most important agent of these works which traditionally belonged to religious. Civil government meets needs which religious cannot meet, but it also takes funds which religious otherwise might get. In addition, there is the quality of modern services, which cannot be rendered by a corps which has nothing to offer except devotion. The training of the religious and the plants in which they work must meet the imposing standards set by government agencies. The problem of meeting these standards is a cause of serious concern to religious, who now wonder whether they can continue what they have been doing. The size of the operations has grown to the point where religious are more and more administrators who hire and direct workers and are less and less personally involved. They are not happy with this, and they are faced with the problem of salaries; in the past it was really the fact that religious are not salaried which made it possible to engage in the operations at all. Hence much of what is still called Catholic charities is not "charity" in the sense that the services are rendered free of charge; the best religious can hope for is to leave room for some cases of genuine need and charge those who can afford it enough to keep some charity in their operations. The situation is far from satisfactory.

Like most other elements of Roman Catholicism, religious life is passing through a crisis at the time of this writing. The obvious signs of the crisis are the same as the signs of the crisis in the priesthood: a diminution of religious vocations and a growth in the number of those who abandon the religious life. It is evident that this trend, unless it is arrested, leads to extinction. As yet not many seem to fear that the trend is definite and irreversible. They see it as one more feature of the contemporary restlessness in Romanism, but, as long as it continues, it compels religious orders to examine their identity and their function in the church. Such an examination cannot do harm, and without an examination of themselves religious communities may be deliberately choosing extinction. The religious life, however, is a sturdy, vigorous plant which has withstood many destructive forces; one should not rashly read its obsequies before its demise. The involvement of religious communities in the ministries of the Catholic Church makes their crisis vitally important for the welfare of the entire church.

All religious communities have at regular or irregular intervals assemblies of delegates from the entire community. Assemblies of large communities are held in Rome and are international in character. Since the conclusion of the Second Vatican Council, the communities have held such assemblies with the express purpose of profound self-study and substantial revisions of their rules, customs, and works, should the study reveal that this must be done. The results have been mixed and furnish a base neither for incautious optimism nor for unrelieved pessimism. Many communities have discovered an irreformable core of conservatism in their older members and most of their officers. They have also discovered a deep dissatisfaction in many of their younger members. In some instances, they have learned how archaic their manner of life and their methods of operation are and have often found that both their leadership and their membership are timid when confronted with the necessity of change. On the positive side, most of them have recognized their situation with candor and hope. Some have been honest enough to ask whether their continued existence is really justified by the needs of the church.

The crisis touches almost every area of religious life, and in particular just those areas that distinguish it from secular life. First of all, there are questions about the very idea of *religious perfection*, of the religious life as a kind of superperfect Christian life. New theological thinking on the Christian vocation and the lay state moves Roman Catholics to ask whether the Christian vocation is not itself a call to perfect Christianity that leaves no room for elite groups. The Roman Church has always tried to state its understanding of the religious life with care, but it has been difficult to state it without implying some denigration of the secular Christian. The problem of defining the place of religious in the church has not yet been solved.

Many religious think that their "poverty" is artificial and unreal. They prefer not only to live as the poor do but to return to their original idea of furnishing their services without charge. They are aware that this would simply wreck most of the work done by religious communities. They believe the worker for the church should provide for his modest needs without any arbitrary standards, often determined simply by customs which come from the past.

The state of celibacy seems so central to the religious life that it has not come under discussion; no one has yet proposed a way in which married couples could live in religious communities. It does not seem to be actually impossible, and there is no reason to think that this may not be the next revolution in the religious life. There is discussion, however, as was noticed in the chapter on the priesthood, on the religious value of celibacy, not so much as an evangelical counsel, but as a component of a life of professional service of the Roman Church.

Dissatisfaction with obedience is so traditional in religious communities that it would seem impossible for a new discussion of the problem to arise. Yet there is a new dimension of discussion, and it deals with what must be called the democratization of religious obedience. As we have seen, the traditional concept of absolute authority is foreign to men and women reared and educated in Western countries; it is strange both to religious and to seculars. Adaptation has occurred here simply by cultural pressure, but what many religious want is a rewriting of the entire idea of obedience in a religious community. They question whether it is an act of virtue simply to submit to the decision of another—in theological language, whether obedience is automatically better than its opposite.

The works of religious communities are no longer done by religious without examination. As will be seen, the entire idea of Roman Catholic education is now submitted to criticism. Education and other works which demand a huge outlay of funds and a large staff composed mostly of seculars are not, for many religious, sufficiently distinguished from the same works conducted under government or other private auspices. They are especially dissatisfied when, for lack of funds or for other reasons, religious communities are unable to conduct these works with the competence and quality achieved by other organizations. They sometimes feel that they are working with things more than with people and that they are dedicated to an impersonal operation rather than to their fellow men. Often they find that their works suffer from a lack of daring and imagination, just the traits exhibited by almost all founders.

Their communities suffer from that conservatism which may be defined as the protection of the investment. The crisis of ministry is perhaps the most serious crisis, for religious, whether as communities or as individuals, have not produced any practical substitutes for the traditional works. It is clear that very few young persons are attracted to a vocation which seems to consist in minding the store. They observe that that since the works of religious communities involve more seculars than religious, religious dedication seems to add little or nothing to the works. They could do as seculars what they do as religious and have more freedom of decision and mobility.

Most religious who intend to remain in their chosen vocation have resigned themselves to the prospect of a much smaller number of religious in a much smaller number of communities. Many allege that the communities have admitted too many unfit and will emerge stronger if their numbers are diminished. It is doubtful that the explanation is that simple; and a community which does not ask itself whether it is unfit for the members has not really faced the crisis of religious life. Whether the religious life will survive if the number of religious is sharply diminished is a serious question which cannot be answered. This way of life, however, has withstood many destructive forces. Historically it has always shown just what it seems to need now, a flexible and resourceful vitality which can accept the movement of history. The crisis of religious life may be in this generation the real test of the vitality of Roman Catholicism.

## 9. *Ecumenical Councils*

The Roman Catholic Church has participated in twenty-one ecumenical councils in the course of its history. Popular interest in this type of ecclesiastical act has been stimulated by the twenty-first council, the Second Vatican Council, which met from 1962 to 1965 and was widely covered by both the secular and the religious press. The first ecumenical council met at Nicaea in 325 and the nineteenth at Trent in 1546–1563. Only the First (1869–1870) and the Second Vatican Councils hav been held in the four hundred years since the Council of Trent. The Roman Church has certainly seen less reason for councils or less usefulness in them in recent centuries. This may be associated with the developed centralization of Roman Church government that has already noticed.

Canon law (CIC 222–229), summarizing the customs and procedures of centuries, prescribes first that no one but the Pope can convoke an ecumenical council and that only he or his delegates can preside. This follows from what we have seen of the Roman Catholic understanding of the papacy. The right of attendance with the power to vote belongs to cardinals (even if they are not bishops), all bishops, whether residential or titular, and the supreme heads of religious communities of men. Others may be summoned as *periti* (Latin, "experts"), but they do not have the power to vote. The acts of the council have no definitive power until they are approved by the Pope.

This last reservation may startle the reader who goes on to read in the canons that the ecumenical council possesses supreme power in the universal church. Here we encounter again the problem of pontifical and episcopal power, discussed above. The question becomes acute in an ecumenical council, for only in such a council is the entire episcopacy assembled, and the collegial aspect of episcopal power emerges with clarity. In modern theology the answer is quite clear: the ecumenical council with the Pope possesses supreme power in the church. The question, however, has not always been so simple. In the fifteenth century, a theory called *conciliarism,* never very satisfactorily defined, arose in Europe.[1] In its extreme form, this theory maintained that an ecumenical council is supreme in the sense that it is superior to the Pope. The problem was sharpened by the Western schism, which at its worst saw three men, each with some good superficial reasons, claiming the papacy. It was perceived early in the schism that an ecumenical council would be needed to rid the Roman Church of this scandal, but it took thirty-seven years to convene the Council of Constance; there was a reluctance to take this step precisely because it might imply that an ecumenical council is a higher authority than the Pope. When the Council convened, it did not move to depose the competitors or even toward deciding their claims; it asked them all, with or without pressure, to resign, and only then was it possible to elect a new pope.[2] The papacy emerged from the schism with a tarnished reputation, and many felt that only a council could take effective action for the reform of the church and the papacy. This desire took form in the Council of Basel, which claimed to be the continuation of the Council of Constance.[3] Without a Pope, however, the Council of Basel was schismatic, and it disappeared after a few years. The conciliar theology, however, did not disappear; and the declaration of the First Vatican Council concerning the Roman primacy was couched in terms which expressly rejected conciliar theology.[4]

The ecumenical council derives its name from the Greek *oikoumenē*, the inhabited (earth). The name was given in Greek and Roman times to the lands of the Mediterranean basin, the only countries in which civilized man was presumed to live. Before the first ecumenical council at Nicaea in 325, regional assemblies of bishops had become a normal way of settling problems which extended beyond a single diocese. It is of more than passing interest that the idea of an assembly of the bishops of the *oikoumenē* came not from the church but from Constantine.[5] When Constantine made Christianity the official religion, its administration became a concern to the imperial government. Constantine was no more sympathetic to dissension in the church than he was to dissension in the provinces. When the Arian heresy seemed to be dividing the Christian community, Constantine decided that an assembly of all the bishops could and ought to find a formula of agreement. When the council met at Nicaea, Constantine saw that Pope Sylvester presided as his own representative, and other imperial officers were present. The solution was imposed by imperial as well as by ecclesiastical authority. The ecumenical councils of the following centuries were almost all called at the request of the emperor or with his support. The Fifth Ecumenical Council, the Second Council of Constantinople, suffered from the interference of Justinian to a degree which was scandalous.[6] In the Middle Ages, the same concern of the secular power for the church was expressed in ecumenical councils by the admission of imperial representatives. This influence was not always wholesome.

The separated Orthodox Churches do not accept any ecumenical councils that have met since the schism. They have a good argument; for as long as the Roman Church recognizes the separated churches as a part of "the body Catholic," a council at which they are not present does not reach ecumenical fullness. The Orthodox Churches were invited to the Council of Florence in 1439; they came, and this council set itself the task of reaching a formula of reunion. The effort failed, and no effort of the same magnitude has been made since.[7] The ecumenical councils of the Roman Church have been and remain councils to which only those who submit themselves to the Roman primacy are admitted with the right to vote. It is thus a council of the bishops and religious superiors of the Latin Church and those few Eastern churches which recognize the Roman primacy. Something is lacking in such a council, and serious efforts were made to admit Protestants as well as the separated Eastern Churches to the Second Vatican Council.[8] The efforts were unsuccessful, not only because of the weight of custom and tradition but also because the Roman Church simply has no structure for such a meeting.

The competence of the ecumenical council covers all the business of the Roman Church, doctrinal and disciplinary. Historically most of the councils have been convoked to meet a serious doctrinal problem, but most of the councils have dealt with discipline as well, and some have dealt almost entirely with discipline. One may contrast the Council of the Lateran, 1512–1517 with the Council of Trent, 1546–1563. About the conditions of the Roman Church from which the Reformation arose, the Lateran Council did practically nothing.[9] Once the event had happened and its consequences became apparent, the Council of Trent instituted a thorough and searching examination of both doctrine and discipline and thus created what is called *the post-Tridentine Church*. Yet the Council of Trent was one of the most poorly attended—and therefore least ecumenical in the proper sense—of all the ecumenical councils.

This statement to some extent answers the question what the Roman Church thinks an ecumenical council is and does. The council is certainly not a normal instrument of ecclesiastical government, and the Roman Church has never looked kindly on any theory that seems to hint that it ought to be. It is the exceptional means, almost the critical means, of achieving an end. Yet it is not true that it is simply a display, a kind of scenic staging to give pomp to pontifical decisions. The Roman Church sees in the pope a power to which an ecumenical council cannot add. In a way the Roman Church sometimes seems embarrassed by a double tradition, the tradition of papal supremacy and the tradition of conciliar supremacy. It is a matter of record that the advisers of John XXIII were surprised and dismayed when he proposed a council, and that no effort to dissuade him was omitted.[10] But John XXIII knew the real power of an ecumenical council, and it was really his personal insistence that brought the Second Vatican Council into being. One may attribute this insistence to his insight into a developing crisis which was recognized by very few others.

An ecumenical council mobilizes the resources in an unparalleled manner. The council is not merely the assembly of the bishops and the gathering of experts. The atmosphere of the council itself generates a new spirit of urgency and of action. In those councils whose history is fully written one can see that the councils went far beyond the agenda proposed by the Roman offices and attacked problems whose existence and importance were not recognized before the council convened. It is evident that the acts of a council have a solemnity not present in the acts of the Holy See. This is not said with reference to the canonical authority of pontifical acts, which needs no support from the assembly of the bishops, but to the impact which a council has on the Roman Catholic world.

It is for reasons such as these that a more or less permanent episcopal synod was recommended by the Second Vatican Council.[11] This synod, which has met once at the time of this writing, would not have the weight of an ecumenical council, but many hope that it will bring something of the perception of the issues and the breadth of view which are associated with ecumenical councils. Should this enterprise succeed, it will be one of the most notable achievements of the Second Vatican Council.

## 10. Church and State

It is impossible to understand Roman Catholicism without some reference to the historic relations between Romanism and civil societies, and it is regrettable that this book does not permit a full examination of such a complex topic.[1] These relations have done much to give Romanism the character which it exhibits, and the forces which have been at work are too numerous to be recited. No more than a sketch can be attempted here and a warning added to the reader that a more extensive study of this problem must be undertaken by any one who desires to know Roman Catholicism. Some areas in which the relations of church and state have affected the development of Roman Catholicism have already been alluded to.

The Christian community of the first three centuries had no relations with the Roman Empire. At times during these centuries, the Empire was officially hostile to the Christian community, but this was the exception rather than the rule. The Christian community formulated no position toward the Empire; and the Empire did not reach a firm legal position toward the Christians. Martin Dibelius once observed that only a few Roman officials and a few Christians perceived that Christianity and the Roman genius were in total opposition to each other and that one must destroy the other.[2] Failure to perceive this allowed the church and the Empire to live with each other in an uneasy peace, with occasional outbursts of persecution.

The conversion of Constantine meant that Christianity was soon to become the official religion of the Empire. It is estimated that when Constantine became a believer, Christianity had already become the faith of the majority in the Empire. The effects of this change were felt by both state and church. Constantine and his successors believed that public authority should exercise some supervision over religion; such supervision was traditional in Roman government, and no one thought that the practice should change when Christianity became the official religion. Furthermore, the emperors believed that Christianity should serve the purposes of public order. On its side, the church accepted this support and came to believe very shortly that the civil government should maintain church order. Put in these terms, which summarize an attitude and are not quotations from contemporary sources, the new relations seemed innocent enough. But what happened if the emperor were an Arian, or if Arian prelates gained his ears? Jerome's saying that the world groaned when it learned that it had become Arian was a theorical exaggeration, but it did express the fact that some emperors were patrons of Arianism.[3] What this meant was that prelates vied with each other to secure the favor of the emperor for their doctrinal side. Constantine and his successors had taught them that the emperor could convoke a council and that the council was likely to declare what it believed the emperor wanted to hear. Politics were invoked to support theological propositions, and politics could be invoked for heterodoxy as well as for orthodoxy. One may suppose that the Arian quarrels would not have dragged out so long had not the contending parties brought the emperor into the quarrels—or allowed him to intrude himself.[4]

The Donatist schism, which began in the reign of Constantine and ended only when the Vandals destroyed African Catholicism, was another instance of the admixture of politics and theology. The schism originated in a controversy that arose after the persecution of Diocletian. The Donatists insisted that any one who had lapsed under the pressure of persecution lost the efficacy both of baptism and ordination, if he were in orders. They would not accept a bishop who had been ordained by a lapsed prelate. Constantine, dedicated to good order, attempted without success to suppress the sect by force. In the time of Augustine, the Donatist schism still divided the African church, and Augustine finally arrived at the acceptance of the use of force by the civil power.[5] There is no doubt that the Donatists conducted a kind of guerrilla warfare against Catholics and that their use of force evoked the use of counterforce. Nevertheless, a principle was established which was to cost the Roman Church dearly.

The principle appeared at its worst in the Eastern churches, which exhibited the phenomenon known as *Caesaropapism*.[6] The Byzantine emperors exercised effective control of the Byzantine church; and it is difficult to assess the degree to which the Eastern schism was doctrinal and the degree to which it was political. It is clear that the Byzantine emperors could not tolerate a head of the church who was not under their control. Prelates, on the other hand, could tolerate a degree of political control because of the share of political power that it gave them. A church which is the church of an entire people is, as we have remarked above, a matter of concern to the government of that people. Because it is the church of a whole people, it can be an instrument of government policy.

The Roman Church was delivered from the Caesaropapism of the Byzantine style, but it did not remain entirely free. In the centuries between the collapse of the Roman Empire and Charlemagne, most of the barbarian tribes which invaded Europe became Roman Catholics. Many of these were mass conversions in the manner of Clovis and the Franks; the kings brought their peoples into Catholicism with them. Again a principle was being established, a principle based on absolute monarchy. The king incorporates the state, and therefore he incorporates the religion of the state. This is the principle of the establishment of religion, or of the union of church and state.

This principle, it seems, began in simple practice; the rationalization of the practice came much later. The Roman Empire had become Christian before its collapse, and it was only natural that the same idea should be preserved in the politics of the Dark Ages. The idea was sustained by Pepin and Charlemagne. The grant of the territory of the papal states made by Pepin was intended to give the pope freedom from political pressure, in particular from Constantinople, but also from any one else who should attempt to turn the papacy to political ends.[7] Charlemagne established a new Roman Empire, distinguished from the old empire by the title of "Holy," and thus created a political-ecclesiastical ideal which endured into modern times.[8] The ideal was "Christendom," a community which was ruled by a single political head, the emperor, and by a single spiritual head, the Roman Pontiff. The Empire was never as effective a political force after Charlemagne as it had been under this extraordinary man, but two important effects of the ideal continued to dominate the relations of Rome with the emerging nation-states of Europe.

The first effect was that the Papal States could not endure without the protection of at least one strong European government. The Pope was indeed a sovereign in the full sense, as much a political sovereign as the emperor or the kings of France and England. In fact, compared to the major continental powers, he was a petty Italian princeling. This meant that the Papacy was engaged in European politics with all its complications of wars and alliances. It is not strange that Europeans were not always able to distinguish between the pope as "spiritual" sovereign and the pope as a rival political power. It is somewhat strange that the popes themselves could not always make this distinction, as will be seen shortly. The efforts of the popes to obtain protection without being dominated can be seen in the history of the papacy from Charlemagne to the Reformation, and since the papacy was politically important, one observes that sovereigns attempted to capture it. The long struggles of the popes with the emperors and the kings of France were directed to maintain freedom from domination by any single power, a domination which would and did alienate other powers.

The second effect was that the popes attempted to combine political sovereignty with ecclesiastical sovereignty in an impossible manner. As supreme priests of Christendom, the popes claimed the power to depose rulers, or at least to excommunicate them, and in Christendom excommunication removed the guilty party from the Christian community. Had the popes not been themselves sovereigns, and had excommunication never been used as a political weapon, the picture of the papacy in Europe would have been different. As it was, the confusion of political with ecclesiastical authority had as a lasting result the loss of respect for ecclesiastical authority. When Protestant sovereigns revolted from their allegiance to the pope in the sixteenth century, they were the heirs of a long European tradition of rebellion against papal authority. In details this can be seen in the incredibly tangled politics of the Italian peninsula. Italy was one of the last modern states to take form, and the Italian revolutionaries judged correctly that the papacy was the major obstacle to their objective.

The attention given to quarrels in this extremely brief summary should not obscure the fact that the union of church and state worked more frequently than it failed. The European states were "the secular arm" of the Roman Church. The men of the Middle Ages did not realize that the idea of Christendom was not the same as the idea of the church. Ecclesiastical and civil authority cooperated to preserve ecclesiastical and civil order; the church supported the throne, and the throne supported the church. Hence the use of political means to further the ends of the church was normal and accepted. The popes could summon European kings to the Crusades, which were politically acceptable as well. Bishops could turn heretics over to the state to be burned, since heresy was a breach of civil as well as ecclesiastical order. On the other hand, kings could expect the popes and bishops to support their wars and to inflict ecclesiastical penalties on civil disorder. Normally the bishops ranked with the nobles, as the popes ranked with the kings, and the prelates were expected to support the landowning nobility.

It is a fact of history that the principle did not endure, and it is not within the scope of this work to analyze the change. What is important for our purpose is that the union of the state with an established church has dominated most Roman Catholic thought and action on the relations of church and state up into the twentieth century.[9] It should be noticed that, when the Protestant churches were formed, they took the principle of the established church with them. The modern separation of church and state is not only the product of Protestant theological thought. After the French Revolution, the established church in most of Europe became a charming anachronism rather than a reality, but as far as the Roman Church is concerned, it has been preserved as an ideal from which existing practice is a deviation, and indeed as an ideal which a kindly Providence might be hoped to restore. The intolerance that accompanied some Catholic pronouncements on the subject led Protestants to fear that the Church looked to a restoration of the medieval church in which dissenters were not tolerated, and the Roman practice in some countries seemed to support this fear.[10]

It was not until the Second Vatican Council that any official Roman document recognized the modern secular, religiously pluralistic state as a legitimate form of society.[11] Critics may judge that the recognition comes late, but in fact it did come; Roman documents have never been noted for hasty acceptance of change. The change is really a return toward the church of the first three centuries, which was in no way a political force. Many have asked whether it is possible for the modern Roman Church to be nonpolitical, and it seems hardly possible for it to return to its pre-Constantinian form. The change means that the Roman Church does not intend to be a political agent; if one may distinguish between force and agent, the distinction may be meaningful. The teachings of the Roman Church are bound to have effects on the political decisions which its members make, but that church intends to influence their decisions by no other means than its teaching. It will not, like the popes before 1870, be one of the sovereign states with its own political interests. It will not claim the right to depose sovereigns, a right which it has not attempted to exercise for some centuries. It will not lend its support to strictly political ends, nor will it ask political support for ecclesiastical ends. The Roman Church may have learned that it can be a powerful political force only by not engaging in politics.

The declaration of the Council has not yet become the factor which entirely determines the relations of the Roman Church to civil societies; one does not rid oneself of a thousand years of tradition by a single statement. It is not expected that the declaration will remove all causes of quarrel between church and state. There will always be doubts about the degree to which the church should influence the political decisions of its members; in such crises as war one can foresee many and grave problems. The traditional union of church and state has meant that the established Roman Church, as such, has taken no position on war; its international character does not allow it to take sides. Piux XII was criticized for not rejecting Nazism more explicitly. In individual nations, the Roman Church in war teaches the duty of patriotism; it is recognized that this may at times not be enough, but the Roman Church will certainly encounter the civil government in any country in which it teaches anything else. Similar problems can arise in internal questions. In some areas of the United States, the Roman Church has experienced dissent approaching rebellion for the liberal stand of certain bishops on racial problems. No one who has any idea of what a church is, however, will deny that war and racial problems are moral as well as political issues and that a church which remains silent on serious moral issues weakens its claim to be taken seriously.

It is in such sensitive areas that the declaration of the Second Vatican Council outlines a position which is really new. The Roman Church, the Council believed, can speak effectively only when it can speak as manifestly detached—that is, with nothing to gain. It may also have a great deal to lose; in most modern countries, the Roman Church depends on the good will, or at least the impersonal tolerance, of the civil government more than its members or the officers of the government realize. The Roman Church has renounced the effort to meet civil governments with the same type of weapons which the civil governments have at hand.

## 11. *The One True Church*

Even in the New Testament, the church appears conscious of its unity. As the gospel was spread through the Mediterranean world and the church began to include Gentiles as well as Jews, threats to unity were seen. Divergences arose which were rooted in ethnic and cultural differences, and points which were trivial were magnified out of all due importance. To anticipate for a moment, in the late second century, the Bishop of Rome was ready to deny communion to a number of older Eastern sees because they did not celebrate Easter at the same date as the Roman See.[1] Paul, who was perhaps more aware of the hidden threat of disunity, coined the expression "the body of Christ" to designate the unity of all true believers.[2] This primitive Christian unity was not structured. Communications between scattered churches seem to have been more frequent than might be expected, and a large number of early Christians in different places were acquainted with each other. But no more rigorous formula of unity is found than appears in Ephesians 4:4–6: "There is one body and one spirit, just as you were called to the one hope that belongs to your call, one Lord, one faith, one baptism, one God and Father of us all, who is above all and through all and in all." When unity needed explicit statement, it was achieved through consensus; so one may deduce from the narratives of Acts 15 and Galatians 2, which give an incomplete picture of the resolution of a major problem faced by the apostolic church.

With Ignàtius of Antioch (†107) a new idea of unity appears within the local church.[3] The focus of unity is the bishop, who preaches, administers the sacraments, and manages the church. Whether the individual Christian is a true member of the church or not is tested by his submission to his bishop. In this way the local church can determine easily who pertains to the unity of the church, and false members can be excluded. The bishop incorporates visibly the one body, one spirit, one hope, one Lord, one faith, one baptism, and one God. He becomes the supreme judge of the unity of the local church. Similarly, the unity of the whole church becomes the unity of the bishops. As we saw in dealing with ecumenical councils, the church in the earlier centuries reached decisions which affected more than one church by regional councils, and after the fourth century by ecumenical councils—although regional councils by no means ceased with the fourth century. The prevailing unity was collegial, in the sense in which it has been described above.

The idea of unity meant that the church was one and that there was only one church. A Christian or a church had to be in communion with other Christians and other churches. It lay with the bishop of the local church and with the assembly of bishops, whether regional or ecumenical, to determine whether the individual or the church was in true communion. If communion were denied, the offending member was simply sheared off; the true unity of the church was found only in the body from which the member was severed. This apparently overrefined distinction is of some importance. There always had to be a church and only one church. It was not conceivable that the church should break up into fragments. When division happened, that body which could most successfully assert its continuity with the church before division maintained itself as the one, holy, catholic, and apostolic church.

There were two threats to unity, heresy and schism. Heresy will be treated in more detail in the chapter on the teaching office of the church; for the moment it is enough to note that heresy was a denial of a belief which was held by the whole church. The purpose of the early ecumenical councils was to discover or to affirm solemnly what it was that the whole church believed. One who did not accept this affirmation severed himself from communion. Schism of itself has nothing to do with belief; it is a refusal to recognize authority in a legitimate officer of the church. Several early schisms, such as the schism of Antioch, arose over a dispute as to who was the legitimately elected bishop of a see.[4] Others, like the schism of the Orthodox Churches, arose because the Eastern bishops thought that the Roman Pontiff arrogated to himself powers which did not belong to him. In schism the identity of the church is really more imperiled than by heresy.

It has been shown that the primacy of Rome began in the fourth century to develop the form which it finally achieved. The Roman primacy then became the test of unity; the one, holy, catholic, and apostolic church adds the word Roman to these titles, for it is that church which recognizes the Bishop of Rome as the bishop of bishops. It is his teaching and his obedience which authenticate the one true church; the Roman is the church which endures, which remains the one true church through all divisions. In fact, history came to the aid of the Roman position. Just as Jewish Christianity was annihilated in the Jewish war of A.D. 70, so the power and influence of the Eastern churches were reduced to insignificance by the Moslem conquests of the lands of the eastern Mediterranean. That body remained the one true church which was best able to affirm its continuity with the undivided church. The Roman Church was the church of the rising nations of Europe, where the brain and the heart of Western civilization were coming to maturity. The one true church was identified with Christendom.

Actually the position was not as clear as it seems. The Roman Church, in spite of some harshness which it has exhibited in its past toward heretics and schismatics, has never renounced the evangelical precept of reconciliation. The Orthodox churches seceded as churches; it was not a secession of individual persons to be dealt with singly. The Roman Church has sought reconciliation with the churches as such. It recognizes that the Orthodox churches retain the sacramental powers and orthodox belief; it asks of them only the one thing which they find most difficult to yield, acknowledgment of the Roman primacy. It does not ask them to renounce the forms and customs which they have retained from their past. In fact Rome does not really assert the doctrine of the one true church toward the Orthodox churches. They are treated as churches within the one true church that are in rebellion.

In the doctrine of the one true church, there is an implicit appeal to the majority. This is reflected in the scoffing question of Optatus addressed to the Donatists, whether they think the one true church is confined to an obscure region of the province of Africa.[5] It is reflected in a quotation from Augustine which John Henry Newman said influenced him deeply when he was thinking about his submission to Rome: "Securus judicat orbis terrarum," which we may roughly paraphrase, "The judgment of the whole world is delivered free from pressure."[6] Roman theology has cherished this implicit appeal while at the same time it has rejected the implication that Roman Catholicism would cease to be the one true church if it should become a minority of the Christian body. The one true church is and must remain the Church of Rome. When the Roman

Church was identical with Christendom, this was easy to maintain. It was with this structured unity that the Roman Church sailed onto the rocks of the Reformation.

Up to the sixteenth century it was difficult to distinguish the unity of the Roman Church from the unity of Europe. The unity of Europe was imperfect, and so was the unity of the Roman Church. In the course of a single generation both unities were shattered, and the structured unity of Christendom could no longer be maintained by the Roman Church. Even the implicit appeal to the majority was threatened. Was it merely an accident that the regions which remained Roman were almost entirely the' Latin and the Mediterranean countries, and that the Saxon and Scandinavian countries largely renounced their allegiance to Rome? The division followed very closely the ancient boundaries of the Roman Empire. Certainly differences in tradition and culture as well as rising nationalism were at work. The speed with which northern Europe ceased to be Roman leads one to ask how deeply Roman these regions had been.

The response of Rome to this division was not the same as its response to the secession of the Orthodox churches, nor did it regard the Protestant churches as schismatic areas within the one true church. Again we observe that the Orthodox churches lay within the ancient territory of the Roman Empire. Rome refused to recognize the new religious groups as churches, and designated them by such unflattering titles as "heretical conventicles." There could be only one true church, and that was the church headed by the bishop of Rome. There could be no reconciliation with the dissident churches, but only with dissident individuals. Rome would not deal with the officers of the Protestant churches as ecclesiastical persons. It dealt only with individual surrenders. This was not a novel policy, for the Roman Church had always dealt with heretical sects as nonexistent in the sense that the Roman Church could not negotiate with them, but never before had this principle been applied on such a massive scale.

The depth of the division has not always been appreciated by Catholics and Protestants. The Orthodox churches rebelled against the authority of the pope to govern them; the Protestant churches rebelled against the authority of the Roman Church to teach them. This is technically the difference between schism and heresy. Both are breaches of unity, but the Roman Church has always regarded schism as a more tolerable and more remediable breach than heresy. The response of the Roman Church to the Protestant revolt was, as we have said, that it did not recognize the Protestant groups as churches. Let us see more closely what this means. It meant in the first place that the Protestants were supposed to have no priesthood; therefore they could have no church government, no sacramental system, and no preaching. As will be seen, the Roman Church believes that baptism is effective independently of the faith or the moral quality of the officiant; this position was worked out in the Donatist controversies of the fourth century, for it was the Donatist thesis that the heretic and the sinner cannot baptize. But the Roman practice has not always agreed with the Roman teaching. Up to a few years ago—and possibly still in some dioceses—it was a common practice to administer conditional baptism to those who entered the Roman Church from a Protestant church. The practice expresses a doubt that the Protestant churches baptize, and this doubt, to express it in its full harshness, is a doubt that the Protestant churches are really Christian. It is a doubt that even the sincere but misguided Protestant can find grace in the Protestant churches—or rather that he can find grace through the Protestant churches. Many theologians have accepted the formula as stated in this second way. The Roman Church interprets the ancient practice of denial of communion as signifying the denial of the Eucharist; it neither gives the Eucharist to Protestants nor receives it from them, since it does not admit that Protestants are capable of celebrating or of receiving the Eucharist. Its laws prohibit marriage between Catholics and Protestants; the laws permit dispensation, but demand that the ceremony be witnessed by a Catholic priest. It is only within the last few years that the Roman Church has thought of abandoning its celebrated pledges that the children shall be baptized and reared in Roman Catholicism. Effectively the Protestant churches and individual Protestants have had a standing in Roman Catholicism not much above the standing of Moslems. Historically Protestants have recognized this, and their reactions have been predictable.

The post-Protestant version of the one true church has solidly identified Christian unity with Roman Catholic unity. The Roman Church has not altered her traditions and her practices in taking this position; it could hardly have taken any other position, but it was not compelled to take it so rigidly before the unprecedented challenge of Protestantism. This version of the one true church is now under examination in Romanism; at this writing it is too early to predict what will emerge, but it seems safe to predict that the rigorous position which endured from the Council of Trent to the Second Vatican Council will not be reaffirmed.

The most significant theological event here is the recognition of the Protestant churches as churches, expressed by the Second Vatican Council.[7] It is remarkable that the Council accepted the term with its implications for the Roman understanding of the one true church. In the Roman understanding, the plural of the word *church* has been no more admissible theologically than the plural of the word *god*. Implied in the declaration is at least the possibility of considering Christian unity as something not perfectly identified with Roman Catholic unity. At this date the Roman Church has no theology into which it can assimilate this development; but many of its theologians believe that such a theology can be constructed. They are well aware that the implications of such a theology (one seems to be dealing almost entirely with implications in this area) may affect deeply the Roman Catholic idea of the church and may lead to developments which cannot be foreseen and which may again lead to dissension.

The Second Vatican Council was the first formal step taken by the Roman Church toward ecumenism, the name given to the search for church unity in the Protestant churches. The movement generally dates back to 1910 and has had some success in healing Protestant disunity. The Roman Church has generally ignored the movement, since it knew no unity except the unity of Rome. Why has the Roman Church changed its stance? It has given no reason, but the theological currents in Romanism over several generations can be traced. One important current is the recognition—expressed by the Council—that the Reformation cannot be understood as a study in black and white; Rome must bear a share of the guilt for divided Christianity.[8] A second current can be called the awareness of the bankruptcy of the Roman position on the one true church. Whatever this position may sustain, it contributes nothing to the restoration of Christian unity. A third current is dissatisfaction with divided Christianity, a doubt whether a divided Christianity can proclaim the gospel, and a fear that anyone who accepts the division as inevitable, irremediable, and tolerable may fail in his duty to the church. A fourth is an awareness of the fact that it is simply false and unrealistic, not to say unkind, to deal with the Protestant churches as nonchurches and with Protestants as doubtful Christians at best.

Much contemporary literature and personal dialogues disclose that the old issues of division are now largely meaningless. The friendly discussion of theological differences with no polemical intention has shown that the doctrinal differences between Romanism and Protestantism generally—with reservations for the separate Protestant churches—are not as deep nor as irreconcilable as they were thought to be. The feeling in the present exchanges is that unity is within reach; it is retarded by fears that the concessions which unity will demand may be more than will be tolerated. Not often mentioned is the existence of a number of religious establishments which may have to face profound modification or even extinction if Christians attain unity. Roman Catholics may feel this fear more deeply than Protestants, but Protestants do feel it also. At this writing, Rome has already made a number of unexpected concessions, and some Roman Catholics feel that Protestants have not made equal concessions. It is true that Protestants do not always realize how much these concessions cost the Roman Church. As we have noticed, the concessions imply that a different idea of church unity may be possible and necessary.

One can hardly conceive an idea of church unity which would include real differences of belief about such things as the Trinity of persons and the sacramental nature of baptism. Hence conversations which are directed to the formulation of statements of belief acceptable to all involved must continue. Such statements must distinguish sharply between the objects of belief and theological interpretations of belief. Roman Catholicism has always tolerated such differences of opinion, although those who defended their opinions have not always been tolerant. The Roman Church affirms that it is its office to resolve ultimately whether such divergences affect the substance of belief or theological opinion. Where it is ascertained that differences between Catholics and Protestants are no deeper than the differences between Roman Catholics, it is clear that such differences do not disrupt the unity of faith. In some questions it now appears that different opinions about the same belief and not differences of belief are the issues of division.

Unity of structure and discipline does not impose itself with the same necessity, but disputes over structure and discipline can be more bitter than disputes over doctrine. The Protestant churches have acquired their own practices and customs over the centuries of division, and they are not willing simply to abandon them. The Roman Church historically has known more diversity in this area than most Catholics recognize, and the diversity can be seen both in development in time and in variety in different areas within the same period. But the Roman Church has usually stood for uniformity in structure and discipline rather than diversity; we have touched upon this problem in discussing the government of the Roman Church. At this moment in history, the Roman Church does not know how much diversity it can tolerate, and the lack of a definite position here is a further obstacle to ecumenical unity. If unity of faith could be assured, there is no reason in the constitution of the Roman Church why it could not accept in the Protestant churches the same diversity which it is ready to accept in the Orthodox churches. If the contemporary mind of the Roman Church can be discerned, there seems to be less insistence on uniformity than at any time since the Protestant Reformation.

# II. Worship

## 1. Religion and Cult

Historically, religion has included ritual cult practiced by a society. The possibility of a purely personal and internal religion with no ritual performance and no association with other persons cannot be denied; as will be seen, Roman Catholic traditions have always left room for the personal, internal element in religion. History offers a sufficient number of examples of philosophical faith, which strictly speaking is a substitute for religion; it is a way of thinking about the deity and the relations of man with the deity, but it does not issue in a social religious act. Roman Catholicism is a society which practices ritual cult, and it attaches great importance to the cult.

Cult is ritualistic, by which is meant that it follows prescribed routine; it is not left to improvisation. The general history of religions shows that there is a constant tendency toward rigorous uniformity in cult which grows as the religion grows older. What originally were spontaneous acts become the model which must be followed in all detail. There is a rational basis for this rigor, irrational as it may seem; its first element is that cult in many religions is believed to have been instituted by the deity directly or through an accredited mediator. The worshiping group is not free to tamper with the details of a rite which has such a sacred origin. Thus in Judaism the cultic institutions were attributed to Moses, and in Roman Catholicism the basic rites are attributed to the institution of Jesus Christ. The second element in the rational basis is the symbolic value of the rite; this demands a fuller exposition.

The basic symbol is the word, and cultic language employs words, but this is not the symbolism which is properly ritual. Cult is not merely the recitation of words but also the performance of actions, and the symbol of the action is not as self-evident as the symbol of the word. The action must be explained. The ritual action, by definition, achieves contact with the deity in some way, and only a symbolic action can achieve this. It is precisely through its symbolism that the action is effective, and therefore the symbolism must remain unaltered. The symbolism of the handshake as a greeting, for

124

example, is divergently explained and widely unknown by those who use it. The original symbolism has been lost because the original gesture has been modified into a merely vestigial trace. Ritual symbolism cannot permit such deviations. Thus even in the ritual of the Roman Mass, which has passed through a number of modifications in its history, the central action preserves the words and the gestures which are described in the New Testament. In Catholicism, as we shall see, the symbolic value of the act is explained in a way which is peculiar to Romanism.

Ritual cult is social, performed in a group for a group. Again, the general history of religions shows that the worshiping group commits the cultic act to one or several authorized members. This has already been mentioned in speaking of sacred personnel, and in later chapters the Roman institution of authorized cultic officers will be examined in more detail. Romanism also provides in its ritual directives that the group—that is, the whole church—be represented at any ritual cultic act. Thus at baptism and confirmation, the church is represented by the sponsors of the candidate. Church law provides that at least one person be present at the celebration of the Eucharist. Penance or auricular confession by its nature involves the penitent, but the modern discipline does not have quite the social symbolism of the earlier rite. For the anointing of the sick, witnesses are desirable but not demanded, and the fact that the recipient is seriously ill generally assures the presence of witnesses. The sacrament of orders is always conferred publicly, and the Roman Church requires two witnesses besides the priest for the sacrament of matrimony.

The presence of the church through representatives is more than window dressing for the spectacle of the liturgy. The church acts through her ritual, and the authorized representative does not represent well without the presence of those whom he represents. Up to recent times, the Roman liturgy has not left much room for active participation of the laity, but their presence has been recognized as giving the cultic act that social solemnity which it ought to have. The Roman Church has only recently recognized that for many of its members the cultic act had no perceptible social character. Roman Catholics worshiped in the same place at the same time, but not really together. Thus one aspect of ritual symbolism, the unity of the group symbolized by the shared cultic act, was often perceived only feebly.

## 2. *The Sacraments*

It is an article of Roman Catholic belief that there are seven and only seven sacraments: baptism, confirmation, Eucharist, penance (sacramental confession), extreme unction (the anointing of the sick), orders, and matrimony. It is further an article of Catholic belief that these rites were instituted by Jesus Christ. From the very beginnings of Protestantism, it was argued by Protestants that not all seven of these rites are found in the New Testament; and Roman Catholics must concede that not all seven are found as clearly as baptism and the Eucharist. It is not necessary here to go over the biblical-historical controversies concerning this question. The Roman Church ultimately appeals to its own traditions rather than to the bible to authenticate the full number of seven, and it affirms that its own history is a valid witness to the belief and practice of the apostolic church. This cardinal principle of Roman teaching will be discussed when the teaching office of the church is considered.

The sacraments are the major ritual actions of the Catholic Church, and the Roman idea of their symbolism has no real parallel in other religions. Roman Catholics have long been resentful that the sacramental rites are so often compared to magic by scholars; however subtle the difference may be, they are certain that there is a difference. The sacraments are effective symbols; and this is more precisely defined by saying that they effect what they signify and that they effect by signifying. Romans point out some analogies in the order of symbolism which, while they are not exactly the same as sacramental symbolism, are nevertheless effective signs which are not magical. Thus symbols are used in political life; there is for any important office a rite of inauguration (as for the President of the United States), and the officer is not considered to have real tenure of the office until this rite is performed. Behind the rite of inauguration is the election which determined the President; but until the inauguration he is called the President-elect, and he can perform no act of government before his inauguration. So behind the sacramental rites, Roman Catholics believe that there is the saving act of Jesus Christ, communicated to the individual Catholic through the performance of a symbolic ritual action. Catholics do not insist that the saving act is exclusively communicated through the ritual action, but that this is the way in which it is communicated through the church. This general theme, it is hoped, will emerge more clearly in the discussion of the separate sacraments.

Roman Catholic belief and theology include the effectiveness of the sacraments in the area of mystery, by which is meant that the action of God cannot be observed or analyzed. It can only be ascertained and that only by some declaration of God himself. Hence there is no single explanation of the effectiveness of the sacraments in Roman theology; a number of theoretical explanations have been proposed, no one of which is entirely convincing. The mysterious quality of the effectiveness is seen most clearly in the celebrated formula *ex opere operato*, which is kept in Latin because it defies translation. It can be paraphrased by saying that the sacraments are effective by the simple performance of the action; and it is this thesis which has so often been compared to magic. Actually the thesis has several reservations; Romans do not consider the sacraments effective for a person who is simply unwilling to receive them. The phrase has reference rather to the officer who performs the sacramental rite. It means that he acts not in his own person but simply as the agent of the church, for the ritual symbolic act is performed in a social group, and in the sacramental rites it is the group which acts through the individual officer. Hence it makes no difference to the rite whether the officer be of good moral character, or even whether he himself believes in the effectiveness of the rite which he performs; all that matters is that he be accredited, and only the church can determine what accreditation is. The condition stated in theology and in church law is that the officer have the intention of doing what the church intends, and this is generally understood to mean that he need intend only to perform the rite. If one seeks an analogy, one may refer again to the rite of inauguration, performed for the President of the United States by the Chief Justice of the Supreme Court. It has happened more than once that the Chief Justice has performed the rite for a man whom he detested and who he wished with all his heart were not President-elect. The rite is effective, nevertheless, because of the election which it symbolizes, even when, as in the hypothesis, it is performed by a minister who would be said theologically to lack faith.

The analogy is imperfect, as all analogies are in this area, for Roman Catholics believe that the acts of God can be perfectly assimilated to no human action. This belief, surely, is not peculiarly Roman. But they believe that the effective symbol as such is not beyond the bounds of intelligibility and that the sacramental symbol escapes comprehension only because of the reality which lies behind it. In a word, it is God who is mysterious, not the sacramental rite as such. The saving act of Jesus Christ is mysterious in its effectiveness under any aspect; it is mysterious in its application to the individual person, whether one think in terms of sacramental rites or in other terms.

It is difficult to speak of a *general* effect of the sacraments, for they are seven in number, each with its *specific* effect. The word *grace,* so long in use in Roman theology and official documents, seems to be yielding in recent writing to other terms. The term grace means little or nothing to most Catholics. The uninstructed often think of it as some kind of spiritual fluid which is transfused through the sacraments like blood or glucose; they will speak in quantitative terms of this fluid, although it can in no way be conceived as mensurable. Even the better instructed are sometimes embarrassed by inquiries concerning the Catholic belief in grace. The present generation of theologians prefers to return to the language of the New Testament and the fathers of the church, where grace is not an important theological term, and speak of life. They are employing an analogy, but an analogy which is easier to grasp. The New Testament speaks of the Christian life as a rebirth. The sacraments are the effective signs through which this new life and its powers are initiated and sustained. But just as life in the large sense is not a simple reality which can be signified by one symbolic rite, so the new life instituted by the saving act of Jesus Christ is symbolized and communicated by the traditional sevenfold sacramental signs.

If the sacraments are considered as the ritual conferring and renewal of the new life in Christ, then they may also be considered as the conferring of power specified for particular needs and occasions. The Christian is "incorporated" into Christ and receives the new life in Christ by his membership in the church; each of the sacraments brings the Christian more profoundly into the church by empowering him to act as a Christian, not merely in general, but in definite circumstances. Thus baptism is the sacrament of initiation into the Christian life. Confirmation is administered at the beginning of maturity. The Eucharist has manifold symbolism, but it is the effective sign of nutrition—that is, of growth and strength. Penance is the ritual forgiveness of sins. The anointing of the sick is the ritual preparation for death. Orders empowers the Christian to fulfill the priestly office. Matrimony empowers the couple to live a Christian married life. Thus there is a ritual sign of Christian life at each of the major critical moments in normal existence.

It will be observed that the enumeration of the situations in which the sacraments are conferred does not follow the order in which the seven sacraments are traditionaly enumerated, and indeed there is no explanation of why this order has prevailed. In Roman Catholic theology, a number of theoretical explanations of the interrelation of the sacraments has been proposed, but none has emerged as superior. In all theories, baptism is first and fundamental; it is the sacrament of rebirth and the necessary condition for the reception of any other sacrament. The late Maurice de la Taille proposed a rather complex theory in which the Eucharist is the central sacrament toward which all others are oriented either as dispositions or consequences of its reception.[1] Even in this carefully elaborated theory, there had to be some nimble theological gymnastics in order to present a relation between the Eucharist and matrimony. On the other hand, no Roman Catholic theologian would quarrel with the central position of the Eucharist in the Roman sacramental system, although no clear way of stating this central position has been found. The intention here is not to fatigue the reader with references to abstruse speculations about which he may know or care nothing, but simply to show that Catholicism makes serious efforts, successful or not, to explain the rites which all of its members witness and in which they participate.

The Roman Catholic Church is rather rigorous in its adherence to the traditional form, perhaps at times more rigorous than it need be; the basis of this rigor was discussed previously. Students of Roman Catholic teaching are sometimes surprised or amused to find that theologians write at length on the definition of "pure, natural water," the only acceptable fluid for baptism, or on the necessity of unleavened bread and the degree of alcoholic content that makes a liquid wine rather than grape juice, the essential qualities of olive oil, and how much one may diverge from the traditional formula of words without making the sacrament ineffective. Such discussions can sometimes make a dispute about the number of angels who can dance on a pinhead look rather serious. One must understand that those who take sacramental signs seriously refuse to tamper with them on the reasonable grounds that they have no right to tamper with them. On this basis, rigorism is

almost inevitable. There is a well-attested story of an entire ordination class in one diocese—most of its members are now deceased—
which was privately reordained because one of the officers appointed
to watch the bishop during the ceremonies thought he had observed a failure of the bishop to make one of the ritual gestures.
The very fact that the ordaining bishop has two men who stand
by him to do nothing except observe him shows the seriousness
with which the ceremony is taken. The integrity of the sign must
be preserved or it loses its effectiveness, and the Roman Church
assures integrity by not altering traditional ritual.

Adherence to the ritual, combined with the belief in the effectiveness of the sign itself, can lead to some bizarre popular beliefs.
The legend of St. Genesius, patron of actors, tells how the saint
was baptized on the stage in mockery, but suddenly declared himself
a Christian and suffered death for his faith. The legend certainly
implies an exaggerated belief in the efficacy of the rite which no
contemporary theologian would share. The Roman Church believes
that one who intends to baptize in jest baptizes in jest—that is, not
at all. In modern times, Genesius, had he lived to be admitted to
the Church, would have been baptized with no conditions attached.
The Church believes that it is a sin scarcely less than blasphemy to
employ the sacramental sign ineffectively. Should one do so without
knowing it, no guilt is incurred, but respect for the sacred sign demands that all reasonable pains be taken to see that it is not employed
in vain.

Hence the Roman Church takes troubles which other Christians
sometimes think fanatical not only to insure the valid administration of the sacraments, but also to insure their recording. In modern
practice, the church of one's baptism is the master file, so to speak.
Every subsequent reception of one of the *permanent* sacraments
(confirmation, orders, matrimony) is recorded in the church of
baptism, and it is to this church that inquiries are directed when a
Catholic wishes to receive holy orders or matrimony. In modern
practice, religious profession, which is not a sacrament but is an
impediment to marriage, is also recorded. If the record is missing,
or if different records are at variance, some trouble may be experienced before the matter is cleared. Church administration is ready
to go to some pains, including not only correspondence but also
personal investigation conducted by the clergy, to ascertain the
fact of baptism or nonbaptism; it will do this rather than repeat the
rite or assume that it has not been administered. This attitude is
not entirely consistent with the readiness to administer conditional

baptism to converts from Protestantism mentioned above; but the conditional baptism was not administered without the investigation. These are by-products, occasionally annoying to individuals, of the Roman respect for the sacredness of the sign and its belief in the efficacy of the sign if it has been ritually administered.

Thomas Aquinas explained the sacramental signs in terms of the Aristotelian theory of matter and form, the component principles of material reality.[2] In this theory, the material substance, such as the water of baptism, the oil of anointing, and the bread and wine of the Eucharist, are the *matter*. The material reality of itself has no sacramental significance; it receives its significance from the verbal utterance, which is the *form*. Both must be ritually correct if the sign is to be valid, and they must be joined by the utterance of the words while the matter is being handled or applied. In baptism, for instance, one can imagine a ritual in which after the water were applied to each candidate, the formula would be uttered for all the candidates at once. In modern Roman Catholic practice, this would simply be invalid. The theory has its uses in the practical administration of the sacraments, since it defines two areas in which a necessary component may be lacking. Even when one understands the words in their philosophical sense—with "matter" as the determined part and "form" as the determining part—such an explanation seems inadequate for an appreciation of penance or matrimony.

The concern for validity appears at its most exaggerated extent when it is applied to the ceremonies which accompany the administration of the sacraments. In any rite, the basic action is brief and can be accomplished within a few seconds, and it is only for this basic action that there can be a question of validity. Traditional ritual, however, encases the basic action in a set of ceremonies which are intended to visualize the solemnity of the action, and these ceremonies can be long and complex. In practice the ceremonies are performed with hardly less scruple than the basic sacramental action. There is, of course, a quite reasonable desire to perform ceremonies correctly if they are to be performed at all, since it is of the essence of ceremonial that it be correct; but there may be also a nearly superstitious fear of omitting even a small detail or deviating from the book.

Catholics believe in the proper performance of the ritual because they recognize that the sacramental ritual, performed correctly and with dignity, is one of the strongest features of the Roman Church. It is the visible symbol of the social nature of the church, even though this symbol is somewhat weakened in the practice of recent centuries. The ritual is intended to symbolize the presence and activity of God, and most Catholics find that it does. This can be called characteristic, in spite of numerous archaisms and unintelligible features which are now being removed from the ritual. No one has ever denied that the Roman ritual creates an atmosphere of reverence. The modern question is whether this is enough, but very few if any wish changes which would take away from the atmosphere of reverence. Roman Catholics have learned from their history that a careless and irreverent performance of ritual has always been accompanied by decay in other areas of Catholic life.

Liturgical renewal has been an active movement in Roman Catholicism since the early nineteenth century, but most Catholics did not think it was important until the Second Vatican Council authorized some changes and experimentation in the liturgy. The movement began with a desire to restore some dignity to the liturgy, which had suffered from improprieties in many areas through the Middle Ages into modern times. Quite often the desire took form in a return to more ancient forms of the liturgy, free from some more recent and less desirable accretions; it is the tendency of ritual to expand, not to contract. But as the movement developed, the goal became less the desire to restore and to maintain dignity than the desire to make the liturgy meaningful to the laity. When the liturgy was examined with this goal in view, a number of superflous and even meaningless archaisms became evident, and it was felt that dignity could be preserved only by simplicity. When archaisms were identified, it was at once obvious that there was no more striking archaism than the use of Latin in the liturgy.

It is not easy to explain the survival of Latin in the liturgy while Latin died as a language and was transformed into the Romance languages of Europe. Latin did survive as the language of learning; and while not all the churchmen of the Dark Ages were learned, all the learned men were churchmen. No doubt also the preservation of the Latin formulae was the only assurance that the integrity of the sacramental signs would be preserved. When the Latin of the Empire broke up into the dialects which became the languages of much of modern Europe, Latin remained the common language in which Rome and the provinces could communicate with each other. Latin did not survive only as a purely sacred language, and probably could not have survived thus. Ritual formulae in other religions often preserve archaic speech forms, but not an entire language. Even Hebrew as a liturgical language in Judaism is a development that occurred after the beginning of the Christian era. There is no real parallel to the growth of Latin as the liturgical language of Roman Catholicism. Before the sixth century it was taken for granted in the Church that the language of ritual was the language of the worshipers.

One may say at once that the survival—or rather the maintenance—of Latin in the liturgy of the Roman Church signified that the liturgy was almost exclusively the concern of the clergy; the laity had become passive spectators. The modern liturgical movement could not make them active participants unless vernacular languages were again employed. Most of the world is aware of the importance that this issue assumed and of the bitterness of the disputes concerning it, and it has found both the importance and the bitterness hard to understand. The Roman unwillingness to tamper with the sacramental signs has been stressed; this may be the most important factor in the reluctance of so many to abandon Latin. Some not too well informed Catholics have created disturbances in churches by asking whether the Eucharist performed in English is a valid sacrament. Others defended the universal uniformity of the Roman ritual, more or less asserting that it was equally unintelligible to the laity whether they attended Mass in New York or in Tokyo. Others have adduced the mystery of the rites conducted in Latin, not observing that a mystery is not much of a mystery simply because it is in a foreign language; this would put the mystery of the rites on the same level of mystery as a timetable on the German railways. Others felt, although they have not said, that the Roman Catholic Church should not make a change which, when examined, evidently should have been made several hundred years ago. Still another unspoken factor was that liturgy in the vernacular has been regarded since the sixteenth century as the mark of heretical sects.

The recital of these factors shows that the Roman Church did not find it as easy to adopt the vernacular in its rites as many people seem to think it should have. It is an instance of a type of change which becomes more difficult the longer it is delayed; the Church has known other changes of this type. To those who are not members, it may seem incredible that Catholics should depart from the Roman Church because it has abandoned Latin in most of its liturgy; and one must agree with the judgment that this cannot really be a serious issue. Yet it is serious, not so much in itself as for what it symbolizes: the timeless changeless reality of Roman

Catholicism, the one stable reality in an unstable world. Of course the Roman Catholic Church has never been timeless and changeless, but this is its image for many of its members.

A few years ago hardly any one would have predicted change in this area. Now that it has happened, it has not proved to be the universal cure for all that ails the Roman liturgy. Unsympathetic and clumsy clergy make the liturgy in the vernacular no more dignified and intelligible than the liturgy in Latin. Roman Catholics, much less accustomed than Protestants to hear their own voices in church, do not always respond with strength to the invitation to participate. The changes are not of great magnitude, but they are sufficient to create moments of uncertainty about procedure both for clergy and laity, and there is no room in ritual worship for the uncertain performer. Some liturgists have said, with a strange mingling of hope and despair, that the reformed liturgy will not be meaningful until enough of the present generation of adults have died to make room for the young who have never known anything but the vernacular liturgy. It is doubtful that those who sought the reform of the liturgy and those in authority who, willingly or unwillingly, approved it, foresaw the reception. It is an instance of the capacity of the Roman Church to make a long delayed change. In the judgment of most observers in the church, the long-term effects of the change will strengthen the unity of the Roman Church.

## 3. Baptism

All Christian churches practice baptism; not all of them believe in its necessity as Roman Catholics do. It is the sacrament of initiation and rebirth which enables the Christian to live as a Christian and to receive the other sacraments. Roman Catholic theology, while it insists on the absolute necessity of baptism, recognizes that baptism cannot be administered without a baptizer. Thus it recognizes what is called *the baptism of desire*, which in its original form was applicable to catechumens, those who were preparing for baptism but had not yet received it. If they died while they were still catechumens, they were buried as members of the Christian community. It was not until the discovery of new continents with millions of people who had never heard of Christianity that the doctrine was modified to meet this reality. The baptism of desire is not understood as a desire of baptism, but as a sincere desire to love and serve God as one knows him. This, Roman Catholics believe, effectively unites a man with God. It does not initiate a man into the church, and should he, on the hypothesis of such a sincere desire, wish to enter the Roman Church, he would be baptized with no examination of his previous disposition. The Church also believes that death inflicted for the Christian faith effectively unites a man with God; this is traditionally known as the baptism of blood. Otherwise the Roman Church insists on baptism, but its belief in the effectiveness of the sacramental sign forbids the Church to insist that the baptism be performed by one of its own ministers. It accepts baptism performed in Protestant churches on assurance that the proper matter and form were employed, and in emergency it accepts any rational human being as the baptizer, as long as the person is willing to act as the agent of the church. The theological formula for this situation is that the baptizer intend what the church intends; he need not know what the church intends nor believe in it. This is an extension of a principle already noted in general. It is also an effect of the Roman Catholic belief in the necessity of baptism.

In Roman Catholicism, baptism is administered by the pouring of water on the head and the use of the formula, "I baptize you in the name of the Father and of the Son and of the Holy Spirit." The Trinitarian formula is derived from Matthew 28:19, and the Roman Church holds that the explicit mention of the three persons is necessary for a valid baptism. There are a few New Testament references to baptism in the name of Jesus, and a few references in early Christian literature which can be understood as referring to the formula, "I baptize you in the name of Jesus." The data do not permit an absolute denial that this formula was ever used; on the other hand, the data do not permit the affirmation that it was ever accepted.[1] The antiquity of the Trinitarian formula is attested beyond doubt, nor can there be doubt that it was the prevailing formula in all periods of which we have any information.

The rite of infusion does not enjoy the same antiquity; and Roman Catholics here find themselves confronted by several Protestant churches which maintain that immersion, the only rite attested for early Christian centuries, is the only valid rite.[2] The Roman Church has certainly modified the rite in this respect; the Roman position is that the sign has not been modified so that it is no longer washing, even though infusion is rather a symbolic washing. Theologians assert that the sign is not complete unless the water *flows*; this is thought to preserve the essential sign. Hence the Roman Church looks with some doubt on the rite of sprinkling, practiced in some Protestant churches, and feels free to baptize conditionally those who have been baptized by aspersion. Historians allege several factors in the introduction of infusion instead of immersion. In the early church, the neophytes were baptized in the nude, and standards of modesty changed after the end of the Roman domination. Besides, baptism by immersion was more cruel in Europe north of the Alps than it was in Mediterranean countries.

The Roman practice of infant baptism has been a point of contention between Romans and some Protestants since the Reformation. Here also the Protestants seem to have antiquity on their side; not only the New Testament but also the catechetical homilies of the fathers of the church presuppose adult candidates.[3] The Orthodox churches, however, practice infant baptism. The early church shows no doubt of its belief in the necessity of baptism, but it is not equally clear about its urgency. Normally baptism was conferred on two major festivals, Easter and Pentecost. The period of instruction of candidates, the catechumens, was rather long, and the catechumenate could endure well into adult life. The delay was probably due, among other things, to the belief that baptism, a single, total purification that could happen only once, might well be postponed to a time when it would do the most good, but the practice of the early church also reflects the conviction that the reception of baptism was an adult decision.

The origins of infant baptism are obscure, but the practice is ancient.[4] It is scarcely possible to present the grounds on which the practice was first adopted, but they could not have been much different from the grounds on which the Roman Church justifies the practice now. The principal reason is the Roman belief that infants share in the hereditary guilt of mankind which is called *original sin*. The sacrament is deemed effective in this respect even for those who are unable to accept it by personal choice; just as the hereditary guilt was not contracted by personal choice, so redemption from the same is achieved without any decision of the subject. The Roman Church does not baptize infants unless there is reasonable certainty that they will be reared in Roman Catholicism. The Church requires the presence of sponsors or godparents other than the natural parents who assume the obligation of rearing the child in defect of others. They also speak for the infant in the baptismal rite. One may say that infant baptism rests on the presumed future consent of the infant.

The Roman practice has long been criticized as a form of what is now called brainwashing. The Roman Church, the objector will say, does everything it can to see that the presumed consent actually occurs; and he will say that the child reared in Roman Catholicism has no genuine option when he becomes an adult. It does not do much good to respond that every child is reared in something which he does not himself determine; and even if he is reared in unbelief, unbelief is a form of belief. If a child is reared to be neutral, normally one should expect him to be neutral, and such a child has no real option either. The objector might respond that the Roman Church would not be unfaithful to its most ancient traditions if it were to rear children in Roman Catholicism, but as catechumens, not as baptized. It is hard to see how the results of this process would differ from the present Roman practice or how it would afford a real option. It would no doubt be a liturgical expression of respect for the freedom of consent which is the ideal attitude of the candidate for baptism. Roman Catholics simply do not see that the Roman practice works any injustice on the child or that it is an irreverent administration of the sacrament on candidates who are incapable of receiving it; and no change in this feature of Roman discipline appears on the horizon at the present moment.

Roman Catholics have to admit that their practice has not always shown due respect either for the sacramental sign or for the free consent of the subject. Missionaries have sometimes baptized converts with almost no instruction on the nature of what was happening to them. The practice of baptizing total strangers who have been rendered unconscious and are medically beyond assistance is questionable and may approach a superstitious regard for the rite. Even in recent times, baptism administered secretly to children who were thought to be dying but did not die has led to some disagreeable legal processes in Roman Catholic countries, when the church claimed the infant on the ground that it has been baptized. To members of other churches or of no church, these are instances of Roman Catholic imperialism. This they are, but they also reflect once again what emerges as the characteristic Roman belief about baptism, the belief in its absolute necessity. When this belief is held so profoundly that it obscures other Roman beliefs about the sacrament, anomalous practices are inevitable.

When baptism is solemnly administered (always the case except in danger of death), it is accompanied by ceremonies which enrich the symbolism of the rite. These include some exorcisms or ritual expulsions of the evil spirit; most modern Catholics would agree that when they are spoken to an infant, they have a disagreeable tone. More impressive are the request for baptism and the profession of faith, spoken by the sponsors in the name of the infant; and it is perhaps unfortunate that the ancient white robe worn by neophytes has become merely the laying on and removal of a small white cloth. This symbolism is better supplied by the traditional white baptismal dress, and this should be incorporated into the ceremony. No Roman Catholic church is complete without its baptistery, which is always separated from the body of the church at least by a screen or a grill; since the sacrament is a sign of initiation into the church, the ceremonies should begin outside the building. In many old European churches, the baptistery is a separate building, constructed with a splendor suitable to this basic sacrament.

It is not possible to return to the practices of the early church, but if one imagines the scene of an ancient church at Easter or Pentecost, when baptism was conferred on a group of adult candidates just before the celebration of the Eucharist, one feels that the external symbolism has been impoverished in contemporary Roman Catholicism. One feels that the ancient candidates had been spared nothing to assure them that this was the most important event in their lives. The modern Catholic must grow into this belief long after the sacrament has been administered to him, and it is not certain that he always arrives at this belief. The place that the symbolism of ritual has in all societies, secular as well as religious, has been noted. Symbolism in religion can turn baroque, but it should also be realized that there can be too little of it.

## 4. Confirmation

In the Acts of the Apostles, there are references to an imposition of hands on the baptized by which the Holy Spirit was conferred (Acts 8:17; 19:1–7). This rite is the biblical basis for the Roman Catholic sacrament of confirmation. Little is known of the historical development of the sacrament.[1] It is accepted in the Orthodox churches, but it is administered at the same time as baptism, and the Orthodox churches accept infant baptism. The rite of confirmation is practiced in a number of Protestant churches, but, except in the Anglican Communion, it is not generally regarded as a sacramental rite, at least not a rite of the same character as baptism.[2] In Roman discipline for the last several hundred years the sacrament of confirmation has been administered at the beginning of adolescence, although this age has more recently been advanced by a few years. The sacrament always followed the first reception of the Eucharist, and since the pontificate of Pius X (1903–1914) the Eucharist has been administered to children at the age of seven.

The administration of confirmation is reserved to the bishop, but it is not reserved to the ordinary; any one in episcopal orders may confirm with the authorization of the ordinary. The *matter* of the sacrament is a mixture of consecrated oils called *chrism*, applied to the forehead while the bishop utters a short liturgical formula. Most Roman Catholics remember most clearly the light blow on the cheek administered after the rite, symbolizing the persecution which the candidate must now be ready to suffer. Since confirmation is a sacrament of maturity, the bishop also listens while some of the children recite from their catechism lessons.

In Roman Catholic theology, confirmation is a somewhat neglected sacrament, and it does not receive much attention in popular instruction. The Roman Church does not require the reception of the sacrament, and no penalty is attached to its omission. It is required for the lawful reception of holy orders, but not for valid ordination, and it is not required even for the lawful reception of matrimony. This apparent indifference to the sacrament has certainly contributed to a lowering of its esteem among Roman Catholics generally. Yet confirmation should be a sacrament of more significance. Together with the Protestant rite of confirmation and the *bar mitzvah* ceremony of Judaism, it is a rite by which a person professes at the beginning of adolescence the religion in which he has been reared from infancy. Thus in Roman Catholicism the Catholic does for himself what was done in his behalf by others at his baptism. Cultural changes have no doubt helped to diminish the obvious significance of confirmation; up to modern times the beginning of adolescence was very nearly the beginning of adult responsibility, but in much of the world this is no longer true. The significance has been further diminished, as we have noticed, by the usual practice of confirmation *after* the first reception of the Eucharist, which means that it may be administered at the age of eight. Furthermore, confirmation is administered to classes which may number as many as fifty; the administration does not impress the individual person in the same way as baptism or the reception of the Eucharist.

While confirmation is an adult profession of faith, at least in theory, it is more than that; the profession is a condition for the reception of the sacrament, not the sacrament itself. The ritual signifies the passage of the person from childhood to maturity, a passage which changes his position in religious society as it changes his position in familial and civil society. The change can be summed up in terms of enlarged freedom and responsibility. Roman Catholics believe that confirmation effects what it signifies. The biological and psychological passage from childhood happens by natural processes without the action of the subject or of any one else, unless the person suffers from retarded natural processes. There are no parallel "supernatural" processes by which growth is inevitable with the passage of time. Arrival at adulthood is often symbolized by domestic or civil ritual, but confirmation is not regarded by Catholics as such a symbolic ritual. They believe that it is the effective rite which imparts spiritual growth to maturity. Yet it receives less attention and regard than it deserves.

While one should not speak of an exaggerated esteem of baptism and the Eucharist, one may speak of an incoherent theology of the sacraments. We have noticed of the number seven that the number has meaning because of the different situations in life toward which the sacraments are directed. Roman Catholic theology has given a great deal of close attention to the explanation of baptism and the Eucharist, so much that it has left little room for the sacrament of maturity. Actually in much of Roman Catholic theology the scholars would have difficulty reconciling their position with the passage in Acts in which the baptized are asked whether they have yet received the Holy Spirit and they answer in the negative. Obviously the passage implies a fullness of membership in the church which is not conferred by baptism alone. Baptism is most certainly the sacrament of initiation; in relation to confirmation it should be conceived after the analogy of birth and adolescence. One acquires all human rights and powers by nativity, but one does not acquire their full use by nativity. Hence one can see that it is fitting that confirmation is reserved to the ordinary, either himself or one whom he directly appoints. Initiation into the church is the right of every one who seeks it; the full use of the powers of membership by an active part in the life of the church can occur only

under the leadership of the ordinary, and it is his office to judge
whether the candidate is ready to assume an adult position in the
church. But in fact, as we have seen and shall see again, Roman
Catholic theology has been weak in defining an adult position in
the church; that is, in distinguishing the adult Catholic from the
infant Catholic. This too may have contributed to the neglect of
the sacrament of confirmation.

## 5. *The Eucharist*

The sacrament of the Eucharist or the Lord's Supper or Holy
Communion is found in almost every church which calls itself
Christian; it is with baptism one of the sacraments most clearly
seen in the New Testament. The name Eucharist is the technical
designation of the sacrament in Roman Catholic official documents
and theology; popularly it is more frequently called Mass or (Holy)
Communion. The designation Eucharist will be employed because
it is rarely used by others than Roman Catholics.

In the controversies of the Protestant Reformation, the Roman
Catholic position that the Eucharist is a sacrifice became a bitter
point of contention. The Protestants affirmed that the death of
Jesus Christ was the one all sufficient sacrifice and that it was
blasphemous to assert that it could be repeated or that any ecclesiastical rite could continue it. Thus the Mass was eliminated from
the Protestant cult; the Eucharist was retained, but it was a commemoration of the death of Jesus. At the Council of Trent, the Roman
Catholic Church declared that the Protestant position was formally
heretical.[1] The Roman Church affirms that the Mass is a genuine
and authentic sacrifice. The Protestant churches retain the Eucharist
as communion, not as sacrifice; the difference between these positions should become clear in the course of the exposition.

*A. The Eucharist as sacrifice: the Mass.* There are certain common elements in every species of Christian belief, and one of these
elements is the efficacious, atoning death of Jesus Christ. Atoning
value is not identical with sacrificial value; but the biblical basis of
the sacrificial character of the death of Jesus is so clear in the
Epistle to the Hebrews that it is not a matter of serious dispute
among Christians. Likewise, all Christian churches accept some
connection between the Last Supper and the death of Jesus; it is
at this point that differences between the Roman belief and other
Christian beliefs appear. The Roman belief is that the death of

Jesus is a sacrifice and that it is a unique sacrifice; that the Mass is also a sacrifice, but not a sacrifice added to the death of Jesus; that the atoning value of the death of Jesus is applied, not expanded in the Mass.

Obviously these statements of belief raise questions about the nature of sacrifice and the relation of the death of Jesus both to the Last Supper of the gospels and to the offering of the Mass, and in answering these questions Roman Catholicism is much less explicit than it is in affirming its belief. In Catholic theology, there have been about twenty-four theological theories proposed to answer these questions, no one of which has been universally accepted. The skeptical observer might say that statements that cannot be satisfactorily explained by twenty-four theories should perhaps be themselves examined; but such a criticism shows a misunderstanding of the Catholic genius—or the Catholic *modus operandi*, if this term be preferred. The Roman Catholic Church believes that the Mass, under this designation or some other, has been celebrated in its communion from the beginning of apostolic times. While the Catholic statement of belief is not synonymous with the biblical understanding of the Eucharistic rite and indeed goes notably beyond it, the Roman Church is not conscious that the understanding of the rite has been altered within its communion since apostolic times. The Church retains its traditional understanding, whether the understanding involves speculative difficulties or not.

The Roman Church believes that the Mass is a true and proper sacrifice, and not merely a rite to which the term sacrifice is applied by analogy. Students of the history of religion know that the rite of sacrifice is found in almost every religion and that its origins are prehistoric. The symbolism of sacrifice is not a single symbolism, and a definition of sacrifice that would be applicable to every sacrificial rite is almost impossible to form. Since the idea of sacrifice in the New Testament arose in a Jewish-Christian milieu, however, one hardly needs to make a complete anthropological investigation of the meaning of sacrificial ritual. The understanding of the death of Jesus as a sacrifice can be related only to Israelite-Jewish sacrificial rites. Within this ritual one sees why the author of the Epistle to the Hebrews called the death of Jesus the perfect sacrifice which ends the Jewish sacrificial system, for it is the sacrifice of communion, the "peace-offering," the sacrifice of atonement and reconciliation, the "sin-offering" and the "guilt-offering," and the sacrifice in which the victim is wholly consumed, the "whole-burnt offering."

Because the victim is the only-begotten Son, no further sacrifice of any value is possible or useful. The author of the Epistle to the Hebrews, one may say, considered the death of Jesus as the one and only genuine sacrifice of which other sacrificial rites were analogies and imitations; they are to be defined in terms of the death of Jesus, not the death of Jesus in terms of them, as theologians usually do. The question is not whether the death of Jesus is sacrificial, but whether the other rites are sacrificial.

The rite of the Last Supper is clearly connected in the New Testament with Jesus' death, and the commission to continue the act is equally clear; this is not a point of controversy between Christians.[2] It is also clear that the rite is a commemoration of the death of Jesus; but the Roman Church rejects the statement that it is no more than a commemoration. If it were a "mere commemoration," it would not be a sacramental rite in the Roman Catholic understanding of sacrament. Maurice de la Taille proposed a theory which distinguished the Supper as the rite of oblation and the death as the rite of immolation; the offering of the unique victim can be repeated, but the immolation can occur only once.[3] The theory was criticized on the ground that the rite of oblation does not fulfill the definition of sacrifice; but if we are dealing with the primary and perfect sacrifice, then the rite, unique in any case, need not be defined in terms of other sacrificial rites. De la Taille thus met the quite valid Protestant objection that the death of Jesus cannot be repeated and that nothing can be added to its value. An older and much more common Roman Catholic theory called the Mass a "mystical mactation," by which was meant a symbolic reenactment of the death of Jesus by the separation of flesh and blood under the species of bread and wine. Grotesque as this theory may seem, it also met the Protestant objections; that it remained so popular so long may illustrate a certain impoverishment of Roman theological theory in the centuries that followed the Reformation.

Apart from these and other theories, the Roman position is that the church repeats what Jesus told it to repeat, the rite of the Supper, and does not repeat what cannot be repeated, the death of Jesus. It believes that Jesus, in offering his body and blood at the Supper, performed a sacrificial act, the efficaciousness of which arises from the atoning death. As long as one understands that the sacrificial rite is a symbolic act in any hypothesis, the Roman position is not indefensible; the Roman Church believes that it retains a symbolic rite which was instituted by its founder, and it does not feel compelled to arrive at a perfect rationalization of the symbolism. If the Roman Church is asked why it insists that the ritual offering of the Supper performed by Jesus was a sacrificial act, it ultimately responds that this is what the Church has always believed it to be. And indeed if the atoning death which is symbolized by the offering at the Supper is a sacrificial act, it is difficult to say that the offering of the Supper is devoid of sacrificial significance.

In Roman Catholic belief and practice, the Mass is the central cultic act which imparts value to all other acts of worship. It is the only cultic act which is of obligation for all Catholics, who must attend Mass each Sunday and "holyday of obligation." In many parts of the world a "practicing Catholic" is one who is faithful to the obligation of attending Mass. The popular definition may be faulty, but it shows the importance which the Roman Church attaches to this act of worship. In the Mass the priesthood of Jesus Christ is operative; the Roman Church regards her priests as visible representatives of the one high priest. The Mass is offered in the name of the entire church, whether many or few worshipers are present. The Roman Church has a solemn ritual of offering the Mass which makes use of music and spectacle; but it does not regard the solemn ritual as any more effective than the simplest celebration under the most austere conditions. Historically, the Roman Church has been ready to make almost any concession to hostile governments except the prohibition of the celebration of the Mass. If the Mass cannot be celebrated, the Roman Church literally believes that it has been forced out of business. Somewhat oddly, the Church is more concerned with the celebration than it is with the attendance of worshipers at the offering, so much does it esteem the inner worth and importance of this ritual act of worship. It does not regard the Mass as a private act, however; every Mass is of itself a public act, and canon law requires the attendance of at least one worshiper for the celebration of Mass. But the church does permit relaxations of this rule, for it believes that it is better that the Mass be celebrated with no worshipers present than not celebrated at all. This belief and practice, sometimes not understood, is really quite consistent. The Mass is the only act of worship instituted and authorized by Jesus Christ. When it is not celebrated the church does not pray as a church; and when the church does not pray it is in serious trouble.

The Roman Church teaches its members that the Mass is the supreme act of adoration, thanksgiving, atonement, and petition,

# THE GOVERNMENT OF THE CHURCH

1 The opening of the Vatican Council at St. Peter's in Rome, October 11, 1962, in the presence of Pope John XXIII

2  Pope Paul VI with Patriarch Athenagoras during his historic visit to the Holy Land in 1967. A Roman Catholic pontiff had not met with an Orthodox Patriarch since 1439.

# SACRAMENTS AND WORSHIP

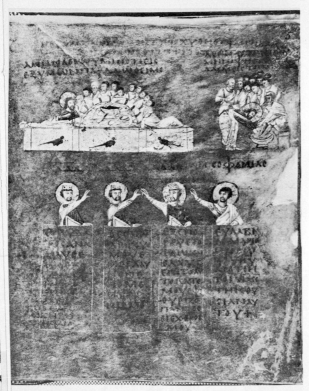

3 "The Last Supper" from a sixth century Greek illuminated manuscript

4 Corpus Christi procession in Toledo

20  A Catholic mission school, the Adelbraka Senior School in Accra

and the only such act in which the worshiper is ritually united with the entire church. One who believes that man must pray at all believes that prayer should express these four sentiments; and one who believes that prayer must be a social act recognizes that the Mass is the social prayer of the Roman Catholic Church. To understand Roman Catholicism even superficially, one must grasp that Catholics do believe this, even in countries (mostly Latin) where the attendance of men at Mass is notoriously poor. Failure to attend does not signify a denial of the traditional value and importance of the Mass; and even those who rarely attend would think it a disaster if the Mass were not celebrated and attended by women and children. We deal with an irrational paradox in such countries, but a paradox between belief and practice does not alter the content of belief, and it is with this content that we are concerned. Those who fail to attend Mass are content that the Mass is offered on their behalf and that it is attended by others on their behalf.

It must be added that the Roman Catholic faith in the Mass is sometimes inarticulate and that Catholics could not easily explain why they attach so much importance to the rite. The Mass is subject to the same problems as any other ritual formula; it can degenerate into a mere routine, it can be performed hastily without care and dignity, and its meaning may not be grasped by those who attend it. Naturally the principal object of the liturgical renewal in the modern church is the Mass. Here appear all the difficulties involved in the retention of Latin as the liturgical language and the passive attendance which has been the rule for several hundred years. Recent discussions make it clear that many Catholics think of the Mass not as a social act of worship but as a period of time which they are obliged to spend in church; they pursue private prayer because they have nothing else to do. This has had rather serious consequences for the Eucharist as the symbol of unity, of which the following section will speak at greater length. Now that the vernacular is being restored, the Mass has become more of a dialogue between priest and people than it was even a few years ago. If the renewal continues—and no one really doubts that it will—the faith of Roman Catholics in the Mass will surely become more articulate, and the basis of the obligation of attendance will be much clearer than it is now. Certainly the ritual which has been traditional since the Middle Ages was calculated to make Catholics think of the Mass as the action of the priest rather than as the action of the church—a form of clericalism that has not been sufficiently noticed. Even the traditional design of churches is clerical in structure; in European cathedrals, the great open spaces which make the churches so impressive are seen to be barriers to community worship, and the altar has now been brought into the middle of the nave. Even the posture of the priest with his back turned to the people was a barrier to communication; it would be hard to think of a more obvious symbol of the exclusion of the congregation from the most sacred of mysteries. The medieval rood screen was a literal as well as a symbolic barrier.

The practice of *stipends* for Mass has often been a scandal to Protestants, who regarded it as the sale of spiritual goods. The origin of the stipend was really quite simple. The Roman Church regards the celebration of Mass as the principal office of its priests, and the stipend was originally the daily support of the priest, who was supported just in order that Mass should be celebrated daily. The medieval practice of foundations (benefices, prebends, and the like) assured the daily celebration of Mass by an endowment which produced fixed revenues. Very few priests have ever lived off an endowment, however. The stipend became the daily offering for the sustenance of the priest, and it was no doubt only natural that the Mass should be celebrated "for the intention" of the donor. In fact the stipend has not been for several centuries enough to support the priest for a day; in the United States the usual offering is two dollars, only recently raised from one. The stipend simply became a cash offering which assured the celebration of Mass for the intention of the donor.

In recent years a number of priests have become uneasy with the practice of stipends, fearing that it may approach commerce in the sacred, and in a few parishes the practice has quietly been abandoned. Where the priest is salaried, it appears that his stipend is already paid, and that he should celebrate the Mass in virtue of his salary. A cash offering should not be necessary to assure the celebration of Mass for one's intentions. There is even some question about the theological theory which permits the Mass to be celebrated for the intentions of one rather than another, or whether such a division is meaningful. In any case, even more priests are uneasy with the price scale of Masses: two dollars for a low Mass, five dollars for a high Mass, ten dollars for a solemn high Mass. No one will be unhappy if these practices are quickly abandoned. In the early church, it was the custom to inscribe particular petitions on tablets which were then read to the entire congregation. In the renewed liturgy this practice is reappearing, and it should make the practice of stipends unnecessary; the priest asks the entire congregation to join in the prayer of the petitioner. The Roman Church could then return to the earlier practice of supporting the priest so that the Mass could be celebrated for all.

These considerations indicate that the Roman Church can and does move in just those areas which might have been thought most neglected. The importance which the Roman Church attaches to its central act of worship makes it imperative that the act be meaningful to all its membership. Recent developments within Romanism have been directed to this end; the developments could have come more quickly, but they did come, and they should make Romanism stronger in its inner structure, the part of the structure which is most genuinely religious.

*B. The Eucharist as sacrament.* It has already been observed that Protestant churches retain the Eucharist as communion but not as sacrifice. Yet in this area of belief Roman and Protestant beliefs seem to diverge at almost every point. The divergence is not as great as it seems to be—so at least recent ecumenical conversations indicate, but Roman belief here is rather definitely formed, and not entirely in response to the Protestant Reformation.

Let it be noticed at the beginning that there is no opposition between the symbolism of sacrifice and the ritual meal. In the Israelite-Jewish sacrificial system, the *peace offering* was consumed by the worshiping group in a sacred banquet.[4] The offering of Jesus was made at the Passover dinner; and the commemorative ritual takes the form of a dinner of the worshiping group, although in practically all Christian churches the meal has become vestigial, in Romanism as much as in any other Christian communion. Yet if the meal disappeared entirely the sacramental sign would be corrupted.

The problem of the presentation of the body and blood of Jesus as food and drink is at least as old as the Gospel of John, Chapter 6, one of the passages on which the Roman Church leans for its own understanding of the sacramental change. The food and drink are given as bread and wine, things which can be consumed by the worshipers. The relation of the bread and wine to the body and blood of Jesus Christ is one of the most intricate theological propositions within the Roman Catholic system, and it is difficult even for a trained theologian to state it accurately. The Catholic understanding is realistic; in most Protestant churches the understanding is symbolic or dynamic.

Since the Fourth Council of the Lateran (1215), the official word for the sacramental change is *transsubstantiation,* a rather barbarous term both in Latin and in English. As the Council defined it, it means that the entire substance of the bread is changed into the substance of the body of Christ, and the entire substance of the wine into the blood of Christ, with only the species of bread and wine remaining. The Latin word *species* here would normally be translated "appearances," but in the cautious language of Roman Catholic theology the Latin word usually goes into English as *species,* and thus becomes unintelligible to the untrained. The Catholic assertion is based on the Aristotelian and medieval philosophy of substance and accident, defined in the schools respectively as that which exists in itself (*substance*) and that which exists in something else (*accident*). The bread and wine become substantially something else, but accidentally they are unchanged. Thus the body and blood of Christ are not seen, touched, or tasted; no substance is the object of the senses. But what is present is the substance, for only a substance can be present. The body and blood of Christ do not take on the sensible qualities of bread and wine. The body of Christ is neither expanded nor contracted nor moved from place to place; it simply becomes present where the transsubstantiation has been effected by the sacramental formula. It is not present in the same manner (called in the schools *local presence*) as it was present in Galilee, however; it is present as a substance. To illustrate, my own presence in this office is not due to my substantial reality, but to "the commensuration of my extension with the extension of the place where I sit." It is all really very simple and almost reasonable if one accepts the theory of substance and accident. I say almost reasonable, for the Roman Church classifies the sacramental presence of Jesus in the area of mystery; there is nothing else like it in the world of experience.

It is not surprising that recent Roman Catholic theologians have become somewhat concerned at the close association of this belief with a medieval theory of the composition of bodies which is no longer accepted either in philosophy or in science. Many say not unreasonably that the miscroscopic and subatomic analysis of matter has not taken words like bread and wine out of the language, and that people, scientists or laymen, will ask for bread and wine and expect that the one who serves them will understand what they mean. In this sense, the "substance" of bread belongs to reality as reality is expressed by language. When Marie Antoinette said, "If

they have no bread, let them eat cake," both Marie and the poor
understood what she meant. If one asks for wine and receives grape
juice or whisky, one says nothing outlandish if one says, "This is
not wine." For what it is worth, the Roman Church does not
accept cake, grape juice, or whisky as an adequate sacramental sign,
simply because no one would call them bread and wine. To put it
briefly, bread and wine are still things which can be identified, and
the belief in transsubstantiation demands no more than this. When
one goes beyond this into medieval cosmology, one may be in
danger of becoming ridiculous. One runs an equal danger if one
discusses bread and wine in terms of atomic and molecular and
chemical compounds.

Nevertheless, the intricacies of the theology of transsubstantiation are beyond most Catholics, and they were sufficient to move
many of the Reformers to propose alternate explanations, ranging
from the purely symbolic, to the dynamic, to *consubstantiation*.
The *purely symbolic* means just that; the body and blood of Christ
are not really present but are symbolized by the elements. *Dynamic
presence* is presence by effect; the body and blood of Christ are not
"really" or "substantially" present, but the worshiper experiences
union with Christ through the consumption of the elements. *Consubstantiation* means that the body and blood of Christ become
present where the elements are present, but with no substantial
change in the bread and wine. Romanism rejected all these variants
and still rejects them; the Council of Trent affirmed in its thirteenth
session, October 11, 1551, that the body and blood of Christ are
"truly, really, and substantially present."

Some more recent efforts at a more refined explanation have not
at this writing been fully developed, nor can it be said that they
have been sympathetically received in Roman theological circles.
The word *transsignification* has made its appearance in Roman
Catholic theology; to the untrained observer it may not seem to be
much better than transsubstantiation to designate what is under
discussion.[5] As we have said, many theologians are unhappy with
the association between the belief and an antiquated philosophical
theory. They would like to find a language which would express
Roman Catholic belief with no affiliation to any philosophical
language, medieval or modern. The task is, of course, difficult; we
are no more likely to find timeless language in the twentieth century than Thomas Aquinas was in the thirteenth century. The
newer theologians are suggesting that more attention be paid to

the sign, for that is the Roman definition of a sacrament. They do not wish to remove the realism of the Roman Catholic belief, but to find other terms for the realism; and they believe one must begin with the reality of the sign. In the Roman ritual, the bread and wine are *signs* of the body and blood of Christ before the sacramental formula of consecration is uttered, but they are not yet sacramental signs. Do they cease to be signs after the formula is uttered? Not entirely, for the species remain the only objects of the senses, and they determine where Christ is sacramentally present. How one is to describe the transformation of the signs—a transformation which does not occur in the other sacraments—and preserve the traditional realism of the Roman belief is not yet clear; but it is altogether probable that Roman Catholic theology will accept the task which some of its scholars have laid upon it.

It is an obvious question, since the formula of institution in the New Testament is so explicit about both the bread and the wine, why Roman Catholics do not receive communion under both species. This was certainly the most ancient practice; but the reception of bread alone goes back well beyond the Council of Constance (1414–1418). Whether the Roman practice was legitimate was a point of the dispute between the Roman Church and the church of Bohemia in the fifteenth century; and no Roman Catholic who knows some of his history could feel entirely comfortable if the Roman Church adopted a liturgical practice for which it burnt John Hus at Constance.[6] The original reasons for the modification of the sign are obscure. It is a quaint feature of Roman practice that the eucharistic bread is made in the size and shape of a coin; the offering made by the worshiper is returned to him changed into the body of Christ. In modern times, reasons of sanitation and convenience can readily be alleged for not restoring the ancient practice; but sanitary and convenient ritual can just as readily be devised. Strictly speaking, there is no reason why each communicant should not drink from his own cup. Convenience is hardly a matter for discussion; the entire liturgy of the sacraments is inconvenient, if one wants to introduce this factor. If the words attributed to Jesus in the Gospel of John (6:51) are taken seriously, "Unless you eat the flesh of the Son of Man and drink his blood you shall not have life in you," then no inconvenience excuses.

The administration of communion under one species only is certainly the most serious modification the Roman Church has made in the sacramental signs. Theologically the practice is justified by the Roman realism of its teaching on the presence of Jesus, a realism which certainly has been influenced by liturgical practice. The Roman Church believes that "the whole body" is present in the whole of the species and in any part of the species after division, as long as the portion is large enough to be perceptible to the senses. Thus it believes that the communicant receives no more of Christ in bread and wine than he does in bread alone, if one will pardon the expression. In the teaching on the presence, this must be conceded; the question is not whether the whole Christ is present, but whether the whole sacramental sign is present. As we shall see, the sign is at least vestigially present and is not modified to such an extent that it becomes a different sign; but no Roman theologian could deny that reception of both species is the original sign. In spite of the ghost of John Hus, there is a serious movement within Roman Catholicism to restore the original sign in its integrity.

It is surprising that the Eucharist, considered in Romanism as the central sacrament, is so lightly imposed upon the members. Canon law prescribes reception of the sacrament once a year during the Paschal season, which for this purpose is extended from Ash Wednesday to Trinity Sunday. Whether the Eucharist be considered as sacramental nutrition or as a sign of Christian unity—and it is considered as both—such infrequent reception is a bare minimum. The Roman Church considers one who omits his "Easter duty" as no longer a practicing member. The law introduces a separation between the Eucharist as sacrifice and the Eucharist as sacrament, and this is another modification of the original sign. In the sacrifice of the peace offering, which was one of the Israelite species of sacrifice associated with the Eucharist, the victim was consumed by the worshipers in a sacrificial banquet, and this was the only sacrificial banquet in the Israelite-Jewish system. In the sin offerings there was no banquet, and no one partook of the victim.

The frequency of the reception of communion in the Roman Church has varied notably over the centuries of its history. In the apostolic church, as far as we know, the Eucharist was always both sacrifice and sacrament, but it was offered only once a week. Penitents were excluded from the sacrament, but they were also excluded from the sacrificial ritual with the catechumens. The daily offering is a more recent development, but in its first phase it seems to have included communion of all those in attendance. By the Middle Ages, when the law of annual communion was promulgated (by the Fourth Council of the Lateran, 1215), reception had become infrequent; and it is difficult to assign reasons for this except a general feeling that most people were not worthy to receive the sacrament. This was connected with the development of auricular confession, which will be treated in the following section, and it was normal that one did not communicate unless one had previously confessed. The general practice was scarcely wholesome, and the reception of the sacrament became even less frequent under the influence of the heresy called Jansenism, which arose in the seventeenth century and continued into the nineteenth. Jansenists regarded no one as worthy to receive the sacrament more than once a year, and their belief was enough in harmony with what had become the traditional practice to influence every European country and, through immigrants, both North and South America.

The practice of frequent communion began in the pontificate of Pius X (1903–1914), the same Pontiff who lowered the age at which communion was first received. Since Pius X, frequent or daily reception of the sacrament is regarded by Roman Catholics generally as a sign of unusual piety but not as something extraordinary. The Roman Church teaches that *mortal sin* renders one unworthy of the sacrament until the sin is absolved by sacramental confession, and the conscience of most Roman Catholics is sufficiently delicate to make many of them feel doubtful about their fitness. In modern Roman Catholic churches, one can see hundreds of people receiving the sacrament on Sundays; but one may not observe that these hundreds are often a minority of the whole membership of the parish. Until quite recently the Roman Church demanded a total fast from the preceding midnight, *total* here including even water; this was not calculated to encourage the frequent reception of the sacrament. This discipline was changed before the Second Vatican Council, and the Roman Catholic may now have breakfast before reception of the sacrament. This seems to have encouraged more frequent reception and suggests that the fast may have been as much a factor as delicacy of conscience.

The sacramental sign of the Eucharist is bread and wine. While it is not obvious in much of the modern world, these were the staples in the ancient world, the food of the poor which was available to every one who could obtain food at all. There is a double symbolism in the sign, and both elements of the symbolism are explicit in the New Testament. One is the symbolism of nutrition, most evident in the Gospel of John, Chapter 6; the other is the symbolism of community, most explicit in the epistles of Paul.[7] The ritual of administration may emphasize either one or the other. Roman Catholic liturgical practice since the Middle Ages and even earlier has emphasized the symbolism of nutrition, and it has been noted that infrequent reception weakens this aspect of the sign. The same emphasis is connected with communion under one species, since bread is a more obvious symbol of nutrition than wine. In most devotional literature, it is certainly the Eucharist as the food of the soul that is explained to Roman Catholics. In some recent theological and liturgical literature, the social symbolism of the Eucharist has received more attention, and there is a feeling that the effectiveness of the sacrament may be diminished because the social symbolism is less apparent in the liturgy.

The Eucharist in the New Testament was instituted as a community meal, and it appears as a community meal wherever it is mentioned. The common meal is a symbol of unity and has been such a symbol since man learned to eat. Sharing of food and table means mutual acceptance, an honor both to the host and to the guest, a symbol of friendship and reconciliation, of devotion to a common cause, and of equality. The common meal creates for the moment an artificial family, or, when the family is the host, the guest is admitted to the family. Roman Catholics must admit that their liturgy symbolizes almost none of this; the sign of the meal is vestigial, the reception of a small portion of bread. Even the administration of the species directly into the mouth of the communicant tends to obscure the social symbolism; this is the way babies are fed, not adults, and the request of many Roman Catholics that the church return to the older practice of placing the species in the hands of the communicant is by no means unreasonable. They urge that if they can consume the species they can touch it and that to deny it to the hands of the laity is an exaggerated reverence for the species. Roman Catholics will have to think of a much more radical revision of their liturgy, however, if the social symbolism is to be restored to something meaningful.

The Roman Church since the Second Vatican Council has become much more liberal in permitting the celebration in private homes or other places where only a small group is present. In the apostolic church, the Eucharist was the sacramental portion of a genuine community dinner. Paul makes it clear in the First Epistle to the Corinthians that abuses crept in almost as soon as the ritual was instituted; but it has not always been noticed that his complaints are directed at those who failed to make the ceremony an effective symbol of unity (1 Corinthians 11:17–34). One has to say that in many modern Roman Catholic parishes a Eucharistic ritual that was a genuine community dinner would be rejected by many of the parishioners simply because they do not believe in the unity which such a ritual would symbolize. Evidently the problems in such parishes go deeper than the liturgy.

Most people are aware of the Roman practice of reserving the sacrament and with the red lamp which shows that the sacrament is reserved. This was not the original practice; food was prepared to be consumed. Reservation is the echo of most of the developments we have mentioned: the realism of the belief in the presence; the infrequency of reception, which created a superfluous amount of consecrated bread; and the emphasis on the bread alone rather than on the bread and wine. The practice of reservation led to a great many paraliturgical or devotional practices that will be treated in the chapter on devotions.

## 6. Penance

Penance is the rather strange name given to the sacrament which most people call "confession." This sacrament is peculiarly Catholic, and the Roman Church has evolved a discipline that is its own. Penance was one of the sacraments rejected by the Reformers, with most emphasis on the claim that the forgiveness of sins is a prerogative of God alone. The Roman Church finds a biblical basis for the sacrament in John 20:23, in which Jesus grants the eleven (of whom one is absent in the narrative) the power to forgive and to retain sins. Protestant churches do something less than justice to this text, even if there are certain obscurities in its meaning.

Most people are at least vaguely acquainted with the Roman practice of confession. The encounter between priest and penitent normally occurs in a small booth in the church, with both priest and penitent concealed by curtains or sometimes by doors. Priest and penitent are also separated from each other by a grill, a very small window-sized opening in a wooden partition with a wooden or metal grating or a curtain or both. This effectively conceals the identity of the penitent and often muffles the voice as well; ideally the priest should not know the identity of the penitent, but it is hardly possible to remain ignorant if a penitent is accustomed to confess to the same priest regularly, a recommended practice. Even in this practice, the priest often knows the penitent only as penitent and does not associate this penitent with an acquaintance known otherwise. The confessional is normally dark, and the penitent and the priest speak in whispers.

Roman Catholics are under no obligation to confess at any time. Confession is required only if one wishes to receive the Eucharist and has committed a *mortal sin*. The obligation of annual communion normally brings Catholics to confession at least once a year, but one who confesses no more than annually is not regarded as more than minimally devout. It is impossible to give any estimate of the average frequency of the reception of this sacrament. Most Catholics do not think that they should 'confess only when they have sinned mortally, as we shall explain below. Confession is taught to children at the age when they receive the Eucharist for the first time, and they are encouraged to form the habit of confessing regularly. For several hundred years, confession has meant not only sacramental absolution, but also whatever direction and guidance the average Catholic receives in problems of conscience.

Most people have also heard of *the seal of confession*, by which is meant the obligation of the priest to protect the secret of the confession. Priests are trained to regard this as their most severe professional obligation, and no hypothesis is admissible that would permit the priest to violate the secrecy *directly*—to use the technical term—by which is meant the clear identification of a particular penitent with a particular sin. The anecdotes of death and imprisonment which priests have suffered for fidelity to this obligation, some historical and some legendary, illustrate the rigor with which this obligation is fulfilled. The priest is also forbidden to violate the secrecy *indirectly*, by which is meant the revelation of information from which the identity of the penitent and the sin could be deduced. Priests are so aware of the severity of the obligation that they follow the obvious means of safety and never talk at all about confessions heard. There are some celebrated anecdotes of indiscretion told in seminary classrooms, such as the priest in middle age who remarked that in his first confession he had heard a murder confessed, only to have a gentleman enter the room and say, "You don't remember me, Father, but I was your first penitent." Such anecdotes are intended to horrify seminary students into perfect discretion. The normal penalty of violation of secrecy would be at least permanent denial of authorization to hear confessions.

The explanation of the sacraments in terms of *matter and form* is not notably successful for the sacrament of penance. Theologians say that the matter is the confession of sins; the form is the formula of absolution uttered by the priest. The Orthodox churches use a form in which the priest prays for forgiveness; the Roman Church insists that in the Roman rite only a declaratory form is valid, and the formula includes the words "I absolve you from your sins." But a mere recital is not considered sufficient for the sacramental sign; the Roman Church demands *contrition*, or sorrow for sin, which is attested by the very fact of confession and in practice by the use of a formula in which contrition is declared. The confession must also be complete; and it is the requirements for completeness which have brought into existence Roman Catholic moral theology.

The Roman Church distinguishes between *mortal* and *venial* sin, a distinction which most of the Reformers rejected. The mortal sin is a moral offense of sufficient seriousness to separate man permanently from union with God—in popular language, it is a sin which renders one fit for hell. The venial sin is indeed a moral fault, but not of the same seriousness; one remains united with God, but not perfectly. Mortal sins must be confessed; venial sins may be confessed but need not be, and one who in good conscience is aware of no mortal sin need not confess, even once a year. Mortal sins must be confessed "according to species and number"; that is, the sin must be described in such terms that it can be distinguished from other types of sin, and the number of times it has been committed must be stated; for each mortal sin is in itself a case for sacramental absolution. For example, one who confessed that he had committed adultery would be considered to have confessed invalidly if he omitted the circumstance that he committed adultery with his sister, for this adds a specifically new moral dimension to the offense.

But what is a *mortal* sin? The science of moral theology arose to answer this question. No one would question the seriousness of blasphemy (in the proper, not the popular sense), murder, and adultery. But how much may one steal before the offense becomes serious? Is the lie a serious sin? The consent of mankind seems to deny that it is serious in itself; but in what circumstances is it serious? What of offenses which are not mentioned in the Bible? Most Catholics thought it was a mortal sin under the old discipline to receive the Eucharist if one had not fasted from midnight. It is doubtful that many would share this judgment now. They also thought it was a mortal sin to eat meat on Friday, and they still think it is a mortal sin to omit Mass on Sunday. Murder is serious, but what degree of personal injury is serious? Fornication and adultery are serious, but is lovemaking serious? And, to illustrate from the last two sins mentioned, what does it mean to say that one sin is more serious than another? *Mortal* seems to admit degrees as little as death does; and if one mortal sin separates one totally from God, how can one be more totally separated? Observe that the word *totally* here does not mean irremediably; this is exactly the significance of the sacrament of penance.

The Roman Catholic Church believes that there is no crime so heinous that it is beyond the sacrament of penance and no sinner so besotted that he cannot receive absolution for his sins. The church insists that it must know what the sins are, and the conscience of the Roman Church since the seventeenth century has been the corps of moral theologians, whose consensus has sometimes become a part of the official documents of the papacy and the hierarchy. The definition of mortal and venial sins comes from the literature of moral theology, particularly in the analysis of particular cases, called *casuistry*. One may ask by what right a body of theologians should become the conscience of the church; and one will answer that they have the right which competence assures to any body of experts. Law, for instance, reflects the opinion of lawyers more than it reflects the opinion of any one else. The corps of moral theologians teaches within the church, and the hierarchy listens to their teaching and advice; but it is important to remember that the corps as such are not *official* teachers in the sense in which the Roman Church understands the term.

Many theologians now think that Roman Catholic moral theology should be substantially overhauled. The qualification of some sins as mortal may not reflect a very accurate moral judgment. One should hesitate to place the eating of meat on Friday or the failure to attend Mass on Sunday, even with full knowledge and reflection, on the same moral level as murder; and Roman moral theology attaches the quality of mortal only to sins which are committed with full knowledge and sufficient reflection. No moralist would say that the two are on the same moral level; but having declared that the omission of Mass is mortal, he really has no place to go for murder, except to promise a hotter fire in hell. It must be said that for most modern Catholics this does not mean much, since the popular mythology of hell makes it a place in which it would be hard to distinguish the more agreeable from the less agreeable areas. A kind of inflation operates in these moral judgments, in which mortal sin is somewhat cheapened by being multiplied. Were it not for the practice of confession, very probably many of these moral judgments would be different. We do not imply that the average Catholic would as readily murder as he would miss Mass on Sunday, but in theory he is no more doomed to hell for the one than he is for the other. It is just this theory which many think needs some revision.

The casuistry breaks down in some other areas, because moral theology is perhaps more wedded to its traditions than any other theological discipline. The writer remembers one distinguished moral theologian, now deceased, who said frankly that he found nothing in the principles of moral theology which compelled him to treat racial segregation as a serious sin. Many who heard this without expert knowledge felt that there must therefore be something wrong with the principles of moral theology. One remembers the ambiguity of moral theologians when they were confronted with the problem of nuclear weapons. Since they had accepted the ethics of the just war, which never analyzed the quality of the weapons, they had no principles by which to judge something which seemed to meet no conceivable military need. Thus casuistry has been charged with taking some things far too seriously and some other things not seriously enough. Magdalene Goffin wrote, with what seems bitter irony, that the Roman Catholic Church, of which she is a member, would have been much more concerned if the United States armed forces had dropped contraceptive pamphlets and devices on Hiroshima than it was when the same United States dropped a bomb which took 70,000 lives.[1] If we were to assume that all those connected with the bombing were Roman Catholics, there would be no consensus among moral theologians that any one of them would have been obliged to confess his part in the affair.

Problems of this sort are the real problems of auricular confession, and they are less problems of auricular confession than problems of the moral teaching of the Roman Catholic Church, which will be discussed in the chapter on the teaching office. The average lay Catholic, however, is confronted with the moral teaching of the church in the confessional more frequently than elsewhere. Old-fashioned Protestant polemic used to say that confession was a license for sin. No one believes this any longer. Catholics are slightly afraid of confession. They are accustomed to "examine their conscience" rather rigorously, and they are sure that a deliberate lie or omission would profane the sacrament and increase their guilt rather than obtain forgiveness. If the penitent reveals that he habitually commits some serious sin, the confessor has the duty of asking him to state explicitly his intention of correcting himself; this is not, of course, a promise or an oath that he will not commit this particular sin again. But Catholics understand that such a declaration shows a more serious purpose than they may have, and they will not make the declaration unless they mean it. If they cannot make the declaration, the priest deniès absolution. The confessor may also conduct some inquiries into the radical problems of conscience of the penitent; instructions for these inquiries are very carefully composed in order that the confessor may not pry into matters which have nothing to do with the case, particularly details which concern another party than the penitent. Only those who have passed through the Roman Catholic seminary training know how often and how much the duty of discretion in this sacrament is inculcated into candidates for the priesthood.

Confession has been associated with Roman Catholicism as characteristic practice so long that it is somewhat surprising and not easily explicable that the practice of frequent confession seems to be decreasing since the Second Vatican Council. This was certainly not an effect intended by the Council and should hardly be regarded as a direct effect of the acts of the Council. Certainly the change in the practice is seen in what are called *confessions of devotion*. As we have pointed out, the sacrament is directed toward mortal sins. Catholics who confess only venial sins confess more frequently than those whose moral practice is more relaxed. In popular belief, the practice rests on the theory of *grace* as something which can be administered or transfused by any sacramental action. This popular belief appears to have lost ground suddenly and widely. The change in practice could ultimately be wholesome, since the sacrament of penance was not always taken with due seriousness in frequent devotional confession; it was cheapened by being used too frequently for a purpose other than the purpose for which it was directly instituted. Those who frequently confessed venial sins found themselves reciting the same faults, some almost trivial in character, at recurring intervals. There was and is a fairly wide dissatisfaction with this practice.

The origins of auricular confession are obscure; it is old, at least as old as the late patristic period, but it was not the original discipline of penance. The literature of the early church speaks only of the public administration of penance, and it dealt only with serious sins. The offender confessed his sin before the entire congregation and received a severe *penance*, which might include fasting, exclusion from the Eucharist, the wearing of sackcloth and ashes, and prostration under the feet of the congregation. Tertullian witnesses to the fact that at least some early Christians believed that murder, adultery, and idolatry could not be forgiven by ecclesiastical penance.[2] The belief was unorthodox, but it did not imply a denial that these sins were forgiven by God; it simply stated that the church was not empowered to absolve them and that those who committed them could never be restored to good standing. The Roman Church has never admitted any restrictions on its power to absolve.

It has been suggested that the earlier penitential discipline be restored without the public confession of particular sins and the austere public penances of the early church. We have mentioned that the Roman Church insists on the confession of sins "according to species and number," but it accepts as valid a confession made in general terms if an emergency permits no more. Such a confession may be made in danger of death, whether from illness or from external danger; general confessions are normally heard by chaplains of armed forces during combat. There is in the rite of the Roman Mass a vestige of the earlier discipline. The Mass begins with a general confession of sin made by the priest, followed by a prayer for forgiveness uttered by the people, then a general confession recited by the congregation together, followed by a prayer for forgiveness uttered by the priest and an additional formula uttered by the priest but not by the people. In the Roman rite, this portion of the Mass does not have sacramental efficacy, but there is nothing in the nature of the sacrament, as the Roman Church has traditionally understood it, which would prevent the rite from having sacramental value. The development of this ritual need not mean the end of auricular confession; it would mean that confession would occur at times when the penitent was conscious of a serious moral need.

Confession has been compared in recent times to psychological counseling and to psychiatry. The comparison is inadequate on several heads. Both counseling and psychiatry have become formal skills for which formal training and accreditation are necessary. The confessor who would attempt to meet a need which he recognized as a need for counseling or psychiatric assistance would be regarded as most imprudent by other priests. There is no doubt that all three treatments overlap in the field of morality, but, strictly speaking, neither counseling nor psychiatry claim to absolve from sin, nor does the sacrament of penance claim to heal psychic weakness or illness. It has long been said that a good confession gives "peace of conscience," which means a serenity based on the assurance that one has done all one can to meet the responsibilities which God had laid upon him. If a confession brings peace of conscience, the penitent seems to need neither psychological counseling nor psychiatric assistance. If it does not bring him peace of conscience, other assistance may be in order. The confessor may be the first to discover that a penitent needs other assistance. A number of priests in modern times have taken graduate training in counseling and even in the longer and more rigorous program of psychiatry in order to discover how the work of the confessor and the work of the professional healer may be joined. Almost all priests who hear confessions have met the strange psychological aberration of *scruples*, the tortured anguished conscience which obstinately sees sin where it is not or doubts that it has confessed properly. Most priests also admit that their own training is little or no help in assisting the scrupulous. They may even suspect that the sacramental discipline creates or aggravates the condition; but it is altogether probable that the scrupulous would break out in some other form of neurotic anxiety if they did not fall prey to their conscience. A very common textbook recommendation for the scrupulous is that they abstain from confession except at rare intervals. We now recognize that this malady is not within the competence of the confessor and demands professional treatment by counseling or even by psychiatry.

Is it true, as many believed so long, that confession is one of the means by which the Roman priesthood retains its power over the consciences of Catholics? No priest of my acquaintance could take this charge seriously. Priests are aware of the traditional respect of Catholics for the sacrament, but they would not confuse this with their own personal influence on penitents. A relationship can grow between a priest and a penitent who confesses regularly to him. It is a relation of confidence basically no different from any other relation of confidence; and any relation of confidence can become a means by which one person exercises power over another.

One who looks for the "key" to the power of the Roman clergy will not find it in the administration of the sacrament of penance.

## 7. Extreme Unction

The fifth of the sacraments goes by its Latinized title, which means the "last anointing." It is perhaps the word "last" which keeps the title Latinized; few priests would care to tell one who is ill that he is going to administer the last anointing, but "extreme unction" is less suggestive. The biblical basis for this sacrament is the visitation of the sick described in James 5:14–15. The *matter* of the sacrament is the consecrated oil, and the *form* is the prayer recited by the priest while he anoints. The sacrament has a full and an abbreviated form, the latter to be used if time presses. In the full form the eyes, the ears, the nostrils, the lips, the hands, and the feet are anointed— that is, the external sense organs. In the old rite, the loins also were anointed; this rather realistic allusion to one of the areas of man's moral weakness has long been omitted from the ritual.

The sacrament is the anointing of the sick, but it is not administered in any and every illness; the illness must be serious and one which can cause death. In modern hospital practice, the priest is summoned when the patient is declared to be critically ill. The Roman Church attempts to educate both clergy and laity not to delay the administration of the sacrament beyond the point when critical illness is recognized; it does not like to have its members under the impression that the priest is the precursor of the undertaker, and certainly critical illness is not a time when the church wishes to generate fear. The sacrament is administered only once while the danger of death endures; if the patient recovers, he may be anointed again if he contracts another serious illness or relapses into the same illness.

The person must be in danger of death from illness, which includes serious injury, and not from an external cause, however certain, which threatens his life but not his health, if one may make this distinction. The writer remembers hearing in his own seminary days a priest recounting his experience as substitute chaplain in a prison. Hanging was still the legal method of execution, and he found it was his assignment to stand with another priest on the floor level below the trap in the gallows to anoint two criminals as soon as the trap had been sprung. His companion fainted and could not perform his part of the task. The practice as well as the story may seem macabre, but every Catholic priest knows that the duty of administering this sacrament may introduce him rather suddenly to views of damaged humanity which are usually seen only by doctors and nurses. A strong stomach is a desirable quality in candidates for the priesthood. In such cases of emergency, the abbreviated form is used, which consists of a single anointing on the forehead.

The rigor of the Roman Church in not anticipating the danger of death from external causes is counterbalanced by its flexible, even loose policy of presuming that life endures even after death in medical terms has occurred. But even in medical terms the moment of death can hardly be determined exactly, and the presumption in most cases has something in its favor. The Roman practice is to administer the sacrament unless the body has been removed. In these cases, the sacrament is administered conditionally, the condition being that the subject is living. Priests have been known to undergo no small risk to themselves to administer the sacrament to those who in medical judgment were corpses; it is the last office of the Roman Church for its members, and priests believe that it is worth some trouble or even risk.

Roman Catholics have great faith in the *last sacraments*, which are confession, Holy Communion (called at this crisis *viaticum*, "provision for the journey"), and the last anointing; and they have a great desire to receive them. In normal procedure, extreme unction is not administered by itself; but normal procedure may be less frequent than abnormal procedure, since critically ill patients are often in shock or coma. The sacramental effect of extreme unction is defined as the removal of "the remains of sin," a term which it is extremely difficult to define; and the Roman Church adminsters it with the belief that it is at the same time a ritual petition for recovery. If the patient cannot confess, the anointing is still administered, again conditionally, with the condition that the patient is properly disposed to receive it; and the anointing is considered to have the effect of sacramental absolution for those who are unable to confess. The proper disposition should be ascertained; and the Roman Church does not administer the sacrament to one who had expressly refused it. But priests sometimes crowd this presumption, perhaps more than they ought; and it is not uncommon where mortal injury has occurred to administer the sacrament to utter strangers, again conditionally. It was noted that the same practice is known for baptism, and one must observe here also that the practice is not well founded in theology. The Roman practice is not a mark of disrespect for the rite or for the personal decision of the patient, but a desire that no sacramental means be left unemployed simply because the person was unable to request them. Priests feel that the presumption for a Catholic in good standing ought to be made with no hesitation; administration which is almost random is much more difficult to justify.

As a positive preparation for death, the Roman ritual of the last sacraments is quite unusual in the history of religions. It has been said that Catholics have faith in these sacraments and a desire to receive them. "To die without a priest" is traditionally in popular belief something of a sign of God's displeasure, and priests find that they must frequently explain that this is a misconception of divine providence. The fear which the appearance of the priest, the harbinger of death, might elicit, is usually more than outweighed by the confidence which his presence arouses. The Roman Catholic really expects the church to accompany him to the last moment, and he wants the visible sign of its presence and activity. One of the less predictable obligations of the Roman Catholic priesthood has long been the duty of answering calls to the ill and dying, and he may easily begin to wonder why the angel of death so often comes at night. It is a call which he is not free to refuse or even to postpone; should he fail to appear when he is reached, it is simply true that the family will never forgive him. Catholics feel that the priest should be there to be reached. It was mentioned earlier that the rectory has to be considered as a twenty-four-hour operation. It is rarely possible to make it this, but no effort is spared. This attitude is difficult to explain; Catholics cannot explain it themselves. They believe that death is the supreme crisis in human life, the last moment of decision. Even if they have lived for years with no conscious need of the services of the Roman Catholic Church, they are likely to feel an urgent need for these services to assist them in doing what no one else can do for them.

## 8. Orders

Orders in Roman Catholic belief is the sacrament which confers power over the sacred, that is, power to administer the other sacraments. That aspect of sacred power which appears in the government of the Roman Church has already been discussed extensively; in canon law only clerics can hold ecclesiastical jurisdiction. Yet there is no inner connection between the two powers, and the person in holy orders does not receive ecclesiastical jurisdiction by his ordination, although he could not receive jurisdiction without it. In this chapter, orders will be considered as the sacrament that confers sacramental power.

While orders would seem to be as obvious in the New Testament as any other sacrament, it is not. There is no doubt that the apostolic church had officers; but references to ordained officers are very few in number. Again, there is no doubt that sacramental power, in the sense of the power to baptize and to perform the Eucharist, was held by church officers and not by every one. The imposition of hands by which one received an office in the church is mentioned for the Seven (Acts 6:6), for elders (Acts 14:23), for Saul and Barnabas (Acts 13:3), for Titus (2 Corinthians 8:19), and for Timothy (1 Timothy 4:14). By the time the First Epistle to Timothy was written, the imposition of hands seems to have been the normal rite of ordination to office (1 Timothy 5:22). What is lacking in these texts is the definition of the sacred power which is conferred by the imposition of hands. The rite of ordination is sufficiently early, however, to remove all doubt of its apostolic origin, and those Christian churches which do not accept ordination are not closely in touch with the earliest Christian traditions.

Traditionally the Roman Church ordains only males, and there is no authenticated instance of orders conferred upon women; Pope Joan is as historical as the unicorn. Some recent complaints have led to a closer investigation of this exclusiveness, and some theologians doubt that there is either biblical or traditional warrant for the exclusion of women from orders; women are not ordained simply because they have never been ordained, which is not in itself a good theological reason. The Roman practice reflects older cultures in which women were subject to men in every respect, including religion. Women do indeed serve as professional religious persons in the Roman Church, but not in orders.

The Roman rite of orders is so complex that theologians are somewhat pressed to defend that it is a single sacrament. There are eight orders, but there is a theological consensus that only the last two or three at most are sacramental in character. One is introduced into the clerical state by the tonsure, which is not an order. The tonsure once meant a complete shaving of the head, but for some centuries it has meant a ceremonial removing of some hair from the crown of the head. One who has been tonsured never leaves the clerical state; but the rite imposes no obligation of advancing to orders, no permanent clerical obligation such as celibacy, and no dispensation is necessary to live as a layman. In the Middle Ages, tonsure was enough to make a man eligible to receive ecclesiastical revenues, and it was quite frequently conferred for this purpose with no advance to subsequent orders.

Of the eight orders, four are called *minor* and four *major*. By tradition the cleric should spend some time in the service of each order before he passes to the next, but modern practice often permits all the minor orders to be conferred at once and the major orders on successive days. The orders are graded according to the propinquity of the service to the Eucharist. The four minor orders of janitor, lector, exorcist, and acolyte represent services (except for the exorcist) which are still performed, but never by persons in minor orders. The *janitor*, "doorman," originally had the custody of the keys of the church; this included the office of admitting only the baptized and catechumens to the Eucharist and of seeing that catechumens and penitents left before the celebration of the Eucharist proper. The *lector* had the office of reading the scriptures in the services, except the gospels, which were read by the deacon. The *exorcist* was empowered to expel evil spirits and to perform the rite of exorcism at baptism. The *acolyte* assisted the priest at the altar by bringing him the materials for the Eucharistic offering. The modern church janitor still has the keys of the church, but his office is to keep the building clean. The office of lector, normally performed by the priest, has in the liturgical renewal become the office of laymen from the congregation. The Roman Church sees a need for the rite of exorcism (outside of baptism) very rarely, and where it is exercised it is not made public; no priest may use this rite without the permission of the ordinary. The service of the acolyte traditionally has been performed by small boys, more rarely by men—never by women. Thus the minor orders may appear to be archaisms, and substantially that is what they have become. One who has received minor orders may depart from the clerical life as easily as one who has received only the tonsure.

The major orders are the orders of subdeacon, deacon, priest, and bishop. The subdeacon and the deacon assist the priest during the actual celebration of the Eucharist. It is the presence of these two officers which defines a Mass as *solemn* in contrast to the Mass celebrated without them, which is *low* (recited) or *high* (sung). The subdeacon reads the epistle (the office of the lector) and handles the vessels of the Eucharist. The deacon stands next to the priest during the celebration and is empowered to distribute Holy Communion; he reads the gospel, and he may preach. Besides his Eucharistic function, he may baptize. In modern practice, a solemn Mass is celebrated by three men in the order of priesthood, since one rarely finds men who have received only the subdiaconate and the diaconate outside of seminaries. Before the reception of the subdiaconate, the candidate pronounces "the deacon's oath" by which he undertakes the obligation of celibacy; but the Roman Church considers the obligation received with the subdiaconate to be more easily dispensable than the obligation which is received with the priesthood.

In the early church, the office of deacon was less concerned with the Eucharistic rite and much more concerned with the temporal possessions of the church. This goes back to the constitution of the Seven (who are not called deacons) in Acts 6. The deacon thus became the almoner of the bishop; the office of almoner endured into later centuries, but it was never an order distinct from the diaconate. Protestant churches sometimes keep the name and the office in the sense of administrators of church property, but they do not treat it as an order. The office of the deacon remained a permanent order longer than the other orders below the priesthood; in the early church the diaconate was the rank immediately below the episcopacy, and therefore permanent unless the deacon were ordained bishop. The priesthood as an order distinct from the episcopacy appears in the second century. In modern times, both the subdiaconate and the diaconate are, like the minor orders, merely grades through which the candidate for the priesthood passes.

The Second Vatican Council in its declaration on missions suggested the restoration of the diaconate as a permanent order. The Council suggests that this order could be conferred on those who now preach by catechizing, preside over scattered communities in the name of the pastor, or engage in charitable and social work. The discretion of establishing the order is left to episcopal conferences. While the institution is mentioned in connection with missionary territories, many see an equal or greater need for the permanent diaconate in established territories. The deacon is empowered to preach, to baptize and to administer the Eucharist.

Except for the celebration of the Eucharist, the hearing of confessions and the ministry to the sick, the deacon can perform the cultic acts performed by the priest. The diaconate could be a partial answer to the diminution of priestly vocations. The deacon would not be a full time professional religious person dependent on the church for his support. A number of observers have extended the scope of the diaconate beyond the scope set forth by the Council. Moves toward the institution of the diaconate have been very slow; the Roman Church does not accept structural modifications easily. The question of the degree of professional training needed by deacons has not been answered. Even more troublesome has been the question whether the permanent deacon must be celibate. If he is not to be a full time religious person, arguments for imposing celibacy are not convincing. At this writing it is difficult to project whether progress toward the permanent diaconate will move more rapidly in the near future.

In modern Romanism, orders for practical purposes means the terminal orders of the priesthood and the episcopacy. The priest has the power to administer all the sacraments except orders and confirmation; a recent modification of the discipline empowers the priest to confirm under certain conditions. This has raised the interesting theological question whether the power to confirm is latent, so to speak, in the priestly power and was not exercised not because the priest did not have it but because the church did not allow him to use it. This in turn raises the question of the relation of priesthood and episcopacy as orders. Is the episcopacy an enlarged priesthood, or is the priesthood a diminished episcopacy? It seems that the second of these is the more accurate way of viewing the relation; and the question may not be significant unless we remember that different orders are found within one sacrament in the Roman Church. The question would have practical import only in the hypothesis that the whole church or extensive regions were deprived of the episcopacy. Theologians ask whether in this case the sacred power of the episcopacy is not already conferred radically by ordination to the priesthood, so that in the hypothesis ordinations could continue. With that love for the hypothetical so characteristic of theologians, they also ask whether a Catholic community hopelessly isolated from the rest of the church could not ordain priests by the imposition of hands by the congregation. Many theologians would deny both hypotheses. Orders have long been considered as something which is conferred only by physical contact from the apostolic age to the present, and these theologians do not consider the power to ordain ministers as radically present in the church.

The Roman Church has been very rigorous in its understanding of the matter, form, and intention in the sacrament of orders. The celebrated question of Anglican orders was resolved negatively by Leo XIII in 1896.[1] Theologians now regard this as a practical decision rather than a speculative and final solution of the problem. The grounds for denying Anglican orders were both notable changes in the ritual of ordination and the explicit denial of the sacrificial character of the Eucharist with an implicit denial that orders empowered a man to offer the Mass as a sacrifice. Some progress in theology is illustrated by the probable fact that the question would not be examined in the same terms if it were taken up now. The Roman Church simply does not recognize orders in churches that do not celebrate the Eucharist as a sacrifice, or at least it has not up to this time.

Against this rigorous background, it is surprising that the Roman Church itself has not been free from ambiguity in the matter and form of ordination. The Council of Florence declared that orders are conferred by the delivery of the instruments; as a part of the rite of ordination the candidate receives in his hands the sacred vessels of the Eucharistic rite, as in the lower orders he receives the symbol of the orders which he receives.[2] In addition to this rite the candidate is also anointed. It is commonly accepted by Roman theologians that the matter of the sacramental rite of ordination is found in none of these but in the imposition of hands by the bishop, the only rite which is attested from apostolic times. The Council of Florence incorporated a monograph of St. Thomas Aquinas into its acts, and for some inexplicable reason St. Thomas did not mention the imposition of hands as the rite of ordination. I say inexplicable because there is no evidence that this rite was not used in the Roman Church at any time.

The qualifications for orders in the modern Roman Church are rigorous in some areas and in others, such as academic achievement, somewhat loose. The qualifications demand both good character and good reputation; and they give witness to the peculiar position of the priest in the Roman Church by excluding almost anyone who has been responsible for the death of another. The qualifications in several instances remain in force after ordination in the sense that one who incurs an *irregularity* or an *impediment* which he did not previously possess is impeded by law from exercising his orders until the irregularity or the impediment has been removed or dispensed by competent authority. The history of Romanism has too many instances of orders conferred upon unworthy men, and the modern Roman Church takes some trouble to assure itself that the candidate is a good risk. The responsibility for making the judgment is reposed upon the ordaining bishop; he is considered to have done his duty if he accepts the recommendation of responsible ecclesiastical superiors.

Orders is a permanent sacrament like baptism and confirmation, and the Roman Church does not believe that sacred power once conferred is ever lost. Thus in "extreme necessity," matters of life and death, an excommunicated priest could celebrate Mass, hear confessions, and anoint the sick; and no blame would be attached to those who required his ministry. Priests who withdraw from the ministry or who are expelled from it are *laicized* by a canonical process. Laicization does not remove the sacred power but forbids the priest to use it. He may live as a layman—that is, outside the type of residence which the ordinary approves for priests, and he may seek secular employment. The Roman Church prefers that the laicized priest live in some place where he was not previously known, and this has sometimes been the condition on which laicization was granted. The priest so laicized, if he has not otherwise violated the obligations of the clerical state—by marriage, for instance—remains in good standing in the church as a layman. Should he return to the clerical state, he is not reordained. He is not subject to the ordinary in any other way than the laity of the diocese where he resides. Laicization may be granted at the request of a priest who can present good reasons why he should no longer exercise the priestly ministry. If a priest withdraws without authorization, he is not by that fact laicized; he simply loses all standing. Laicization means that the priest joins the lay state, not simply that he ceases to act as a priest.

## 9. *Matrimony*

While Protestant churches celebrate marriage in the church before a minister, with the exception of the Anglican Communion, they do not consider that matrimony is a sacrament. The Roman affirmation at first glance seems to involve serious difficulties. Marriage is a ceremony and a state that exists independently of religion.

Civil society legislates concerning marriage and empowers certain
officers to officiate at the ceremony. The captain of a ship can officiate at a marriage on board his ship. Thus marriage exists as a
secular reality, and the question is one of how a secular reality can
become a symbol of the sacred while it retains its secular nature.
The Roman Church recognizes marriages celebrated outside its own
communion, whether they are performed under religious or secular
auspices; one who had contracted such a marriage cannot be married
to a Catholic even after a civil divorce. Yet the Roman Church has
maintained the sacramental character of marriage between baptized
persons, although this is less clear for the early centuries than for
most of the other sacraments. A passage in Ephesians (5:21–33)
which compares the union of Christ and the church to the union of
husband and wife does not really establish the sacramental character
of Christian marriage, although it does suggest its holiness. This holiness does not imply a sacrament any more than the holiness of
religious profession implies a sacrament.

The Roman Church identifies the sacrament with matrimonial
consent, not with any ceremony apart from the consent. Thus the
sacrament is administered not by the priest but by the spouses; the
priest is merely an official witness. The *matter* of the sacrament is
considered to be the consent offered, the *form* the consent accepted;
obviously the theory of matter and form has a very weak application
here. The contract is sacramental only when it is executed between
two baptized persons; the Roman Church extends this to all baptized,
whether they are Roman Catholics or not. The immediate and important consequence of this is that the Roman Church affirms indissolubility only of sacramental marriage.

The Roman identification of the sacrament with consent has
had repercussions in the relations of the Roman Church with some
European states. The Roman Church claims complete jurisdiction
over sacramental marriage, allowing the state jurisdiction over what
it calls "the civil effects" of the contract. Since the contract and the
sacrament are the same, it is clear that not much is left for the
state. This has been a point of quarrel between the Roman Church
and the Catholic states of Europe since the seventeenth century,
although the quarrel has not been unremitting. The modern "lay
states" resolved the problem by denying all jurisdiction to the church
and recognizing no marriage which was not performed by a civil
officer, in some instances requiring that the civil ceremony precede
the religious ceremony. Theologians sympathetic to the claims of the

states devised various theories of the contract and the sacrament, usually affirming that the priestly blessing was the sacrament. The Roman Church could not accept this without denying its own traditions. The church in modern times has not urged its claims to exclusive jurisdiction, tolerating the claims of the state where it could not combat them, and not penalizing its own members for complying with the civil law.

The presence of a priest at a marriage was not required before the Council of Trent, and in wide areas of the church, such as most of North America, not even until the twentieth century. This older practice recognized that a priest might not be always available, especially in newly settled countries. Since the Council of Trent the Roman Church has demanded the presence of two witnesses for the marriage of Catholics. This feature of canon law shows that the theory that the priestly blessing was the sacrament was out of harmony with traditional practice. Since the code of canon law of 1918, the church has demanded the presence of a priest except in danger of death or in case of the foreseen absence of a priest for a month.

A bewildering mass of law has grown up around Roman Catholic marriage which it is impossible even to summarize; but it is of interest because the non-Catholic encounters this law whenever the marriage of Catholic and non-Catholic occurs. Up to the Second Vatican Council, the encounter was often hostile. The non-Catholic party, if the marriage was to be recognized by the Roman Church, had to accept marriage before a priest and to sign written promises that the children would be baptized and reared in the Roman Catholic faith. These conditions have been somewhat relaxed, at least to the extent of permitting a Protestant minister to share in the ceremony with the priest, and the direction of Catholicism at present is to abandon the written promises. Until a few years ago, the "mixed" marriage could not be performed in the church nor in the home of the bride, where Protestant marriages are frequently celebrated. It was performed in the parlor of the rectory, often a dingy and dismal place, and was done with all brevity. The entire ceremony expressed disapproval of the Roman Church that one of her sons or daughters had been so weak in faith as to fall in love with one not of the fold. Considerable clerical cordiality—which was not always present—was necessary to throw some warmth into a ceremony which was designed to keep the atmosphere cold. In the more recent discipline, a "mixed" marriage may be performed in the church, and Mass is celebrated.

The laws of the Roman Church do exhibit a pattern, not discernible on the surface. They are intended to assure that the marriage once contracted will not be subject to dissolution on the grounds that some element necessary for validity was missing. This has as a somewhat unintended effect that it is difficult to perform a hasty marriage in the Roman Catholic Church and thus adds assurance that those who desire to marry have made a firm decision to do so. The Church requires the officiating priest or the pastor in whose church the ceremony takes place to make an investigation whether both parties are free to marry. In law this means a letter from the pastor of every parish in which either party has resided as long as six months since the minimum legal age of marriage. It includes establishing the fact of baptism or nonbaptism and the exclusion, as absolute as one can make it, of any previous marriage with a person still living. It means that the priest must assure himself that none of the eleven impediments which may render the marriage invalid are present. The pattern of assuring the marriage is seen also in the maxim of legal practice which governs ecclesiastical courts before which marriage cases are brought: "In doubt the presumption is in favor of the marriage." Convincing evidence is necessary to show that a marriage is invalid; no evidence except the record is needed to show that it is valid.

There are eleven conditions (*diriment impediments*) which render a marriage invalid whether they are known or not. A marriage contracted in ignorance of these is called *putative*, which means that certain effects of invalid marriage do not follow; for instance, the children of a putative marriage are reckoned as legitimate. If the impediment is discovered, it must be removed or the parties must separate. The Roman Church shows its humanity in difficult cases by the extralegal practice of leaving the parties "in good faith," which means that they are not told all the facts. Each of the impediments would admit a lengthy treatment, and we can do no more than enumerate them. Some the Roman Church believes it is empowered to dispense, others it does not.

The impediment of age (sixteen years for men, fourteen for women) is dispensable. Impotence is not dispensable; but it must be proved that it is a permanent condition and that it existed before the marriage. An existing marriage bond, whether sacramental or civil, is not dispensable, with the exception of what is called the Pauline privilege, based on 1 Corinthians 7:15. If one of the parties in a civil marriage becomes a Catholic and the other party refuses to accept the conversion (*cohabit peacefully* is the technical term), the new Catholic is free to marry a Catholic if the non-Catholic party has *left*, in the technical sense of the term. The privilege is operative when both parties were unbaptized, but in some Roman decisions the privilege has been extended to marriages in which one of the parties was baptized in a Protestant church. The privilege does not reach a marriage between two baptized Protestants, for in Roman theology this marriage is as sacramental as a marriage between two Roman Catholics. Lack of baptism in one of the parties is a dispensable impediment. Solemn religious profession is a dispensable impediment. Major orders is a dispensable impediment; but the practice has long been not to dispense from it. In recent years, the dispensation has been granted normally to priests who have contracted marriage, but not to priests who wish to contract marriage. Rape in the canonical sense, not the legal sense, is not dispensable. Canonical rape means the forcible detention of a woman for the purpose of marriage; the Roman Church here and elsewhere is careful to make certain that both parties contract the marriage freely. The somewhat strange impediment of *crime* arises from adultery with a promise of marriage or from cooperation in the murder of a spouse, with or without adultery. Thus the moving picture "Divorce Italian Style" was faithful to church law, which Italian civil law accepts by the Concordat of 1929; there was murder, but neither adultery nor promise nor cooperation. Crime is dispensable. Blood kinship is not dispensable in the direct line of descent nor between brothers and sisters; it is dispensable for first cousins. Affinity, a relationship contracted by marriage, is not dispensable in the direct line, but it is dispensable for brothers-in-law and sisters-in-law. *Public honesty*, another strange impediment, places the same obstacle to marriage with relatives by blood or marriage of a person with whom one has cohabited in an invalid marriage or in "public and notorious concubinage" as is placed by the impediments of blood kinship and affinity, and it is dispensable in the same way.

Although they are not classified as impediments, certain *defects of consent* render a marriage invalid, even if they are proved years after the marriage was celebrated. *Error about the person* nullifies the marriage; the Roman law is thinking not so much about the kind of deception which Laban practiced on Jacob when he gave

him Leah instead of Rachel (Genesis 29:16–26), a rather unlikely
device in modern times, but if the wrong twin were to appear at a
marriage, the Roman Church would declare the marriage null
with no difficulty. The impediment also affects the *quality of the
person*, and the law illustrates by the example of one who marries a
slave believing that the person is free. In earlier European society,
this defect would affect a marriage of a noble who in error married
a commoner. Fear which arises from some external threat *unjustly
caused* is a defect of consent; it was on this ground that the once
famous annulment of the marriage between the Duke of Marl-
borough and the former Consuelo Vanderbilt was granted by the
Roman Rota. Hence the Roman Church really does not recognize
the "shotgun" marriage, since any compulsion to marry even a girl
whom one had made pregnant would be unjust. In practice the
Roman Church recognizes the *mores* to the degree that it would
be very slow to accept the testimony of such compulsion. If the
parties attach a condition to marriage which, in the words of the
law, is contrary to the substance of marriage, the condition nullifies the consent. Thus an explicit condition of divorce would in-
validate the marriage. The practice of the Roman courts is to be
very slow in recognizing such conditions and never without convincing evidence. The courts are realistic enough to recognize that
if a man need do no more than swear that something was in his
mind, many will perjure themselves to obtain their liberty. It is
presumed that the parties meant what the words of the matrimonial
consent say unless they can prove that they meant something else.

The Roman Catholic Church teaches that the primary purpose
of marriage is the procreation and education of children. It admits
as secondary purposes—meaning that they are achieved only within
the primary purpose—the mutual assistance of the spouses and the
somewhat strange purpose called in Latin *remedium concupiscentiae,*
"the remedy of concupiscence." The Roman Church readily admits
that the sex urge is too powerful for most men to restrain; marriage removes the need of total restraint. The theory of the nature
of marriage reflects earlier European culture, in which the
preservation of the family was far more important than the individual fulfilment of persons in marriage. It is only in recent
times that marriage has been contracted by the wishes of the parties
themselves rather than by mutual arrangement of the two families.
In such marriages it was not important whether the two parties
loved each other, and the social structure, dominated in most

countries by Roman Catholic tradition, assured the stability of marriages. It did not, of course, assure either mutual love or fidelity. The Roman position against contraception. is based on its understanding of the primary purpose of marriage.

Both the theology of marriage and the theology of contraception have been seriously examined in recent years, and the Holy See reserved to itself a statement on these questions. The papal statement on contraception (July 29, 1968) has elicited confusion rather than clarity. It has been disclosed that a majority of the advisers of the Pope believed that the statement should not have reiterated earlier teaching. The theology of contraception cannot be discussed without a discussion of the entire structure of marriage; this is now recognized. Modern culture demands that marriage bring personal fulfilment as well as preservation of the family; in the terms of Roman theology, it would make this end equally primary, if one can speak of more than one primary end. One may say that modern culture believes that the family must be achieved in love, and this in such a way that if there is no love, there is no genuine family. It is evident that many Roman theologians, including some who are highly respected, are ready to move in this direction.

The Roman teaching on divorce is rigid, and it rests on a biblical base which seems no less rigid.[1] Recently questions have been raised whether the biblical base is as rigid as it has long seemed to be, but at this writing no firm conclusions have been reached. Yet the Roman teaching does not affirm the absolute indissolubility of any marriage except that which has been contracted between two baptized persons and has been consummated by sexual union. The Roman Church does dissolve marriages in which it is proved that carnal commerce has not occurred. The element of *consummation* has no biblical base, and it reflects a traditional belief, never formally proposed, that two people are not really married until they have known each other carnally—after the marriage ceremony, one must add. The Roman Church has never taught that the matrimonial consent actually consists in coitus, but it certainly requires coitus as an element of indissolubility. The Roman Church does not believe that any religious or civil power has the authority to divorce what it calls a *legitimate* marriage, that is, a marriage of two eligible people of whom one or neither is baptized, witnessed by a recognized religious or civil officer. The only divorce which the Roman Church recognizes is the Pauline privilege mentioned above; and it will be observed that this divorce is not "decreed" by church authority but simply recognized. The previous marriage is not dissolved by the baptism of one of the parties but by the following marriage. The Roman Church appeals to the Bible for the indissolubility of sacramental marriage, and to "the natural law" for the indissolubility of other marriages; obviously its position is stronger in the first case than it is in the second.

What many people think are divorces granted by ecclesiastical courts are really declarations of nullity; in these cases investigation shows that the marriage was defective from the beginning because of some impediment or some defect in consent. The distinction may seem subtle, but to the Roman Church it is serious; the Roman Church simply does not divorce. A marriage which is invalid can be validated if the impediment or defect can be removed; but the parties are under no obligation to have it validated any more than they were obliged to marry in the first place. At almost regular intervals, one reads in the press of annulments granted to people of wealth and aristocracy, and certain conclusions are drawn from these reports. In fairness to the Roman courts, it must be said that these news reports say nothing about annulments granted to people who have neither wealth nor aristocratic birth nor of petitions denied to people of wealth and status. The process is rather slow and discouraging. The case must be heard in two diocesan courts; if the decisions are for nullity, it must be referred to the pontifical court for final adjudication. Some degree of wealth may help to hasten the process, but it will not affect the judgment. The only way to influence an ecclesiastical court is by perjured testimony; and ecclesiastical courts, like civil courts, are aware of this possibility and not unequipped to deal with it.

The Roman Church authorizes "separation from bed and board" of couples who find that they cannot live together; cohabitation is a serious obligation of marriage in Roman Catholic teaching, and the married person sins by unauthorized departure. Separation gives no freedom to marry again. A married person may separate without authorization if the other party commits adultery, but this likewise includes no freedom to remarry. The Roman Church here departs from the Orthodox churches, which permit divorce for adultery on the somewhat doubtful biblical basis of Matthew 5:32 and 19:9; but it must be admitted that these difficult verses have no generally accepted interpretation.

The practical effect of the mass of Roman law and the prevailing Roman practice is that Roman Catholics enter marriage with the idea that the marriage will endure until death, whatever problems may arise. It is an established fact that the rate of divorce is lower among Roman Catholics than it is in the general population; the Roman Catholic who remarries after divorce loses good standing in the church. Whether this means that Roman Catholics marry more cautiously than others or that they are willing to make greater efforts to sustain the marriage is not so easily concluded. But the teaching of the Roman Church seems to have some success as far as the stability of marriage is concerned. One cannot deduce from this that Roman Catholics are more happily married than others; the primary purpose of marriage is not concerned with happiness in marriage. But the Roman Church is aware that unhappy marriages are not likely to procreate and rear happy children, and in pastoral guidance this is considered. In marriage as in the sacrament of penance the modern Roman Church recognizes that professional counseling may be demanded in addition to pastoral counseling, and priests will invoke the professional counselor for problems which lie beyond their own training and experience.

## 10. Devotions

Under this obscure rubric are included those Roman Catholic cultic practices which lie outside the sacraments; the liturgy proper is the liturgy of the sacraments. These cultic practices are now often called *paraliturgical*, by which is meant not only that they lie outside the liturgy but also that they are in some sense in opposition to it. The name *devotions* or *devotional practices* signifies to Catholics that these practices are taken up by free choice; in Roman Catholic idiom, "to do something from devotion" is to do something which one is not obliged to do. Thus one attends Mass on Sunday from obligation but on weekdays "from devotion"; yet the Mass is not a devotion.

A large area of devotions arise in connection with the Eucharist; and here it must be recalled that for many centuries it was normal for Roman Catholics to receive the Eucharist rarely. The rarity of communion was compensated by other venerations of the Eucharist that were based on the practice of reservation of the Eucharist in the church. Reservation itself is a substitute for communion; prayers are addressed to Jesus in his Eucharistic presence, either by private individuals or by the entire congregation. The best known and most common of these practices are Benediction of the Blessed Sacrament and exposition of the Blessed Sacrament, particularly the Italian form of exposition practiced through the entire Roman Church, called the Exposition of Forty Hours. In Benediction and in exposition a consecrated wafer, made larger than usual for this purpose, is placed in a vessel called a monstrance, usually decorated with radiate spikes, so that it can be seen by the congregation. Incense is used, the congregation sings a few hymns, and the priest presents the monstrance to view making the sign of the cross facing the people. Benediction is thus the blessing of Jesus himself, and the priest wears a veil which conceals his hands in order to remove his own blessing. In exposition, the same vessel is displayed in an elevated position on the high altar for most of the day, sometimes during the night as well. In exposition, it is arranged that worshipers will always be present. Flowers, incense, and candles are used generously.

It seems obvious that the idea of the Eucharist either as sacrifice or as food becomes quite remote in these devotions. The Eucharist is rather the visible presence of Jesus, who is invoked in hymns and prayers common and private, but not consumed. One old and well-known Latin Eucharistic hymn, attributed to Bernard of Clairvaux, begins with the lines (roughly translated), "The sweet thought of Jesus gives true joy to the heart, but better than honey or anything else is his sweet *presence*." The emphasis on presence rather than on sacrifice or communion is manifest. In the centuries of infrequent communion, the devout could remain in the church for hours whether the sacrament was exposed or not; they certainly had a spiritual experience, but in Roman Catholic theology it was not a sacramental experience. It is no more than a slight exaggeration to say that in those centuries the Eucharist was consecrated to be stored and not to be consumed. It is in this devotional atmosphere that such phrases as "the prisoner of the tabernacle" arose, a phrase which is theologically inaccurate in its understanding of the real presence as well as innocent of any reference to sacrifice and sacrament.

In 1264 the festival of Corpus Christi (the body of Christ) was instituted by Pope Urban IV, and the liturgy was composed by Thomas Aquinas. Only in Roman Catholic countries can one witness the solemn Corpus Christi procession through towns and villages, and even through the open fields. The festival was something of a response to the void left in Roman Catholic life by infrequent communion; but it is strange that the festival is almost entirely one of exposition and veneration and not of Mass and communion. The hymns written by Thomas Aquinas, like the hymn mentioned above, are hymns of presence rather than of sacrifice and sacrament. Yet in the Roman Catholic communities of Europe and Latin America, this festival is the greatest and most visible manifestation of faith in the entire year. Modern Roman Catholic liturgists regard these practices as substitutes for Mass and communion and not to be encouraged. It is rather striking that since the Second Vatican Council, which made no explicit move in this direction, these particular paraliturgical practices have begun to disappear. A better understanding of the Eucharist widely diffused through the Catholic laity has restored the sacramental rites to their original significance. Where the sacrament is celebrated and received, no substitutes are necessary; indeed the substitutes may detract from the genuine understanding of the sacrament.

Other devotional practices venerate the Incarnate Word under certain particular aspects or *mysteries*. The Roman Catholic practice of naming churches and schools after these mysteries or saints has led to some headlines in the sports pages of United States newspapers which bewilder non-Catholics: "Sacred Heart Wallops St. Joseph," "Mother of God Whitewashes Christ the King," and other quaint locutions. Yet the writer remembers a friend, who spent a few years at the University of Cambridge, telling of the surprise with which he heard at his first boat race the cheers of "Bump them, Jesus;" but most of the colleges of Oxford and Cambridge were named by Roman Catholics, and the names illustrate something which is not immediately obvious in this area of devotions. I mean the familiarity with the sacred which is often expressed in Roman Catholic devotions.

By a scruple not unlike the scruple which led postexilic Jews to abandon the pronunciation of the divine name Yahweh, Roman Catholics, as any one who knows them recognizes, have a reluctance to speak of Jesus and even of Mary, preferring to speak of Our Lord and his Blessed Mother and similar paraphrases. There is an anecdote, very improbably historical, of an elderly priest who attended an ecumenical service and squirmed impatiently while the preacher, a Protestant minister, spoke at length and eloquently of Jesus; the priest finally whispered to his companion, "He might at least call him Mr. Jesus." The scruple is slightly irrational, but it is compensated, if not overcompensated, by Roman Catholic devotions. One has to compare the scruple of the names with the Chapel of the Milk at Bethlehem, which is so candid that Roman Catholics usually try to detour Protestant visitors in some other direction. The prayer of spinsters, "Good St. Ann, get me a man," does not suffer from exaggerated reverence. Nor did Teresa of Avila who, disappointed at the failure of a series of prayers to St. Joseph, turned the face of the statue of the saint to the wall. She claims that her prayer was answered the next day, and the saint was taken out of the corner.

Devotions directed to the Incarnate Word are again paraliturgical approaches to Jesus Christ which meet needs not met by the liturgy at particular times and places. It has already been noted that for centuries the Roman Mass was celebrated in Latin as a sacerdotal action with little or no participation by the laity. Devotions present Jesus Christ under some particular aspect attractive in a particular time and place, but they often spread to much of the Roman Church. Devotion to the Sacred Heart is perhaps the best example. Like many others, it originated in what is called a *private revelation*, by which is meant the mystical experiences of a private person. The devotion arose in France in the seventeenth century from the experiences of a nun of the Order of the Visitation named Marguerite Marie Alacoque. The devotion emphasizes the humanity of Jesus, of which the heart is a symbol. Students of the Bible know that the heart is not a symbol of the emotions in biblical language; but in modern language the dialogue with Jesus "heart to heart" is a recognition of the emotional dimensions not only of the Christian faith but also of the Incarnate Word. One may wonder why, if the New Testament were read, it was necessary to have a private revelation to restore the mystery of love to its primacy, but this seems to be the peculiar quality of Roman Catholic devotions; they fasten on aspects of biblical revelation which for various reasons have been obscured. Like the devotion to the Sacred Heart, they often recover these aspects without recourse to biblical documents. Devotion to the Sacred Heart, whatever be its theological weaknesses, has made many Catholics better aware of the historical reality of the man Jesus and of his emotional components. The danger in such devotions is an excess of sentimentality, and devotion to the Sacred Heart has not been free from this excess. But there is also a danger of depriving religion of its emotional content, which neither Roman Catholicism nor Protestantism has escaped entirely. In addition, there is a danger that such devotions may come to mean for Catholics what the authentic sources of the Bible and tradition ought to mean, and the danger is real. Perhaps more serious is the danger that the devotion may come to have a super-stitious efficacy.

Devotions, we have said, respond to particular needs; and one can see in the history of devotions that they rise and fall with develop-ments in history and culture. They thus illustrate the capacity of the Roman Church to adapt itself to different times and places. One must add that there is a certain competitive element in devotions. They are usually attached to some particular religious group or religious order which promotes them, and no Roman Catholic could honestly deny that devotions exhibit some unpleasant aspects of commercialism. The traffic in pictures, medals, and the like barely escapes the scandalous in some instances. Devotional liter-ature is proverbial among Roman Catholics for its triviality and its innocence of sound theology. It is scarcely an excuse to say that it reaches the simple and the unlearned on their own level. The New Testament does that too, but it is not open to this peculiar exploitation, and it makes demands which the devotions sometimes fail to make. One cannot say that devotions are an unmixed good or an unmixed evil; one can say that the Catholicism which springs up after the Second Vatican Council seems inclined to search for its devotional experience in the liturgy and theology rather than in devotions. Those who think that devotions represent the trivial and the peripheral rather than the substantial may take comfort; those who think that most of the laity cannot have a religious experience above the level of the devotions will find this development discourag-ing.

Devotions to the saints are a characteristic Roman Catholic belief which was rejected by the Reformers. The primary position here, of course, belongs to devotion to Mary. The Roman Catholic venera-tion of the saints is very simple, and it can be considered under two aspects. In the first aspect, the saints are believed to represent the most notable successes in the effort of the church to lead the Christian life. Honor and imitation of the saints for this achievement do not differ in kind from the honor paid to the memory of any civic or cultural hero. Under the second aspect, the saints are con-sidered as intercessors, and this is what Protestantism rejected. But the Roman position here is equally simple; the saints are the friends of God, and God is on good terms with his friends. This may be a naive anthropomorphism, but it does not, as early Protestants said, derogate from the unique mediatorship of Christ. Roman Catholics do not consider that the saints have redeemed us by a saving act; they are themselves redeemed by the saving act. The cult of saints is based on belief in survival after death and *the communion of the saints*; the saints are believed to have in an eminent degree that power of intercessory prayer which Christians have in the church and which the Bible, Old and New Testaments, attributes to great persons. One does not leave the church by death but rather joins the perfect, eschatological church.

Roman Catholics consider that the mother of Jesus is closer to him than any other human being. This' belief is based less on biblical evidence than on the natural relation between mother and son. In Roman Catholic theology, the basic *prerogative* of Mary is the divine maternity; all other beliefs concerning her intercessory power, her conception free from original sin, and most recently the assumption of her body into heaven, flow from the belief that these things are worthy of the mother of God, who must have been a privileged person before God. Roman Catholics believe that this privilege, like the friendship of the saints with God, does not end with death.

Within this rather modest theological framework Roman Catholicism has found room for various manifestations of Marian cult, which even Roman theologians have found excessive. They agree, with reservations, that Mary represents the feminine element in religion, which appears in no other place in Roman Catholicism. It is well known that Catholicism of the Middle Ages venerated Mary with a chivalric devotion formed by the ideal of knightly behavior to the ideal woman and that much of this chivalry has survived into modern devotion, where it no longer has the meaning it once had. Mary unites the two features which Roman Catholicism from early periods has presented as the ideals of womanhood: dedicated virginity and motherhood. The meager biblical evidence about the life and person of Mary has left ample room for the imagination of the devout to create details about a person that are not known to have existed.

The multiplication of Madonnas has sometimes been compared to the multiplication of gods in ancient paganism. The comparison shows a poor understanding of Roman Catholic devotion, even in its most ignorant and superstitious forms. Roman Catholics no more believe in several Marys than they believe in several Christs. What is multiplied is not Marys but *apparitions*. Private revelation has been more active in Mariology than it has in Christology, which in itself may indicate some instinctive reserve in Roman Catholic devotion. Almost every great Marian cult arose from an alleged apparition of Mary to some person or group. As a result of the apparition, some devotion such as the Rosary, according to legend given to St. Dominic by Mary herself, or some place such as Lourdes or Fatima becomes peculiarly sacred and recommended as a means or a place of effective intercession. It is not at all remarkable that most of the apparitions have some national affiliation; they are almost a way of naturalizing the Virgin, and one would not expect the Catholic nations of Europe to venerate the Virgin under a title which belonged to some other country. Most of the apparitions do not stand up well under rigorous historical examination—most of which has been conducted by Roman Catholic scholars, such as the Bollandists of Brussels. These good men have exploded so many legends of the saints that they have often been thought subversive. These reservations hold not only as well but even better for the most recent apparition at Fatima in Portugal, which achieved legendary status in modern times even while some of the original witnesses were still alive.

The non-Catholic may ask whether any devotion can be solid that rests upon an unhistorical foundation, but to ask the question is to answer it. The question the Roman Church asks is not whether the alleged vision or apparition can be critically validated, since it does not believe that such a validation is possible. It asks whether the devotion is in harmony with Roman Catholic belief and standards of life. If the devotion meets these criteria, the Roman Church will neither affirm the critically validated historical reality of the event nor forbid its members to practice the devotion. It is, as was said at the beginning of this section, a matter of personal choice. No devotion accepted in the Roman Church is imposed upon any Catholic.

The observer who witnesses some devotional manifestations at places like Lourdes or Guadalupe or Fatima may be puzzled or alarmed. It is possible that he may look no further than the crass commercialism which can be seen. He may also think that he is seeing manifest superstition in action; and it would be idle to deny that Catholics are ever superstitious in their devotions. His critical instincts may be offended by a serene indifference to the known facts of history. Such demonstrations are a peculiar religious experience which is not typical of normal Roman Catholic worship. They are also deeply affected by the quality of the culture in which the shrine is located. They are, like the Eucharistic devotions, substitutes for the liturgical cult. In addition, they allow room for *enthusiasm*, an element to which Roman Catholic cult historically has not been sympathetic. Catholics too are somewhat puzzled and bewildered by these demonstrations, but ultimately they can judge them in no other way than the church judges them. If they are faithful to orthodox belief and orthodox morality, one may really criticize them only on grounds of taste. A Catholic who attaches more importance to his devotions than to the liturgical cult of the sacraments is certainly a poorly instructed Catholic, and he may be in danger of becoming a superstitious Catholic. But many Roman Catholics have professed their faith through devotions; it may have been an inferior profession of faith, but the Roman Church believes that this is better than no profession at all.

## 11. *Mysticism*

The history of Roman Catholic mysticism has been studied extensively by scholars both Roman Catholic and other, and the reader should consult some of these works for a complete treatment.[1] The subject is too large to do more here than relate the phenomenon of mysticism to the general structure and spirit of Roman Catholicism.

Mysticism is not a peculiarly Catholic phenomenon; it appears in a great many religions of the world, and mystical phenomena in different religions have a striking resemblance to each other. The mystical experience can be described in general terms as a direct experience of the reality of the divine, comparable to the direct experience of external reality through sense perception. Mystics who have attempted to analyze their experience insist that it is not comparable to any other human experience. It is not the awareness of the divine which comes through faith, for faith is not a direct experience. But it is not the same as awareness of external reality which we have through the senses, for the object of the experience is not sensible. Mystics compare it to the awareness of the near presence of another person with whom one has the most intimate personal relations. One who has not had the experience must leave the description to others, unless he wishes to study the writings of the mystics closely.

The Bible itself, Old and New Testaments, relates experiences that can be called mystical. The Old Testament is faithful to the Israelite belief that no man can see Yahweh and live; but man can see manifestations of the divine presence and activity that are not normal sense perceptions. He can hear the voice of Yahweh and feel Yahweh's hand laid upon him. If the mystics said no more than this, one could conclude that their experiences were created from their reading of the Bible; but many of the mystics knew little about the Bible, they did say more, and their experiences have other sources.

The early Roman Church shows little evidence of mystical experience. The introduction of Platonic and Neoplatonic philosophical contemplation into Christianity by Christian scholars approaches a discipline for mysticism but does not suggest the extraordinary phenomena associated with medieval and modern Christian mystics. Almost all of the mysticism recorded comes from the Middle Ages and since, and it is this mysticism which is typically Roman Catholic.

It is typical of Roman Catholic mysticism, although not universal, that it is Christocentric. Most mystics experience one or several apparitions of Jesus Christ. Teresa of Avila believed that sensible apparitions are a lower, introductory form of mysticism which leads one to a higher nonsensible perception of divine reality.[2] When the mystics claim to have received information from Jesus himself about details of his life, especially detailed accounts of his passion, criticism demands a very reserved attitude. Some mystical accounts of the passion are so far out of line with known historical facts that they are simply incredible. In other cases, the mystic may receive a message for the church or some of its officers. The message may direct that a new devotion be instituted; thus the institution of the festival of Corpus Christi, the devotions of the Sacred Heart, the Rosary, the scapular, and several others are credited to mystical revelations. The message may deal with the problems of the church. Catherine of Siena, the counselor of popes, was a mystic; no one has ever questioned the soundness of her utterances. Some celebrated mystics, such as Teresa of Avila and John of the Cross, had no message for anyone and founded no new devotions.

Apparitions of Mary, as we have seen, have also been frequent; one may mention Lourdes, Guadalupe, and Fatima among the better known. These revelations all dealt with the institution of new devotions. Marian apparitions are even more characteristically Roman

Catholic than Christocentric apparitions. Both types are often mentioned in connection with the foundation of new religious orders.

In spite of the frequency of mystical experiences, the official Roman Catholic Church is not sympathetic to mysticism and never has been. Its first response to mystical claims is to doubt them and to submit them to rigorous examination. The mystics have something in common with the Israelite prophets; they often criticized the institutional church and came under the suspicion of the authorities. The history of mysticism shows a sufficient number of mystical claims that have been proved false to justify reasonable doubt. The majority of the most respected mystics had at least a period of their life when they fell under suspicion. The Roman Church has no way to test the validity of mystical claims except the biblical maxim that the mystic is to be known by his or her fruits. If the mystical experience issues in a genuine growth of faith and love in the mystic and others, the Roman Church will still not certify that the experiences are genuine; it will certify that the mystic is sincere in his faith. When the Roman Church canonizes men and women, it studies their mystical experiences as closely as the material will permit; but the study is directed to the orthodoxy of the experiences, not to their reality. Evidently the Roman Church admits that one may be sincerely deceived about the quality of one's mystical experience without suffering any harm, as long as orthodox faith and the preservation of Roman Catholic moral standards are proved.

Mysticism, like other things in Roman Catholicism, changes with time and culture. It is extremely rare in the modern world. It may indeed have been relatively rare in the Middle Ages and the Renaissance, but there is certainly more literary evidence of it from those periods. One may ask whether the experience is really at home in an age of reason; and while one hesitates to call the modern age an age of reason, it is certainly an age in which reason has achieved a technology that it never achieved before. The mystical experience sprang from a faith situated in a culture; whatever it was, the culture provided both the needs which the mystical experience met and the impulse to mystical experience. Neither the needs nor the means seem to be normal for the Roman Catholic in the modern world. If the word credulous can be used in a neutral sense, one can say that mysticism presupposes credulity. One may allege that Paul, who had a notable mystical experience, was by his own account incredulous; but Paul lived in a credulous culture, and his incredulity was limited to the new sect. If a modern Paul were to experience a similar sudden reversal, it would not take the same form which Paul's experience took and probably would not be recognized either by the person himself or by others as mystical.

Teresa of Avila in the sixteenth century seemed to be moving toward something like this in her own reflections. In her day mysticism was normally accompanied by external abnormalities, such as the trance and levitation, or at least these abnormalities were alleged. Teresa, a daughter of her times, accepted these things, but felt that they revealed imperfection rather than perfection. When the mystic arrived at as clear a perception of the divine reality as is possible, the result, she thought, was a great tranquillity and serenity and an inflexible confidence that one could do whatever it was that God wanted one to do.[3] Such an experience would not be perceived by others, and unless the person had learned it from others he would not realize that his experience should be classified as mystical. It may therefore be not that mysticism has disappeared in modern times, but that it takes a modern form.

# III. The Beliefs of the Roman Catholic Church

## 1. Faith

It is impossible within the scope of this book to present even a sketch of the major beliefs of the Roman Catholic Church. These beliefs can be studied in some recent theological works to which the reader is recommended.[1] One who even glances at these works will wonder how much of doctrine reaches the average Roman Catholic layman, and he will correctly assume that the amount is not much. The basic means of doctrinal instruction for the layman is the catechism. The use of the question and answer method in this form is associated with the names of two theologians of the sixteenth century, Peter Canisius (1521–1597), who wrote in German, and Robert Bellarmine (1542–1621), who wrote in Italian. Both were motivated by the losses the Roman Church suffered in the Reformation. A longer and more detailed work was the Catechism of the Council of Trent, produced in 1566 in response to a decree of the Council. The modern Roman Catholic who has received secondary and higher education will very probably have received instruction above the elementary level of the catechism, but even such instruction does not approach a full exposition of Roman Catholic doctrine. Such full instruction is given only in seminaries for the training of candidates for the priesthood. Our purpose here is not to summarize the doctrine but to set forth the place which doctrine occupies in the structure and life of Roman Catholicism. It is much more important than doctrine is in any Protestant church, and faith occupies a central role.

The Roman Catholic understanding of faith has been notably evolved from the New Testament idea of faith, and it differs from the usual Protestant understanding no less notably. Since the work of Thomas Aquinas, whose explanation of faith was substantially incorporated into the acts of the First Vatican Council, Roman Catholics have understood faith to be an intellectual assent under the impulse of the will.[2] The proper object of faith is truth revealed by God; the motive of belief is the authority of God who reveals. The Catholic thinks of faith as that act of the mind by which he accepts some proposition as true, and he thinks of the object of his faith as the articles of belief. Faith is thus distinguished from faith in a person, illustrated in the English idiom, "I have faith in you." But in English, faith and belief are also used to express the assent to some proposition as true, with this sharp difference: when one says he believes something is true, one usually implies that one is not certain that it is true. In this use of the term, belief is opposed to certain knowledge. Roman Catholic faith is contrasted to knowledge gained by experience or deduction; but it is not regarded as uncertain. It is rather like the faith which one gives to the witness of a fact, but Roman Catholic theology does not like to have this analogy pushed too far. A witness becomes credible because upon examination he is proved to be informed and veracious. God is not submitted to this type of examination. Roman Catholicism believes that once the fact of God's revelation is established, faith is imposed. Thus the motive of faith is not the divine reality in its fullness, but precisely God as all-knowing and perfectly truthful.

In Roman Catholic teaching, the proper object of faith is *mystery*, by which is meant a truth revealed by God which is beyond human comprehension. Mystery does not mean that which is unknown or unknowable because the resources are lacking to ascertain it; the textbook example is the number of fish in the sea, which cannot be known but would be quite comprehensible if it were ascertained. Nor does it mean something which is unknown because of historical conditions, as electricity was unknown until recent times; the *mysteries of faith* will remain mysteries whatever be the future progress of human knowledge. The reason is simply that the mystery is a revelation of God, who remains beyond human comprehension. Thus the mystery is always to some degree irrational, in the sense that it cannot be explained and understood, and suprarational, in the sense that it belongs to an order of reality that is impenetrable to reason. The mystery retains a degree of incredibility. It is open neither to rational demonstration nor to rational objection, for, in the hypothesis, no one knows it well enough to object to it. The Roman Church, however, does not present the mysteries as entirely incredible and as contrary to human reason. In its teaching it is at pains to relate the mysteries to analogies drawn from experience and to show that the revelation of God which emerges in them is possessed of a higher unity and coherence in which all becomes credible, if never entirely intelligible.

How does the Roman Church suppose that the revelation of the unknown that remains unknown adds to man's understanding of God and himself? At the base of the mystery is an unspoken belief that man and the world taken by themselves are ultimately irrational and meaningless and that they acquire meaning and value only when they are seen illuminated by the divine reality. This light is dim to man's vision, but it is the only light in a world of total darkness, and it gives man a goal toward which he can move. The mysterious is known to the fullness of man's capacity only when he attains it; and in this attainment it will be manifested as the supreme truth, not understood only because it lay beyond unredeemed man's capacity.

It is an easy passage from this to think that the Roman Catholic is saved by what he knows; but Roman Catholicism, even in somewhat primitive forms of popular belief, does not fall to this level of Gnosticism. The famous and usually misunderstood Lutheran formula, "justification by faith alone," could easily mean to a Catholic "justification by knowledge alone." The Roman Church rejected the Lutheran formula and insisted on justification by faith and works. The Roman Catholic is saved by what he believes and by what he does; his knowledge is supposed to give form and character to his life.

The fact that God has revealed is established for the Roman Catholic by his church, which becomes in one order of logic the primary object of his faith. The Roman Catholic learns as a child to profess his faith by saying that he believes all that the Catholic Church believes and teaches. He learns what God has revealed from the church, and only from the church. What this presupposes will be discussed when the teaching office of the Roman Church is treated. If the Catholic is not well instructed, he may lump together a number of ill assorted propositions to all of which he gives the one assent of faith. He may attach the same quality to his belief that baptism is a sacrament that he attaches to his belief that baptism should be conferred by infusion of water; both are taught and practiced by the church whose belief and teaching he accepts. If he is neither well instructed nor endowed with even average intelligence, he is very likely to misunderstand the propositions to which he gives his faith. Since his faith is sacred to him, he will react violently against any person who seems to attack or threaten it, and verify without knowing it the gospel text which says that men will kill others thinking that they are doing service to God (John 16:2).

Such excesses as one sees in the execution of heretics and witches are not characteristic of Roman Catholicism; they are—fortunately— isolated examples of a pathology of faith. Other milder and more subtle types of pathology are both more common and more difficult to analyze. One may group them under two headings, both of which come from the fact that the Roman Catholic thinks of faith as a total commitment to the truths which the Church teaches. One effect is a credulity toward the church which can be excessive. The Roman doctrine of infallibility will be spoken of later; for many Catholics it means simply that nothing which the church does or allows can really be wrong. Occasionally this opens the door to superstition. At other times it leads to an overvaluation of certain beliefs and practices. A scholar who expresses a doubt that Mary really appeared at Fatima will be thought by many Catholics to be attacking the faith. It is difficult to explain this attitude because it is basically irrational, but if one were to rationalize it, it arises from the implicit conviction that the church would never permit the Fatima cult if Mary had not appeared at Fatima.

At this point, one may ask whether there is more anti-intellectualism in the Roman Church than there is elsewhere and whether the Roman Catholic idea of faith contributes to anti-intellectualism. For what it is worth, the observations of this writer do not permit the conclusion that the Roman Church is more anti-intellectual than any other group or that the idea of faith contributes to it. Anti-intellectualism is a general human response that can occur anywhere and can feed on anything. If it does not feed on the Roman idea of faith, it will find something else to feed on. The Roman Catholic Church is in a difficult position when a notable number of its higher offices are filled by anti-intellectuals, but its position is no more difficult than that of any other organization in which this might happen. The tendency toward anti-intellectualism is countered by the second of the milder types of pathology, which is rationalism.

Strange as it may seem, rationalism does appear in the Roman Church, and at times quite strongly. In the first place, Roman Catholics match their total commitment to the truths which their church teaches them with an almost unlimited freedom outside the area of this teaching. They are usually quick to point out that the church or some of its officers have spoken outside the area of faith, and they assert that the church has no authority in these matters whatever. Where questions of politics and social conditions touch morality, the relations between Catholics and their prelates can become hostile. Since these areas of public interest do touch the order of morality, the Roman Church often has something which it ought to say; to say it is as difficult as any task which the Roman Church has to perform. The difficulty is compounded by the fact that in the past the statements of churchmen on these problems have been at times political rather than moral.

Rationalism also appears in the legacy which the Roman Church holds from the intellectual movement of the Middle Ages. An almost constant tendency can be observed in Roman theology which attempts to put everything on the basis of sheer logic. Many theologians speak as if articles of faith, including the system in which the Roman Church becomes the speaker of faith, can and ought to be proved beyond all reasonable doubt. They are much concerned with the "evidence" of faith. Unless this evidence attains the quality which would stand up in a court of law or even in a laboratory, they do not think that the faith should be imposed upon any one. During the nineteenth century, the century of science and criticism, theologians attempted to respond by showing that the affirmations of faith stand up under scientific and critical analysis. Anyone who believes knows that they do stand, but not as conclusions of science and criticism, rather as truths which simply lie above these disciplines. One who believes cannot adduce scientific and critical evidence for his faith; if he could, it would not be faith as Roman Catholics understand the term.

The Roman idea of faith, especially after the controversies of the Reformation, left little room for emotional reaction, and thus contributed to the rationalist approach to faith. Roman Catholic apologetic rarely moved by speaking to the heart, and this has been recognized as a weakness. Emotions, as has been seen, belong to devotions and to mysticism. In fact, however, most Catholics have never been capable of a really rationalist approach to their faith, and the assent has often been a cultural as well as a religious assent. Roman Catholics do not think that their credulity is any more excessive in their religious faith than it is in their cultural assent. Normally a man accepts his country, his own people, his own traditions. A critical examination of the culture would disclose many features which make it less admirable than he thinks; but he does not make the critical examination, and if he did, it would remain true that a man must have a country. If he·adopts a new country, as so many Europeans did during the nineteenth century, he gives to the new country not only the same loyalty he gave the mother country, but usually much more and much more loudly professed. If his religious faith is closely identified with his culture— one may cite Ireland and Poland—or if, as in the United States, his religious faith is guaranteed a freedom which it did not have in the mother country, the two faiths come so close together that many fail to distinguish them. The two assents resemble each other closely enough for the analogy to be useful. The educated American Catholic, for instance, sees no more reason to question his faith than he sees to question his allegiance. Both form the most important parts of the cultural framework in which he was born and reared and in which he expects to spend his life and find his personal fulfilment. He sees the charge of credulity as being no more valid for one than for the other, and no obligation to submit either loyalty to a critical examination to assure himself that his assent is valid.

The opposite of faith is heresy, the denial of an article of faith. In the Roman Church from the early patristic age this has been the chief sin against the church. The idea of heresy exhibits a development parallel to the development of the teaching office; but the sin of heresy can hardly be conceived before faith is considered an assent to certain propositions. Heresy casts doubt on the entire idea of divine revelation because it casts doubt on the one authentic source of divine revelation, the church, and assumes that there is another superior source. Technically heresy does not arise until one expressly denies a truth which the church presents as divinely revealed. As long as the discussion continues, no one is guilty of formal heresy; one becomes heretic only when one refuses to submit to the declaration of the church and thus becomes contumacious. One may commit *material* heresy without formal guilt; by this is meant a declaration contrary to revealed doctrine made in ignorance. Obviously there has been and still is considerable material heresy in the Roman Church. As the Roman Church regards itself as the one authentic spokesman of divinely revealed truth, so it is also the only authority that can declare that a proposition is heretical.

The seriousness with which heresy was taken can be seen in the medieval penalty of death by burning. In modern times this seems barbarous, and it was. We spoke earlier of the identification of faith with culture; and the identification was never as close as it was in medieval Christendom. Religion was one of the unifying elements of the structure, and one who attacked the unity of faith attacked the social structure. Heresy was a crime in civil law as well as in canon law, and the penalty was inflicted by the civil authority. This does not excuse ecclesiastical authority, which cooperated with civil authority in full knowledge of what it would do. The strange designation of the execution of heretics in Spain was *auto da fé*, an act of faith. Surely no more outlandish profession of faith was ever devised, and modern Roman Catholics find it difficult to share the faith which was professed in such a way. The same attitude toward heresy was borrowed by the Protestant churches, which have their own history of executions for heresy. In Protestantism also, faith was identified with the culture; and in many of the early Protestant churches a confession of definite articles was required for membership in good standing.

In Roman Catholic teaching, faith is a basic virtue as no other virtue is; and this teaching is in some ways difficult to reconcile with the primacy of love which appears in the New Testament. Faith is one of the three *theological* virtues received in baptism (hope and love being the others), and it is considered the base of the other two. Thus faith is the last Christian virtue to perish; but if it perishes, all other Christian virtues perish with it. The Roman Church has sometimes taken a very rigorous understanding of the words of the Epistle to the Hebrews, "Without faith it is impossible to please God" (11:6). When faith is understood as assent to certain propositions, the possibility of pleasing God does not exist for most people in the world. Modern Roman Catholic theology is not as austere on this question as earlier theologians were; the expression "in good faith" is used paradoxically of those who have never heard of the revealed propositions. Earlier theologians assumed quite simply that those who did not profess the true faith were damned, whatever be the reason for their failure to profess it.

The catechism as the means of instruction used in the modern Roman Church was mentioned previously. The most ancient form of profession of faith was the creed, and the Apostles' Creed, retained by many Protestant churches, is the best-known formula. The Roman Church uses in the liturgy of the Mass the Nicene Creed, developed from the formula of Nicaea which condemned

Arius in 325. The Nicene Creed is expanded from the Apostles' Creed by a number of Christological propositions which come from the councils of the fourth and fifth centuries. The Apostles' Creed consists mainly of the recital of the saving event, the birth, passion, death, and resurrection of Jesus Christ. It resembles closely the primitive proclamation of the gospel in the apostolic church; but it too is expanded from this proclamation by the addition of the concluding statements concerning belief in the Holy Spirit, the church, the resurrection of the body, and life everlasting. The profession of faith by the recital of a saving event is found in the Old Testament confessions of the saving acts of Yahweh. The climactic saving act is performed by God in Christ Jesus, and this is what the early Christian was asked to believe. Nor does the Roman Church deny that this is still the central object of faith, that Jesus Christ is savior and lord. Further developments were intended to protect the central statement from misunderstanding and distortion. The protection of the faith by declarations concerning the meaning of the central object of faith was inevitable, and it should not be regarded as entirely unwholesome. Had the church paid no attention to refinements of belief in the saving act, it would have had members who did not believe that Jesus was really the Son of God or really the son of man. In either hypothesis, the central object of faith disappears with the savior, and man is not really saved. The Apostles' Creed is still the formula used by the Roman Church at baptism, and the catechetical homilies of the Fathers of the Church, addressed to catechumens, explain the articles of the creed. Many of these homilies were delivered against the background of heresies, and it is remarkable how far the explanation of single articles could be carried. It was not enough in the fifth century to say that one believed in God's only son, Jesus Christ our Lord; one had to know that he is consubstantial with the Father, truly born, not made, really conceived of the Holy Spirit and made man from the Virgin Mary.

When one compares the Apostles' Creed with the profession of faith composed by the Council of Trent and the oath against Modernism imposed by Pius X (1903–1914), one sees how the recital of the saving act has been transformed into a compendium of doctrine.[3] It takes about twenty minutes to read the two documents aloud. The average Catholic never encounters these formulae. They are recited and an oath of belief is taken by all candidates to major orders (including the episcopacy), by all who enter upon any major ecclesiastical office, and annually by professors of theology and philosophy in Roman Catholic seminaries. This last obligation suggests that the professors are a particularly untrustworthy class, and in recent years the formula has been called "the loyalty oath." That is just what it is. The two documents together represent what the modern Roman Church regards as the minimum of propositions which one must believe in order to profess the Roman Catholic faith in its integrity. It is not employed for the laity, but every member of the clergy takes it at least once in his life, most of the clergy several times. I have pronounced it about twenty-five times, but most of my colleagues approach forty. The oath is intended to safeguard the orthodoxy of faith of those who are in the best position to pervert the faith.

At this point the Protestant critic may ask—indeed has asked many times—whether the Roman Church has not passed the limits of tolerance in the number of propositions which it proposes for belief. The question is better answered in discussing the teaching office, for the expansion of the objects of faith is not as great as it appears to be, and the propositions have different values in the scheme of Catholic doctrine. The same Protestant critic may have an unfavorable impression of the monolithic structure of Roman belief. There is no good answer to this except that it is not as monolithic as it appears from the outside. It is not a system of thought control, although the Roman Church has had and still has members who tried to make it so. It will be seen in the chapter on theology that the principle of rationalism permits differences wide enough to be surprising. On the other hand, the Roman Church since the Reformation has made every effort to see that its members, whether they teach or learn, know and accept those beliefs which it takes as basic; and the number of such beliefs is notably larger than it was in the early church.

A number of contemporary theologians have asked whether the doctrinal emphasis in Roman faith may not have obscured the New Testament idea of faith; Dewart has called it Greek rather than biblical.[4] Belief is for all men, whether learned or unlearned, old or young, intelligent or simple; and it is a personal commitment which is within the grasp of all. These theologians attempt to recover something of the faith which the apostles called for when they proclaimed the gospel, a kind of faith which is not given by a mere assent to doctrine. Such attempts to rethink faith are not directed to the annihilation of doctrine and its development, but it has to be confessed that it is not easy to rethink faith. The modern Roman Catholic does have questions and problems which can have only doctrinal answers; he accepts the answers from the church because he believes in the church. Does he thus attain "faith which works through love" (Galatians 5:6)? He even less obviously attains the faith which moves mountains (1 Corinthians 13:2). The modern Roman Catholic does not really understand what this kind of faith is; and the rethinking of faith must restore it for him. Assent to doctrine is not of itself dynamic, and biblical faith is dynamic before all else.

## 2. The Teaching Office of the Church

If the teaching office of the Roman Church were defined as the office of presenting divinely revealed truths, it might be incredible but not complex. The teaching office is understood as having wider scope, however, and the problems of the teaching office arise from its complexity, not from its incredibility. But the incredibility is not to be dismissed without comment; when the Protestant churches seceded from Rome, they seceded from the teaching office, and the Roman understanding of the teaching office was not adopted in the Protestant churches. The abandonment was not total; the Protestant churches wrote confessions of faith, they reached doctrinal decisions by synods of bishops or of ministers, and they enforced doctrinal conformity at times with a rigidity equal to the rigidity of Rome. It has never been true that the Protestant churches embraced without reservation the principle of private judgment, but they did not think of their teaching as authoritative in the sense in which the Roman Church thinks of its teaching.

The Roman Church claims to teach with authority, and the idea deserves some preliminary reflection. Teaching is an old and honored profession, and any teacher can be said to teach with authority. The authority can in the first place be considered as conferred upon him by the state or the educational institution which authorizes him to lecture in classrooms. This authorization in turn rests upon a more fundamental "authority," which is based on his competence to deal with the material of his instruction. In modern times, this means that his competence has been certified by some examining body, and he may have in addition that proof of competence which comes from experience. He does therefore teach with authority.

The teacher may exercise his authority in several ways, some of which are regarded as abuses in the teaching profession. He is within his authority if he insists on silence and attention while he lectures and if he ejects students who refuse to give him silent attention. He is within his authority if he presents to his students a body of knowledge on which they must pass a successful examination and if he assigns work to be done. Most teachers feel that he exceeds his authority if he imposes mere opinion on the students or if he presents opinion as established truth. Most teachers likewise feel that he exceeds his authority if he refuses to entertain inquiries and objections concerning his presentation.

The analogy of the authority of the teacher does not entirely fit the Roman conception of authoritative teaching, although it resembles it in many respects. The "competence" of the Roman Church lies in its possession of divinely revealed truths, a possession which the Roman Church claims is exclusive for the totality of these truths. Its "certification" comes from the commission it has received from Jesus Christ to teach these truths to all men. It exercises its authority by insisting that its members accept these truths on pain of failure or ejection. It imposes these truths with a deeper conviction that they are indisputable than the conviction of the teacher who may allow his students to dispute whether Columbus was the first European to "discover" America, but not to dispute whether Columbus first reached America in 1492.

The analogy breaks down in three important respects. First, any teacher and any school are engaged in a cooperative activity; they depend on other teachers and schools. The Roman Church claims to be the only teacher of revealed truth, and it cooperates with no one and learns from no one. Secondly, its commission is universal. No particular teacher is obliged to be a teacher, and no one is obliged to become a student. The Roman Church addresses all mankind and has a duty to address them. Consequently, all mankind has a duty to listen, and to refuse to listen is a sin from which one is excused only by ignorance "in good faith." Thirdly, the Roman Church teaches with an assurance which no teacher or school can have. This will be treated at greater length; it is the claim of infallibility. Hence the Roman Church imposes its teaching in a unique manner.

The assent which the Roman Church imposes is the assent of faith, discussed in the preceding section. Faith is given to God and to the church as the channel through which the revelation of God comes. Yet there is of course a faith in the church, a faith that the church is the authentic spokesman of God revealing. The Roman

Church claims its credibility on its historic continuity with the apostles, on the unity of its teaching with apostolic teaching, and, according to the First Vatican Council, on its historic reality as a manifest sign of God at work. All these claims have been disputed; it is not our purpose here to vindicate them, but simply to set forth the base of the Roman claims. Ultimately the base is that no other church can vindicate the same claim, and the Protestant churches have somewhat implicitly acknowledged this by denying that either Rome or the Protestant churches can make the claim.

The Roman Church locates the subjects of the teaching authority very precisely, and here some of the elements of the structure discussed previously must be recalled. The teaching church consists of the college of the bishops with the Pope at its head. The Pope, however, may teach independently of the college in the sense that he need not consult them or seek their approval; it is not an admissible hypothesis in Romanism that he could teach in opposition to them. This is the normal exercise of the teaching authority; the ecumenical council which assembles all the bishops of the world is an extraordinary teaching authority. The Pope is the teacher of the whole church; the bishop, and only the bishop, is the authoritative teacher in his diocese. The clergy are empowered to assist the bishop in his office of teaching, but he remains the sole authoritative teacher. Technically the clergy as well as the laity belong to the learning church, not the teaching church. The position of theological scholars will be discussed in the chapter on theology and doctrine.

The objects of authoritative teaching are not so precisely defined, and from this imprecision many problems have arisen. I have several times used the term "divinely revealed truths" to designate the object of authoritative teaching, but the object goes beyond these in the strict sense. To return to the analogy of the teacher, these are all that the church learns from God, and therefore all that the church can teach. The official phrase in Roman doctrine is *faith and morals*. Faith, meaning here the object of faith, means in the first place revealed truths. Morals refer to *works*; the Roman Church imposes faith and works. It claims to be the sole authoritative judge of Christian moral conduct, and it therefore claims the right to direct the individual conscience. Yet under both headings the Church teaches propositions which neither it nor anyone else considers divinely revealed, and the basis on which this authority is claimed is somewhat subtle.

To begin with faith: from its first century, the Roman Church encountered the fact that belief in any proposition implies belief in other propositions. An early heresy was Docetism, which taught that the body of Jesus was an optical illusion, that the Son of God did not really become man. The heresy actually denies nothing of the Gospels and admits fully the historical record of the words and deeds of Jesus. It simply interposes an absurd presupposition with which the external record taken by itself is compatible. When the church rejected Docetism, it had to go beyond the Gospels to do it and to affirm explicitly something which the Gospels imply. Similarly when Arius said that the Son was a creature of like substance with the Father, he said something which could not be refuted by simply quoting the New Testament. When the church affirmed that the Son is *consubstantial* with the Father, it used a term unknown to the Bible to define a biblical reality. In these early heresies, the church acted as teacher rather than proclaimer, explaining the content and meaning of the proclamation. Had heretics not introduced the language of Greek philosophy to define the content of their belief, the church would not have had to employ the same language to define Catholic belief. The church had to choose one type of philosophical language against another; and one may say that the very idea of the teaching church is born when this happens. But it seems self-evident that the church can claim no commission from Jesus Christ to teach philosophy; yet who else is empowered to determine whether a philosophical statement of Christian belief is faithful to that belief?

The church then becomes aware that, if its belief is to be safeguarded, other propositions not directly belonging to belief must also be safeguarded. The principle is something like the rabbinical maxim that one must build a fence around the Law. One does not directly violate the Law by crossing the fence, but one is in greater danger of violating it; therefore to breach the fence comes to mean almost the same thing as breaking the Law. Mystery was spoken of as the object of faith. To illustrate from the Christological controversies, the church does not claim to understand the personal relationship of Jesus with the Father. Yet it claims to be able to define when a statement of that relationship is false; but the definition cannot be based on an understanding of the mystery. It can be based only on the consciousness which the church has of the way in which it has interpreted the mystery; the novel statement can be measured only against this, which is exactly to measure it against the teaching of the church. The teaching authority then empowers the church to judge the validity of both scientific and philosophical conclusions, if these conclusions seem to make it impossible to retain some article of faith. Thus, in the Christological and Trinitarian controversies of the fourth and fifth centuries, the simple statement of belief that Jesus is the Son of God was not enough; the church also arrived at fairly precise definitions of nature, substance, and person, which permitted it to formulate its Christological and Trinitarian beliefs as belief that God is three persons subsisting in one nature. Was it necessary that belief be formulated in these terms? Absolutely speaking, it would seem that it was not, but one can rarely speak absolutely in history and cover all the facts. So many erroneous ways of stating belief appeared that the church settled on a single formula which would remove the errors which it knew. The formula would not necessarily protect it against errors which it did not know.

I have tried to set forth a principle implicit in the historic experience of the church, the principle that the church could not teach its belief without expressing itself on propositions which are not objects of belief. One could go on from here to the principle that the church alone ultimately knows where its field of competence ends, for it must admit limits. Certain episodes in the history of the church, however, do not permit this principle to be stated without reservations; the case of Galileo is recognized as an instance when an authoritative ecclesiastical body exceeded its competence. There are other instances where the excess is less noticed only because it was less obvious. The attitude of the Roman Church toward the theory of evolution in the nineteenth century nearly furnished another Galileo case. Yet the principle that the church can reject what is contrary to its belief must remain, for otherwise it has no teaching authority at all. The question then arises whether the church always knows what it believes, and it is clear that the church must examine its own belief as well as the statements that seem to contradict its belief. With this reservation, one may maintain the principle that the church is the sole judge of its own competence, for only the church knows what it believes. One can hardly say that the church has always possessed this knowledge in its perfection.

Hence the church has engaged in learning; this seems inevitable, but it has no commission to engage in learning, and one ought to assume that when the church is so engaged, its learning will be only as good as its research. The engagement in learning was

easier in those centuries when almost all learned men were churchmen and when learning made little progress beyond the point
which it had reached in Hellenistic and Roman times. With
the new learning of the Middle Ages and the Renaissance, and
more urgently with the explosion of learning since the seventeenth
century, the church was hopelessly outdistanced. Anything like the
Galileo case or the evolution controversy seems most unlikely in the
modern Roman Church.

In the field of morals, the same development can be observed.
One does not find a moral "code" in the proper sense in the New
Testament; the Christian moral ideal is the ideal of love, illustrated
by obvious fulfilments of the ideal in the affairs of daily life. In the
centuries since the apostolic church, however, problems of conduct
have arisen which early Christians did not have and to which the
proclamation of love gives no concrete answer. Yet the Roman
Church claims to be the supreme director of the Christian conscience and it must answer questions of the Christian conscience.
An enumeration of some questions which have been evaded or
answered ambiguously will illustrate uncertainties in this area. May
a Christian go to war? May a Christian own slaves? May a Christian
lend money at interest? May a Christian burn heretics and witches?
May a Christian practice contraception? If the teaching office of faith
is influenced by the culture in which the faith is professed, the influence of the culture on morals is even more profound. The classic
example is the abandonment of the medieval prohibition of lend-
ing money at interest. This was abandoned because money came
to be viewed as a productive good and not as a consumptible good.
One observes that the change here was not in belief but in economic
theory, surely an area in which the church has no commission to
teach.

When such questions arise, they may deal not with Christian
morality but with ethics—that is, principles of conduct which are
formed by man's reasoning about his condition and not from divine
revelation. As the church has no authority in philosophy and
science, so it has no authority in the morality of reason; its statements again will be as good as its research. It may indeed find that
certain ethical principles are contrary to the principle of Christian
love, but here also it may have to examine its own beliefs as well
as the ethical principles. One must admit that the distinction between morals and manners is even more subtle than the difference
between philosophy and theology. It is only a few generations since

most Roman Catholic moral theologians (who are not the official teaching church) affirmed that the waltz was sinful. Roman Catholics here taught the moral theologians by ignoring this affirmation. In morals as in faith, the teaching of the church has been extended to questions which lie outside its competence, but it remains true that the church can hardly speak on morals at all without touching ethics.

It must be admitted that the teaching authority of the Roman Church has sometimes been exercised with imperialism, nor can it be denied that the Roman Church is the very model of conservatism, in that it almost never withdraws from a position once stated. It has never reversed its condemnation of Galileo; it has simply allowed the condemnation to fall into oblivion, and this is its normal way of handling such problems.[1] The teaching authority of the Roman Church is vested at any given moment in men, who are not all of equal virtue and competence. The Roman Church believes it has certain built-in safeguards against vice and incompetence, but these safeguards are minimal; they assure survival, but they do not guarantee immunity from serious trouble. Pius V was and is respected as a holy and learned man, but his deposition of Elizabeth I of England is recognized as one of the greatest blunders in the history of the Papacy.[2] Leo X, celebrated neither for virtue nor for learning, refused to take Martin Luther seriously, and the Roman Church has had to take him seriously ever since. These are not precisely examples of the teaching authority, but they touch it closely. Pius V, as the arbiter of the Catholic conscience, released English Catholics from their allegiance to their sovereign. Leo X did not examine Luther's complaints about the practice and the doctrinal implications of indulgences; there is no doubt that both the practice and the doctrinal implications needed to be examined very carefully.

The Roman Church, as was said, has never had the knowledge of what it believed in its perfection. If one observes that the teaching office has exhibited imperialism, one must also notice that the Roman Church has not always spoken at times when the mature judgment of history is that it should have spoken. It is difficult to understand how the Roman Church, even in medieval Christianity, could have accepted the Crusades. It is difficult to understand how it has never officially declared that slavery is immoral. In spite of its reputation for a certain rigor in its dogmatic and moral teaching, the Roman Church has sometimes shown a remarkable tolerance of human weakness. One must say that it has often been less of a force for Christian belief and Christian morality than it was instituted to be.

The Roman Church does believe that the learning or listening church can be a source of its teaching. It accepts "the consent of the faithful" as one of the factors which determine its belief, but in the history of Roman belief this has been a theoretical rather than a practical consideration. The consent of the faithful must be a consent maintained under the leadership of the pastors and teachers, and it is difficult to understand how a consent could be meaningful with this condition added. It is normal for Catholics to believe what they have been taught.

A less defensible aspect of the teaching office is the supervision which the Roman Church has exercised over Catholic learning since the Protestant Reformation, especially over learning in which priests are engaged. Priests who write on any subject must submit their manuscripts to episcopal authority for approval (CIC 1386). Lay scholars are under the same supervision for works on the Bible, theology, canon law, and ecclesiastical history (CIC 1385). The practice of censorship has been submitted to criticism quite often in recent times, and it is probable that the Roman Church will abandon this particular form of imperialism in learning. The history of censorship is not an attractive narrative, and nowhere is it more evident that the teaching authority is vested in men. In the late nineteenth and early twentieth centuries, Roman authorities issued declarations and directives concerning biblical criticism which have now been consigned to oblivion; as we noticed, the Roman Church does not withdraw from stated positions. These declarations should simply never have been made, for they were made without investigation. That Catholics have always believed that Moses wrote the Pentateuch and John the fourth Gospel proves nothing critically until one has examined the basis of the belief. If the belief is not based on divinely revealed truth it has no value at all. Like the Galileo case, these declarations illustrate the abuse of the teaching authority. It must be added that the present mood and temper of the Roman Church is less sympathetic to such abuses, although some flagrant examples have occurred within the last twenty years. The examples are now so widely recognized for what they are that the probability of other examples in the near future seems remote.

It is such examples more than anything else which have contributed to what many view apprehensively as a growing disrespect for the teaching authority, and surely no authority enhances itself by abusing its powers. That the present generation of the Roman Church is really disrespectful, insubmissive, ready to voice all sorts of doubts and questions, is not certainly an accurate description of the situation. On the other hand, the former respect and submissiveness are much less in evidence. To some Catholics this seems a healthy development; they believe it manifests a more mature Catholicism, a Catholicism whose faith will be more intelligent and more firmly founded than the faith of their elders. They hope that the doubts and questions will compel the teaching authority to accept its responsibility more fully and that the response to genuine leadership will be more sincere and hearty. Others see in the present the seeds of future disaster, even on the scale of the Protestant Reformation. Still others see the phenomenon as inevitable but refrain from prognostications of the future. One may say surely no more than that Roman Catholicism will take a somewhat different form both in the teaching church and in the learning church; this is a critical development, whatever its future course may be.

The unique assurance with which the Roman Church teaches has been mentioned; this is the charisma of infallibility, the one feature of the Roman teaching office which is most offensive to the rest of the world. The explicit claim dates only from the First Vatican Council, which defined that the Pope enjoys the same infallibility in defining teaching on faith and morals which the Catholic Church enjoys.[3] The point of the definition was the infallibility of the Pope; but the infallibility of the Church had not been previously declared in such explicit terms. The claim was not really as novel as many said at the time; the Roman Church had always acted as if it were infallible, and it was not a difficult step to put the action into a formula. Very few Roman Catholics at the time felt that the Roman Church had made an unfounded claim and those who were deeply convinced of this left the Roman communion.

The declaration of infallibility was put in precise terms, and it is important that the precision be understood. The claim is actually quite restrained and in Roman belief no more than the church must claim if it believes in its own survival. The object of infallibility is defined as faith and morals, terms which have already been discussed, and a statement is not considered infallible unless it is uttered under certain conditions. It must be a *solemn* utterance. There is no agreement on what external solemnities must be present, but the casual utterance is excluded. One may say that the matter must be important enough to deserve solemnity, that some deliberation must have been made, and that the statement must be couched in such terms that its seriousness is evident. It is not expected that the Pope will say, "This is an infallible declaration," and no Pope has ever said it.

The declaration must be concerned with faith and morals; it should be clear from the preceding discussion that this is the least precise part of the definition. Roman theologians believe that the terms should be taken in the narrow sense, that is, the church and the Pope are infallible when they declare that something is of faith, that it is a divinely revealed truth. If the declaration deals with anything else, it is, as was said, as good as its research.

The Pope is infallible only when he speaks to the entire church formally and of set purpose; this is meant by the phrase *ex cathedra*, "from the throne." He is the primate of the entire Roman Church, and he must make it clear that he speaks in this capacity. Again there is no set formality; most pontifical documents are addressed to the whole church, but a large number of them are addressed to particular countries or even particular dioceses, and these cannot be invoked as infallible documents.

Within these terms it seems that there is ample room for papal declarations which are not infallible, and in fact Roman theologians agree that the number of infallible declarations is far smaller than the number of declarations for which infallibility is not claimed. But here one encounters another aspect of infallibility. Theologians distinguish between the *extraordinary* teaching office, which is exercised in solemn declarations, and the *ordinary* teaching office, which is exercised in the normal operations of the Roman Church. Infallibility is asserted here also in the area of faith and morals, defined in the same way, but to ascertain whether a proposition has always been presented as an article of faith in the ordinary teaching of the Roman Church can be a research problem of some magnitude; and if doubt arises over such a proposition the doubt would most probably be resolved by a solemn declaration. The omission of a declaration in such a question would be an equivalent denial that the Roman Church presents the proposition as an article of faith. This is illustrated in the discussion of contraception, still unresolved at this writing. If it were assured that the encyclical *Casti Connubii* of Pius XI were a solemn declaration of the type described, or if it were established that the prohibition of contraception had always been taught in the Roman Catholic Church as an article of faith, no further discussion would be possible. But neither hypothesis is verified, and the discussion continues.

The teaching authority of the Roman Church, consequently, is not primarily exercised by infallible declarations; yet an assent is imposed for the ordinary teaching, even when by hypothesis it is subject to change. The definition of this authority is difficult to state in terms which give it neither more nor less weight than the Roman Church means to claim for it. In general Roman Catholics are expected to accept the teaching authority of the Roman Church because it is a safe guide, even if it is not perfectly free from error and because in the critical areas of faith and morals it will not fail them. There is no other guide to whom they can turn, and they are not personally responsible if they submit to the church, even when in a particular case the position of the church could change. The ambiguity in the definition of such authority appears when one tries to distinguish it from the authority of one's physician or attorney, to whom one normally submits in professional questions. One can always go to another physician or attorney, and the Roman Church would not accept this analogy. Assent to the Roman Church is a kind of assent which admits reservations, but the principle of the reservations is not stated. The technical phrase used in theology to describe the response of the Catholic to the teaching authority is *internal religious assent*, so defined to distinguish it from mere external submission and from assent given simply because the teaching authority seems to have sufficient evidence for what it says. The hypothesis that one might have good reasons for doubting or denying a proposition of the teaching authority is admitted in the Roman Church as long as the proposition has not been solemnly declared; one who has such reasons is recommended to make his position known to the teaching authority.

It has been seen that not all propositions of the teaching authority are presented with the same weight. The pompous and turgid quality of ecclesiastical Latin prose can make the simplest statement sound like the promulgation of the Decalogue on Sinai, and a part of professional Roman theological training is to learn to read, or rather to decode, ecclesiastical documents. When the Roman Church wishes to affirm that something is an article of faith, it is quite capable of doing it clearly and unambiguously, and in what it considers vital issues it usually exhibits these virtues of language. The Roman Church may cross the line which separates belief from learning, as has been discussed; here also the Roman Church can make itself clear, but it does not always do so. Theologians understand that infallibility in faith does not extend to infallibility of reasoning and that the basis of statements made at any particular time can be eroded as learning advances. Teaching which deals with a definite contemporary situation or with a definite local problem are limited to the time and the place. This is obvious when a Pope addresses a country or a diocese; it is less obvious when a statement concerning a contemporary problem is couched in the Roman prose of eternal verities. In the notorious syllabus of errors of 1864, Pius IX condemned eighty propositions almost all of which have since become commonplaces in scholarship, Roman Catholic as well as others.[4] Viewed simply from the point of language, the student and lover of good language finds that the Roman Church habitually overstates its case.

The description given above is bound to suggest, especially to an unsympathetic reader, a cumbersome and inefficient system of thought control. One can respond only in terms used already, that it is not what it appears to be from the outside. For some generations now the posture of the Roman Church since the Reformation has been described as the mentality of the beleaguered fortress. In the area of the teaching authority, this has meant a certain timidity toward anything which even remotely resembled the movements which issued in the Protestant revolt. Effectively this has meant that the Roman Church has been unsympathetic to the progress of learning, secular or sacred. The attitude springs from no deliberate hostility to the progress, but simply from a desire to maintain that security which rests on a community agreement on the teachings of the Roman Church. The structure of the teaching authority of the Roman Church has experienced no change from the times when Augustine and Thomas Aquinas wrote with a freedom enjoyed by no Roman Catholic scholar since the Council of Trent. One can never escape the fact, mentioned several times, that the teaching authority at any given time is vested in men who respond to situations according to their training and habits. The response of the Roman Church to the Reformation can now be recognized as withdrawal, not an attitude sympathetic to freedom and adventure, intellectual or any other variety. Unfortunately this meant that the Roman Church confronted the nineteenth and twentieth centuries not with an antiquated faith but with antiquated teachings. The process of adjustment has been painful. It has probably ended. The documents of the Second Vatican Council do not express the mentality of the beleaguered fortress.

## 3. Tradition and Scripture

The problem designated by this subtitle may seem rather theologically recondite for a summary exposition of Roman Catholicism, but the relation of Scripture and tradition in the teaching office of the Roman Catholic Church was raised in the Reformation, debated in the Council of Trent, and most recently has again been discussed in Roman Catholic theology. Even an outline study of the teaching office must include some remarks on this problem.

All Christian churches accept the Bible as the word of God, however they may differ in their understanding of this term. Jews also accept the Old Testament of the Christians, which they call the Bible, as the word of God. Roman Catholics do not differ from Protestants in identifying anything else as the word of God. To give the book this value is to accept it as divinely revealed truth to be believed and lived.

All Christian churches likewise substantially agree that the Bible must be read in the church, but modal differences in the interpretation of this principle can diverge rather broadly. Protestantism has never admitted that a man and his Bible can constitute a church. The Bible itself describes a Christian community, and it leaves no room for purely private and personal religion. If the Christian community failed to exist, then the Bible itself would be proved to be not the word of God. If the believer in the Bible is honest in his belief, he will find his way into a church.

All Christian churches agree that the church is older than the New Testament, as the community of Israel is older than the Old Testament. The Bible is not only to be read in a community, it was produced in a community for the community. It cannot be heard apart from the community for which it speaks. The Bible is the word of God, but it was the church which uttered this word. It is the church which gives the believer the Bible, not the Bible which gives him the church.

This summary of agreement may be somewhat overstated, and it may appear that it leaves little room for difference between Roman

Catholics and Protestants. In fact, precisely this aspect of the teaching authority may have been the major point of division in the Reformation, and the division has grown wider since. Only very recent discussions have begun to suggest that the division may not be really as wide as it appears. Protestant churches do not deny the existence and value of church tradition; but they deny that it has the weight which Roman Catholics give it. In early Protestantism, one of the slogans was *Scriptura sola*, the Bible by itself, often misunderstood by both Catholics and Protestants. The Reformers never denied that the Bible had to be read in the church.

The Council of Trent considered the question important enough to be placed first on its agenda, and the debates disclosed a notable lack of unanimity on the meaning and value of tradition. Some of those who spoke in the debates used language much like the language of the Reformers, but their colleagues did not accuse them of heresy. No Roman Catholic in the sixteenth century or at any other time could deny that the Bible alone is the word of God. It was necessary to assert it with more than usual firmness against the Protestant charges that Romanism did not give proper respect to the word of God. But the Council also had centuries of Roman Catholic tradition which it could not repudiate without conceding everything to the Protestants. Finding an agreeable formula turned out to be a long and difficult task.

The formula finally adopted had a deliberate ambiguity which has left room for the most recent discussions.[1] The Council said that the Roman Church derived its doctrines both from the Bible and from tradition and that it venerated both these sources with equal affection and reverence. It affirmed that the Bible is the inspired word of God, which tradition is not; but tradition is a source of faith equal to the Bible in that it is a true source and that it imposes the assent of faith. This was the answer to the Protestant charge so often expressed in popular language as "The Romans teach things that are not in the Bible." It would be hard to think of any Protestant church which does not teach things that are not in the Bible; but the Protestant churches do not venerate these teachings "with equal affection and reverence." That is, the Protestant churches do not claim a teaching authority equal to the Roman authority. The Protestant opposes the Bible to the teaching authority of the Roman Church, not to the teaching authority of his own church.

The meaning of tradition is not entirely precise in Roman

Catholic theology. Tradition can be viewed as channel and as content, to use a modern phrase. As content, it is a body of doctrine. The Council of Trent called this body of doctrine "unwritten" in contrast to the written word of the Bible; "unwritten" does not mean that the doctrine is not found in literature. But the word "unwritten" is of importance. In the definition of the Mariological dogmas of the Immaculate Conception (Pius IX, 1854) and the Assumption (Pius XII, 1950), it was evident that literary evidence of these beliefs was lacking for the earliest centuries. The Roman Church concluded from the literary evidence in which the beliefs are found that the beliefs were as old, at least in an implicit form, as the church itself, and thus was enabled to declare that these articles had always been believed in the church. No proposition can be declared an article of faith unless perpetual belief in the church can be affirmed of it. The Roman Church, however, does not depend solely on literary and historical evidence; it depends on its own consciousness of its belief, and it must be admitted that the analysis of this consciousness can be subtle. In the two dogmas mentioned, it was the consciousness of perpetual beliefs which are in harmony with these dogmas and which are themselves confirmed by these dogmas. Tradition as content, then, is simply the body of Roman Catholic belief taught by the teaching authority.

Tradition as channel thus becomes the teaching authority, the only authentic spokesman of Roman Catholic belief. Tradition can therefore be called "living," for at any given moment it exists in the teaching authority. It is not merely the record of the past; for the teaching church in the past proclaimed its belief with no more authority than the church has now. The line here is drawn at the apostolic age, for only the apostles were in direct communication with Jesus, the climax and consummation of divine revelation.

The Council of Trent admitted frankly that the Roman tradition contains propositions which cannot be found in the Bible. It countered the Protestant charge by asserting itself, so to speak; it denied that either in the Bible or in its own traditions is there any affirmation that the Bible is the sole source of revealed truth. It appealed to the historic behavior of the Roman Church from apostolic times and equivalently said that the Roman Church confirmed itself by its very reality. The divine truths are contained in Scripture and tradition, and they have always been found there.

An unresolved question in contemporary theology is whether the Council of Trent meant that Scripture and tradition are two sources of revealed truth. Certainly the Council did not mean that they are two unrelated sources. The weight of opinion in Roman theology since the Council of Trent has been that the Council did mean two sources. The Bible is superior in dignity, but tradition is superior in completeness. The Bible needs the church as interpreter, and there is no other authentic interpreter. Probably no Protestant would accept this as equivalent to the principle that the Bible must be read in the church, but it is equivalent, although far from synonymous.

Some recent theologians have questioned the theory of the two sources, and their objections seem to be gaining ground.[2] No doubt they would gain ground more rapidly if their formulation were as neat as the common opinion. They observe that the common opinion achieves neatness by a false oversimplification. To attempt a formulation which has not been made, one might say that tradition is the reading of the Bible in the church. One may ask how diligently one must read the Bible in order to arrive at the dogma of the Immaculate Conception, and it is at this point that the newer opinion has less clarity than the older, but it is precisely the Bible as read in the church which one must consider, and not merely the Bible detached from its place in the church. And since Protestants can share the statement put in this way, a number of theologians think that agreement on this ancient and fundamental question may be possible. The aim of the theologians who propose the newer opinion is to rid the Roman Church of what seems to be a false dualism in its view of the sources of its faith.

The question is not really different from the question which was agitated in the nineteenth century under the rubric of "development of dogma" or "development of doctrine." It was when he satisfied his own mind on this question that John Henry Newman felt he owed submission to Rome, and his own contribution to the problem is still a classic in the field.[3] Even without the Protestant revolt, one thinks, the Roman Church would sooner or later have had to explain to itself the expansion of its belief from the belief of the apostolic church. In most of the theories, the development of dogma is a development of understanding or perception rather than an accretion of knowledge. One may compare it to the growth of a person's self-knowledge as opposed to the growth of his knowledge through schooling. The Roman Church simply does not admit that any article of faith can be proposed which was not contained in the apostolic preaching, and it is aware of the Protestant objections to the dogmas of Mariology and purgatory and some others. Since it cannot admit an *objective* expansion of the content of its faith, it must appeal to the *subjective* expansion. But it has been difficult to find a satisfactory formula for this.

The formula of *explicit-implicit*, employed by many theologians, does not really meet the problem. If Jesus is the Son of God in a way different from other men, it merely makes the belief explicit to say that he is the natural son; otherwise he would be an adopted son, for there is no other alternative. Is it equally implicit to say that, because Mary is the mother of God (a truth implicit in the divine sonship of Jesus), she is therefore immaculately conceived? Whatever be the process, it cannot be a process of deduction. Thomas Aquinas, by what he thought flawless logic, proved that Mary could not have been immaculately conceived; even the prince of theologians had his blind spots. Duns Scotus, by an argument which does not so much defy logic as ignore it, was convinced that she was. The Roman Church does not conceive that it arrives at such beliefs by logic. Newman alluded to the universal belief that Great Britain is an island, although very few men have proved it to themselves experimentally. It is just that if Great Britain is not an island, one does not know what one can believe. The Roman Church uses a similar process in arriving at some of its beliefs, but in order to follow the process one must be acquainted with certain presuppositions. Regarding both the Immaculate Conception and the Assumption, the Roman Church experienced a constant surging in itself toward the affirmation of these dogmas. At the risk of hypostatizing the institution, one can say that this surging, which went on for centuries before the declarations, gave the Roman Church a kind of inner compulsion to declare itself. It recognized the pulse of its own faith, to carry on the metaphor. There are pious beliefs beyond counting in the Roman Church where no such inner compulsion has been felt. Perhaps because the religious experience involved in such a process—and it is good to remember that it is a religious experience—has no parallel in other experience, the Roman Church will never find a formula for it. It is only fair to the Roman Church, however, to point out that such declarations have never been impulsive or hasty.

Reference has already been made to other instances of development which can generally be described as cases in which the Roman Church had to solve a problem proposed in terms that it had not used before. The formula of explicit-implicit is even less applicable to these cases; they are translations of apostolic or biblical belief into another terminology, and they are subject to no more and no less danger of perversion than any translation is. The question is whether the translation is an accurate statement of belief, not whether it is a perfect reproduction of the primitive statement. One who believes that Jesus is consubstantial with the Father says something which is certainly not explicit in the New Testament, and the New Testament writers would not have understood the question if one had asked them whether consubstantial described their belief. The Incarnation is conceived in an ideology which is not the ideology of the New Testament and which cannot be deduced from the New Testament. It is a well-known fact in the history of theology that the term consubstantial gave an occasion to the heresy of the Monophysites; to that extent it is not an entirely good term.

Development of doctrine means that the Roman affirmations of belief are in a way open and in a way closed. They are closed in that the Roman Church does not admit the possibility of another statement which would negate them. They are open in that further statements about the same belief are always possible. The proper object of faith, as has been said, is mystery, and mystery is never so well understood that it cannot be better understood. In fact the conservatism of the Roman Church has always made it slow to accept new formulas which added something to the old, still more if they seemed to change the old. But development is not a process which has halted. On the other hand, its course cannot be predicted. Development more frequently than not arises from a factor outside the Roman Church.

It was noted that the Roman Church regards itself as the sole authentic interpreter of the Bible. The claim has many reservations which must be remembered. The interpretation of the church deals with the Bible as the rule of faith; here as elsewhere the general commission of the church deals with revelation. Up to the nineteenth century, the entire Bible was regarded by most Christians, Protestant as well as Catholic, as the word of God which came to the human authors by dictation; hence the whole Bible was revelation and, as such, the proper object of authentic interpretation. A much more complex view, which we need not detail here, makes it clear now that most biblical questions can be answered without any reference to the rule of faith, indeed that the rule of faith supplies no answer to them. Hence the interpretation of the church moves in broad outline rather than in details. The Roman Church is not competent by its teaching office to write an exegetical commentary on the Bible. It is not competent to settle critical and historical questions; the failure of some attempts to do this has been mentioned. It is competent to point out what the Bible says about the belief and the life of Christians; tradition, as was said, can be described as the church reading the Bible. Theologians do not agree on the number of biblical texts which have been the object of definitive interpretation, but there is general agreement that the number is small—less than ten. It may appear that the Roman Church has used this claim very sparingly, and it has. Its interpretation appears rather in what is called the *analogy of faith*, by which is meant the simple fact that the Roman Catholic who reads or studies the Bible reads it as a Roman Catholic. This religious background does not assure him that he will always understand the Bible correctly; it assures him that the book he reads is the book of the church, which gives it to him as the source of the belief which he has from the church. Neither the Roman Catholic nor any one else is able to read the Bible as if his mind were entirely vacant. The analogy of faith describes what is in the mind of the Roman Catholic.

## 4. *Theology and Doctrine*

The preceding exposition is intended to present the Roman Catholic understanding of doctrine and its place in the church. The Roman Church makes a distinction between theology and doctrine, although the two are very closely related. No assent is imposed by the church for theological propositions, and complete liberty is granted to theological opinion as long as the opinion is not contrary to doctrine. Naturally this restriction seems to negate the term "complete," but here again the situation looks different from the outside. Only a review of the whole history of theology would show the degree to which liberty of theological opinion has prevailed in the Roman Church, and such a review is not possible here. Undue restrictions upon theological liberty occur when the Roman Church finds itself in unusually tense and threatening situations, as it did during and after the Reformation and the Modernist crisis of the early twentieth century. In such periods, apprehension reaches a high pitch, not only among the officers of the Roman Church but also among its members. Apprehension issues in "witch-hunting" or "heresy-hunting," often with fatal results to the victims.

Theology as a learned discipline really came into existence in the Roman Catholic Church. The Greek word *theologia*, "discourse about the gods," was a philosophical term and designated a type of philosophical investigation. Catholic theology too is a philosophical investigation, but not in the same sense as Greek philosophy. The material of Roman Catholic theology is the doctrine that we have been considering; this doctrine is investigated according to a philosophical method.

The first name usually mentioned in this connection is Justin (†165), who prepared a vindication of the Christian faith in philosophical language—not with profound philosophical insight, in the opinion of most scholars. The first enduring theological tradition is associated with the school of Alexandria, dominated by the names of Pantaenus (†190), Clement (†215), and Origen (185–254). It can be said of this school, as of Justin, that theology was born of controversy. The early generations of the church had no members who would be called intellectuals; if it did have them, they were silent, and silence is not characteristic of intellectuals. Some fragments have been preserved of the pagan scoffing at Christianity as the religion of the ignorant and superstitious. When intellectuals became Christians, they felt the need of presenting a reasoned defense of the faith which they had accepted. The philosophical language adopted by the school of Alexandria was the language of Platonism and Neoplatonism, and this became the language that dominated theological writing for the centuries before the Middle Ages.

It was no accident that the school arose in Alexandria, the most respected center of learning in the Hellenistic-Roman world. Antioch, also a major center of learning, appears as a theological center not much later than Alexandria. After Constantine, Christians in great number attended the great schools of the Roman world; a number of the Fathers of the church have left accounts of their travels to various centers of learning, and they show in their writing that they were thoroughly acquainted with the standard equipment of the learned man of the time. It was this learning which precipitated the doctrinal controversies of the fourth and fifth centuries, and it was this same learning which resolved the controversies. Theological principles and methods emerged; they could be employed by the heterodox as well as the orthodox, but the important fact was that a theological pattern of thought and language existed which was nearly universally understood.

Like the rest of Roman civilization, theological learning went into an eclipse during the Dark Ages of the barbarian invasions; the only achievement of these centuries was to preserve the literary monuments of the age of the Fathers. It was a mark of their interest that the men of this period preserved the writings of the Fathers much more extensively than they preserved the literature of classical antiquity, but theology made no positive advances until the revival of learning of the Middle Ages.

This revival is one of those mysterious movements which defies analysis. It began in philosophy and issued in efforts to restate Christian belief in a new philosophical language. Interest in theology was primarily responsible for the foundation of all the great European universities which date from the twelfth and thirteenth centuries. All of them were founded by ecclesiastical authorities and were originally staffed entirely or mostly by clerics; the very word *clerk*, which designated a learned man, is a corruption of cleric. The most important and lasting element of this movement was the recovery of the works of Aristotle; the employment of these works by Thomas Aquinas gave Roman Catholic theology an Aristotelian pattern which it has not yet lost. The new theological movement, however, was already well under way when Aquinas wrote; without his predecessors it is hard to imagine how he could have achieved what he did. Curiously the Aristotelian pattern is not entirely faithful to Aristotle. The works of Aristotle reached Europe through Latin translations of Arabic translations of the original Greek, as tortuous and obscure as any Greek which has been left from the ancient world. The framework is properly called Thomistic, for it is a framework which Aquinas devised using Aristotle as he knew him.

Thomism is not the only intellectual movement of the Middle Ages; the number of writers of the period called Scholastic is quite large, and names like Bonaventure and Duns Scotus are almost as venerated as Thomas Aquinas. Their influence is less because they did not achieve as systematic an exposition as Aquinas; this was his great strength and explains the endurance of his work. The system of Thomism is more rigorous than the system of Aristotelianism; it is an effort to impose rationalism upon the entire system of Catholic doctrine. Aquinas did not intend to remove the mystery from Roman Catholic faith, but he was much concerned to show that belief is *reasonable* in the sense that it fits into the universe as Aquinas saw the universe through Aristotelian lenses. It is, of course, just this identification of theological interpretation with a world view conditioned by time which has become the weakness of Thomism in contemporary theology, but no similar effort has been made since to erect a philosophical structure in terms of which every item of Catholic doctrine can be expressed. The coherence comes from the philosophical framework.

Just as theology decayed after the golden age of the Fathers, so it decayed after the golden age of the thirteenth century; theology is not the only learned discipline which has a tendency to live off its investments, but the tendency seems to be more pronounced. The Reformation broke upon a theological world which had not had a truly great and original thinker for two centuries and upon schools which were content to parrot textbook phrases. Unfortunately the Reformation was nearly simultaneous with the birth of modern scientific learning, which shattered the Aristotelian world view, and Roman theology simply turned its back on the learned world. The queen of sciences was deposed or expelled from the universities which she had founded; when the general attitude of theologians toward "the new learning" is considered, no other course of action would have been appropriate. Very little theology of permanent value was produced in the tons of polemical writing which responded to the Reformation. Roman Catholic theology remained sullen, defensive, and derivative until the twentieth century, with a few exceptions. It may still exhibit these characteristics, but it is difficult for one to judge his own times. Effectively up to the Second Vatican Council, again with a few exceptions, it had nothing to say to the world outside the Roman Church and very little to say to the members of that Church. Theologians were like mandarins and spoke only to each other. Many if not most people with no church affiliation would rank theology with alchemy and astrology.

This extremely summary sketch can do no more than suggest some features of the relations of theology and doctrine, but suggestions can be made, and those which follow are not presented in the order of importance. Theology arises in part from the need of the intellectual or the educated man in ancient and modern times to justify his faith to himself and to others. He is rarely able to compartmentalize his mind and put his beliefs in a category by themselves where knowledge and experience do not touch them. If he does this, his faith will become meaningless. He asks questions which the simple and the unlearned do not ask. When he answers the questions, he does not restate his faith, but he believes he says something which makes it easier for him to continue believing and to relate his belief to the world and to life. Roman Catholics have become aware of the fact that a highly educated man cannot maintain his faith on the same level as he did when he was ten years of age, for then his belief in God, the Father of our Lord Jesus Christ, might be only as meaningful as a child's belief in Santa Claus.

Theology also develops in response to heresy, a point which Newman thought of capital importance. Heresy asks questions and gives an answer which the church finds intolerable; but the church cannot explain itself unless it thinks through its belief theologically. Here the church does reach new statements of its belief in the sense that the language is new, as has already been observed. The heresy may be the creative factor—which is not meant to imply that heresy is ultimately a good thing; but the historic response of the church to heresy has been to fight the battle on the heretics' ground, because if it is not fought there it is not won. Simple refusal to speak the language of the heretics would be to withdraw from an area of human discourse and thus to become meaningless to all who speak in that area. The Roman Church has been charged with such withdrawal an ample number of times. Its responses to heresy keep the faith from dissolving into completely bland and ambiguous formulas.

Here perhaps the Roman Church may manifest that it is still substantially a European church with Greek antecedents. Other "world religions" have no system of doctrine; it was noted that the Protestant churches retained this Roman feature in a less rigorous form. Judaism, according to its exponents, is a religion without dogma. Traditional Judaism has its own body of learning, which is rabbinical; but it is exactly here that the contrast appears. Rabbinical learning is altogether unstructured. Roman Catholic theology arose in the European intellectual tradition that began with the Greeks, a tradition in which all learning is structured. This structured learning has accompanied the Roman Church where it has been established outside Europe; many theologians wonder whether it will survive in cultures which do not share the European intellectual tradition. One imagines that an Indian or Chinese theology would be as different from Roman theology as Indian and Chinese learning differ from European learning. There is nothing in Roman belief as such, which the Roman Church claims is universal in scope, that would be incompatible with a rabbinical or a Chinese or an Indian type of theology, but as Roman theology exists, it has arisen from the Greek and European need for structure, and this is the third factor.

This factor may be illustrated from this very book, written in the European intellectual tradition. The writer is much more consciously derivative than creative; he is aware that he pumps constantly from a stream of theological tradition in which most of his life has been spent. He cannot talk about the Roman Church in any other language. Possibly this presentation of the Roman Church would be unintelligible in other cultures; perhaps it might even repel readers from other cultures, should they happen to fall upon it.

A fourth factor, also Greek and European, is the drive for philosophical and scientific rationalism. If Thales said that everything is water, he was the first to ask and answer the question. Historically, European man had to ask the same questions about what he believed; like Thales, he may have had the wrong answer more frequently than the right answer. Theological rationalism in the Roman Church is much older than scientific rationalism, and it may be asked whether the second did not develop from the first. As man's knowledge and techniques expand, however, the area of rationalism grows at the expense of the area of theology; it is important to notice that I say the area of theology, not the area of belief. The belief that certain pathological conditions are due to an indwelling demon who can be expelled by exorcism is not really a belief, but an antiquated piece of theological rationalism. As an explanation of the phenomenon, it is on the same level as the panhydrism of Thales. This particular example, it is true, is not a product of Greek rationalism; it is much older than Greek culture, but it illustrates the point. Theological rationalism appears at its most ingenious and its worst when it attempts to rationalize such ideas after philosophical and scientific rationalism have dispossessed them. Theology is at its best when it draws a precise line between what is believed and what is thought; it is a guardian against ignorance and superstition, and it is faithful to this charge to the degree to which it is rational. Like philosophical and scientific rationalism, it sometimes fails to explain the phenomenon. Thomas Aquinas is not commonly called a rationalist; in fact he was one of the most "rationalistic" thinkers of all times, if confidence in the powers of reason makes one a rationalist. A major problem of more recent theology had been that the drive for rationalism has been slowed.

Many Roman Catholics now believe that theology is entering a period of revival comparable to the golden ages of the Fathers and the Scholastics; and perhaps this revival is more advanced than it appears to be. Most observers say that the Second Vatican Council incorporated into its acts much theological work done during the last twenty to thirty years; most of the writers who have done this work are still living, and most of them were present at the Council as *periti*, experts. Their theological work was largely responsible for the tone of the Council, a tone quite different from the tone of earlier councils. One extremely interesting result of this work is the fact that theological literature has become popular among Roman Catholics, popular here meaning that it is widely read by the educated. The level of this literature, which is produced by the most respected theologians of this generation, is remarkably high. Nothing could contribute more to keep the theological revival alive than a wide popular interest in theology. As was said, for several hundred years theology has had very little to say to the Roman Church at large. This revival could not have come about without relaxation of the "siege mentality" and an increase in the amount of working freedom of theologians.

If the revival should turn out to be genuine and lasting, it will illustrate both the sturdiness of theology and its mission. I have tried to show that theology is the principal agent in the process called *development of doctrine*, but this is no longer the proper term for what theology should accomplish. Faith must be constantly examined and reinterpreted, not because traditional interpretations are erroneous but because the church and its members constantly move with history. It was said that Thomas Aquinas tried to set the faith in a comprehensive and coherent world view. He may have been too ambitious, but the effort has to go on. The church lives in the world, speaks to the world, listens to the world. Theology is its interpreter in both directions. The task of theology is never finished unless the world stops changing. St. Augustine coined a celebrated phrase, "faith seeking understanding." He did not mean merely an understanding of the articles of faith, or at least one need not understand the phrase in such a restricted sense. Faith seeks the understanding of the world and of man and of the self, and those who believe are convinced that there is no true understanding of any of these without faith. In recent times, the late Teilhard de Chardin has become the very model of faith seeking understanding, of the theologian who attempts, like Thomas Aquinas, to set his faith in a comprehensive world view. Like Thomas Aquinas, he may have been too ambitious; his work, like the work of Thomas Aquinas, will probably stand until some one else produces something equally comprehensive. In both cases, the world view was hoped to be able to give a deeper understanding of what is believed.

It may be a false generalization to say that the revivals of theology have always been associated with revivals of learning, but the statement is historically true. The decline of theology since the sixteenth century—some would place the date earlier—is associated with a lack of communication between theology and other learned disciplines. Teilhard, who many think is the most influential theological writer of this century, was not a trained theologian; his field of competence was anthropology and paleontology. He also enjoyed a fine understanding of the general principles and methods of the natural sciences. Up to the present generation, there has been no mutual enrichment between theology and other disciplines. The theologian became a custodian of the records of the past and a policeman of orthodox doctrine, orthodox here meaning doctrine the safety of which is assured because it has been said so often that it is safe to repeat it. Theologians did not engage in discourse with other learned men and could not; they simply have not been members of the community of scholars. In the popular mind, they are associated with "church talk", the kind of questions in which no one but a professional churchman could be interested. The Galileo case has had no parallel, but the conditions have not been changed until recently. By unchanged conditions I mean that the Galileo case was possible only because the judges in the case were totally unacquainted with the methods of the natural sciences and did not think that these methods deserved investigation. Theology could not learn from the natural sciences; it was the duty of the natural sciences to learn from theology. In fact it was not theology but the current world view which Galileo threatened. That medieval world view has long since disappeared, but theology has not developed along with the world view that replaced it.

The Council of Trent may be largely responsible for this, although its intentions were good. The Reformation was inevitable for many reasons, but one of the things that made it possible was the lamentable state of education and morality in much of the Roman clergy. The Council wished seminaries to be established, schools in which the clergy would be educated in theology and trained in good habits under close episcopal supervision.[1] This did not happen at once, but it became the prevailing practice. It must be understood that the Council decreed some education instead of none, not seminaries instead of universities. Since theology historically has been the learning of the clergy, however, it meant that theology has been studied in schools isolated from the rest of the learned world. The desire to protect students from some obvious dangers of student life assured that any contact of seminarians with others, whether academic or nonacademic, would be rare and safeguarded.

The history of theology shows a wide variation of quality; and in the long-term analysis one has to say that the Roman Church has had more bad theology than good. Bad theology is not necessarily a theology which exceeds the limits of tolerable error; there has always been room for error in Roman theology, as long as it was not proved to be error in doctrine. But the desire of theologians to achieve something akin to the infallibility claimed by the Roman Church can have pathological effects. Among the most obvious of these defects one may mention timidity and ancestor worship. "Novelty," a word of compliment in most human activities, is a politely insulting word in theology. It has long been more of a theological virtue to cite older writers supporting one's view than to propose a new view for which older writers cannot be cited. This leads to the evasion of questions which older writers did not treat or to the distortion of their statements to fit new situations. It leads, as has been seen, to a preoccupation with "church talk," which involves no discourse with laymen or with those outside the Roman communion. Theology has long been charged with being an authoritarian discipline, both in the sense that it relies on authorities rather than on investigation and in the sense that it proposes its conclusions with an authority that illegitimately imitates the teaching authority of the Roman Church. The culture lag of theology nowhere appears more clearly than in these characteristics; the whole trend of modern learning and education moves away from reliance on "authorities" and from imposing the conclusions of scholars with no other motivation of assent than "because we say so."

If there is a revival of theology, these traits must disappear, and they have disappeared in the writings of those men who represent the contemporary revival. They have not disappeared from theology entirely, and they never will; they appear in other learned disciplines, too. In other learned disciplines, however, they do not lead to promotion; in Roman Catholic theology they still do. There seems to be a kind of Gresham's Law by which bad theology drives out good theology. No previous revival has endured. The present revival must go beyond earlier revivals if it is to endure longer than they did.

Theology and theologians, then, are not members of *the teaching church* in the technical sense; they depend on the teaching church, and the teaching church depends on them. They depend on the teaching church for their authorization and for the material of their discipline. The teaching church depends on them to prepare its own statements of its teaching. The Pope traditionally has a theological adviser drawn from the Order of Preachers, called the *Master of the Sacred Palace*. Each bishop is entitled to a theological adviser (although this officer is not included among the canonical officers), and many bishops do have them. Others consult them as need arises. Occasional public statements made by bishops confirm the utility of a theological adviser for bishops who do not have one. It is evident that such an adviser can reach a position of influence which no scholar as such can earn and retain, and it is unfortunate that the chief and operative qualification for such advisers is so often that they be "safe," meaning that they have never said anything controversial. This may mean that they have never said anything.

That theologians should be an arm of the teaching church is neither entirely good nor entirely bad. They may be kept scholars, submitted to a control which scholarship in general rejects. It is easy to understand why the teaching church thinks that theology should be closely supervised, and in principle there is no reason why it should not be; it is not the fact of supervision but the manner of supervision which raises questions and doubts. It was observed in a previous chapter that the Roman Church cherishes archaic ceremonial practices beyond need and utility. Most of these practices should be abandoned, but if some must be retained, there is an archaic ceremony of theology which deserves consideration. This was the ceremonial which invested the doctor of theology with some of the insignia of the bishop. Most doctors of my acquaintance would shudder at the thought, and many bishops would shudder even more, but theologians would not shudder at some formal external recognition of the worth and dignity of theology, symbolized in the persons who have proved their academic competence in the discipline. They would prefer a real recognition of their ability to do the work of theology over a symbolic ceremonial which might conceal a golden chain and fetters. They would certainly prefer that the world of theology should imitate the academic world in recognizing that the scholar is certified by what he knows rather than whom he knows. The ring, the four-peaked biretta, and the scarlet did not make the theologian a bishop; they did indicate that he was a teacher who enjoyed the only freedom a teacher needs and desires.

# IV. The Works of the Church

## 1. The Saints

It may seem strange that we should reckon the saints first in speaking of the works of the Roman Church; but if we follow the thinking of the Church, we must recognize that this church believes that saints are its finest product, the product which most authenticates it. It should be noticed that they are "products"; neither the Roman Church nor the saints themselves thought of saints as self-made persons. Strictly speaking, a saint is one who has been *canonized*, that is, the title of saint is awarded to a deceased person after a long legal process. The Roman Church does not think that the canonized saints are its only successful products. They are eminently successful products, and the success is defined in the heroic practice of Christian virtue. The process of canonization includes a thorough investigation of the life and papers of the candidate. One officer, properly called the promoter of the faith but popularly known as the devil's advocate, has the duty of seeking flaws in the candidate. The Roman Church does not expect its heroes to be free from fault, but it does expect them to be free from nonheroic flaws. The divine approval of the candidate is proved by miracles worked through the intercession of the candidate. The modern man may find this aspect of the process a bit medieval, to say the least, but a large number of cases have been pending for many years, not because there are no proved miracles but because there are not enough. The Roman Church in all simplicity expects this sign of approval, and the fact that canonizations occur show that miracles are attested. One can say only that the miracles are submitted to a very searching examination, and most claims do not pass.

The candidate must normally pass through several stages of approval. The first step is approval of his cult. If the examination proceeds well, he can be declared *venerable*. If it continues well—this means miracles—he is *beatified*, given the title of *blessed*. Many have stopped there. If more miracles are produced, canonization follows. According to the procedure established by Benedict XIV (1740–1758), the process may not be initiated until fifty years have elapsed after the death of the candidate, and further intervals must be observed during the rest of the process. The Pope may shorten this for a favored candidate. The Carmelite nun of Lisieux, Sister Thérèse of the Child Jesus, known popularly as The Little Flower, died in 1897 and was canonized in 1925. Before the rules of Benedict XIV, the procedure was much more relaxed, and in earlier centuries canonization sometimes occurred by popular acclamation. The early casual practices resulted in a few embarrassments: nonexistent saints like Philomena and George (a Christian reincarnation of the Marduk-Tiamat, Baal-Mot, and Perseus-Andromeda myths), and John Nepomuk, who conflated more than one person. Yet in spite of these embarrassments the Roman Church claims infallibility in the canonization of saints— more correctly, it permits its theologians to teach that it is infallible. In such cases, the infallibility is seen to relate to the quality of the heroism proposed for veneration rather than to the historical reality of the person.

What is the heroic practice of Christian virtue? The list of the saints shows that it is not attached to any particular vocation, state of life, age, sex, or condition. The liturgical classification of saints sorts them out as apostles, martyrs, confessors (subdivided into bishops and nonbishops), virgins (martyrs and nonmartyrs), and "holy women not virgins" (martyrs and nonmartyrs). The somewhat negative classification of "holy woman neither virgin nor martyr" sometimes causes irreverent amusement. Apostles are those who receive the title in the New Testament; although they head the list after Mary, who is in a class by herself, almost nothing is known of the lives of most of the apostles. The cult of the saints began with the martyrs of the Roman persecutions; the early church, like the modern church, believes that one can show no greater heroism in Christian virtue than to die for its sake, but for canonization the Roman Church demands proof that death was inflicted "in hatred of the faith." If any other motive intervened, the martyrdom remains doubtful. This doubt delayed the processes of Roman Catholics executed for high treason in England and Scotland during the sixteenth and seventeenth centuries. The twentieth century, which may be producing more martyrs than any century that preceded it, will produce very few canonized martyrs; in most cases a political motive was operative, although the degree of its influence can never be measured. Confessors originally were those who in the Roman persecutions professed their faith but did not die for it. The term has come to mean any man whose heroic virtue was not consummated by martyrdom. The same standards are applied to women in the classifications of virgins and nonvirgins.

The classifications, however, do not disclose the variety of the saints. The implication of the veneration of the saints is that the Roman Church knows no human condition, no honest profession, no degree of education or ignorance, no social class in which it is impossible to practice heroic virtue. There is hardly any profession or trade which does not have its *patron saint;* even bandits and prostitutes are represented by saints who repented of their participation in these unwholesome professions. The connection between the patron and the occupant is sometimes remote (for example, St. Barbara and artillery), but the lesson is that the Christian artillerist is in the company of the saints. Obviously this connection arose when artillery was in higher esteem than it is now, but the Roman Church recognizes now as it always has that the soldier who serves his country is not excluded from Christian holiness, and he may venerate as his patron St. Sebastian, an officer of the Roman legions. The catalogue of the saints is a true cross-section of the Roman Church in space and time. Some quite famous historical figures, such as Innocent III, are not in the catalogue, and some extremely obscure persons, such as Sister Thérèse of the Child Jesus, are there.

The catalogue is weak in married persons; many of the married saints, if not most of them, were widowers or widows or, in rare instances, were credited with a mutual vow of chastity in marriage. The Roman ideal of celibacy has already been discussed, and the number of married persons who have been canonized hints that the Roman Church believes not only that marriage is less heroic than chastity, but that it is rarely heroic at all. There is a modern witticism in the Roman Church, somewhat unkind, which says that to become a saint one should be either a member of a religious order or an Italian. Behind the witticism is the fact that religious orders are able and willing to maintain the long cases of their members, and that the Roman Curia is largely Italian and sympathetic to the cases of their fellow countrymen. Personal holiness does not depend on the strength of a lobby, but canonical recognition of personal holiness does depend on a group which is strong enough and persevering enough to carry a case for perhaps more than a hundred years.

The saints vary as persons as much as they vary in states and conditions. Some were more amiable than others, some were more intelligent than others; a few notable examples like Joseph of Cupertino and Jean Marie Vianney, the Curé of Ars, were of extreme simplicity, to put it kindly. Thomas Aquinas by contrast would have to be reckoned one of the best minds over a period of several hundred years. Both rich and poor have been recognized, but the rich saint was one who gave generously of his goods, in some cases to the total abdication of them. Jerome in his own writings exhibits a temper which, if the devil's advocate had existed in his day, would probably have been a block to his canonization. Robert Bellarmine, one of the saints who has a reputation as a wit, said three months after he received the cardinal's hat that, while many bishops had been canonized, no cardinal except Bonaventure (in 1482) had ever been.[1] This was true at the time (1599); by a coincidence the College of Cardinals in Bellarmine's period had another future saint in its complement, Charles Borromeo, Archbishop of Milan. Bellarmine received the hat for services to the Pope which were cited in his case by the devil's advocate as evidence against him. Borromeo's appointment to Milan was a typical scandalous example of family patronage; he had given no reason to suspect that he would become a truly great bishop. Francis of Assisi has become a universal favorite, Philip Neri and Thomas More have become almost legendary as lovable. On the other hand, Ignatius Loyola opened his heart to very few and projected a cold and harsh personality. In fact, Ignatius was very probably neither cold nor harsh; he suffered from chronic gallstones most of his adult life, and the fact that he accomplished as much as he did with nearly unremitting stomach pains may enhance his heroism. It is one of the legends of the saints that Ignatius damaged his digestion by excessive fasting; he may have done so, but the plain fact is that the sufferer from acute biliary colic is unable to take food.

Peter of Alcantara, with Jerome one of the least amiable of the saints, was against nearly everything. Edward the Confessor and Louis IX, two sainted kings, would not have been canonized if the recognition depended on the quality of their government. Peter Celestine was canonized simply because he resigned from the papacy; it was assumed that this was an act of heroism, especially in the period when a legendary Renaissance Pope is related to have said, "Now that God had given us the papacy, let us enjoy it." His resignation was also a service to the Roman Church, which may enhance his heroism too; the Roman Church has known few prelates who resigned because they recognized their incapacity. Bernard of Clairvaux wrote sweetly of the love of Jesus and attracted many to his monastery by his personal charm; he was also a party to the condemnation of Abelard by a process which fell notably short of justice.[2] Ambrose had two complaints against Theodosius, and on one occasion refused to admit the emperor into the church. One complaint was that the emperor had permitted the massacre of some prisoners of war, the other was that Theodosius had compelled the Christians of a city in Asia Minor to restore a synagogue which they had burnt down.[3] Aloysius Gonzaga interpreted his vow of chastity so strictly that he never looked his mother in the face; one hopes that this is one of the legends of the saints, but since Aloysius died at twenty-five, it can be forgiven as a youthful indiscretion, frightfully boorish as it was.[4]

The women are no less varied and interesting than the men, but they are not as well reported. Jeanne Françoise Fremiot de Chantal is venerated as a woman who achieved heroism in four states of life (virgin, wife, widow, and professed religious). When she had decided to leave her grown children to found a religious community (the Order of the Visitation), her eldest son prostrated himself at the door of the house in an "over my dead body" gesture. Jeanne stepped over him and walked out; the breach was not permanent. Her spiritual counselor, Francis de Sales, is known as one of the more charming and accomplished saints. He had a vile temper when he was a young law student and nearly killed a fellow student. The story, fact or legend, is that he was so appalled at what he had nearly done that he never lost his temper again. His books, intended to recommend "the devout life" to people who lived as seculars, insist constantly that their piety must be such as not to offend those who are less devout.[5] One could only wish that his principles were more widely known. Teresa of Avila, mentioned in the chapter on mysticism, founded a large number of convents of the reformed Carmelite observance. This meant obtaining financial and moral support for an unpopular cause. Her *Book of The Foundations* reveals that she was a hard-nosed business woman and manager; yet this same business woman wrote of mystical experiences which approach the incredible.[6] Catherine of Siena devoted much of her short life to persuading the Pope to resign so that the Western schism could be healed; he did not, and the schism was not healed until a later pope did resign under pressure at the Council of Constance.

What, then, does the Roman Church mean by *heroic virtue?* The Roman Church believes that when it appears it will be recognized. There is no pattern which the saint must meet; he can do what he must do wherever he is and whatever he does. The heroism of the peasant or the housewife is less manifest than the heroism of the bishop or the king; but the Roman Church not only admits the peasant and the housewife to heroism, the Roman Church believes that their heroism can attain public recognition. The Roman Church does not tell the saints how to practice heroic virtue; it learns from them how to practice such virtue. They are charismatic figures who see and act according to the fullness of the gospel proclaimed in the church, and they may do it even when they do not hear the full proclamation of the gospel. Thomas More had the support of only one English bishop for his position; it must be remembered that the papacy did not mean in his days what it has come to mean since. More, another wit among the saints, disclaimed any pretense that he was doing any more than he had to do as a lawyer. Like the other martyrs, More's heroism comes to a clear focus in a great crisis. The heroism of the confessors is a more subtle type.

Perhaps one of the best introductions to the genius and spirit of Roman Catholicism is through the saints. These are the best representatives of the Roman Church, and they are authenticated. Most Roman Catholics are acquainted with the lives of some of the saints, and they accept them as patrons and models. It is true that some of the saints are an acquired taste; but it is remarkable that they come through a close examination very well. They were all children of their culture, usually in advance of it but not out of touch with it. The men and women of the Middle Ages and the Renaissance show most of the limitations of the Middle Ages and the Renaissance; one may say that they are canonized precisely for the limitations which they do not show. Some examples of unenlightened conduct have been mentioned, but it is not in these that the saints showed their heroism. They are models in their attitudes and habits rather than in particular actions. They did not recognize the limitations of their culture as we do not recognize ours. Some years ago two historians had a dispute over whether Francis Borgia—not a very sympathetic saint—did or did not attend an *auto da fé* in Spain. He was expected to be there, he should have been there, and in his time one did not easily absent oneself from these proceedings; the absence might be imputed against one. One historian proved to his satisfaction that Francis was several miles away when the process was carried on.[7] He did not prove how Francis managed his absence, but the context suggests that he did manage. In his time, attendance at an *auto da fé* would not have been an objection to his holiness; absence might have been.

Some of the worst enemies of the saints have been their admirers. Hagiography, the writing of the lives of the saints, has rarely been an exact science in the Roman Church. The earlier saints acquired legends even during their lives, and after their deaths the legends grew more fantastic. It must be admitted that the legends had much to do with the institution and completion of the process of canonization. Typical legends had to do with the thaumaturgic powers of the saints and the mystical qualities of their prayers. One would have to conclude that many of their admirers spent much time peeping through keyholes. Such legends do not so much describe heroic virtue as its supernatural attestation. When historical criticism studies the legends, it finds that the saints are heavily encased in plaster, and the recovery of the historical person may sometimes be impossible with the material available.

A seventeenth-century Flemish Jesuit named Jan Bolland founded an institute for the study of the legends of the saints. His purpose was to go through the calendar (each saint has a commemorative day in the year) and find out the facts about each one. One may still visit the institute, its library, and its museum at the College St-Michel in Brussels, for the task is unfinished, and the Bollandists continue the publication of the *Acta Sanctorum*. To many legends they have been positively cruel, and they are unpopular in many quarters of the Roman Church. It is their work and the work of modern scholars who follow the same principles and methods which permits us to say that the saints stand up well under close examination. Heroic Christian virtue does appear, perhaps in a form quite different from the legends, but more credible and more convincing. Very few historical figures have been submitted to so rigorous an examination, and many great men have lost stature from a less searching examination. The Roman Church does not choose or honor its saints carelessly.

The saints were called "products" of the Roman Catholic Church. Implicit in the cult of the saints is the belief that the Roman Church affords to each of its members the resources of heroism in Christian virtue. It is their choice whether they make full use of the resources or not, but no member is excluded from the resources. This may seem to be in strange contrast to the realism—some would say corruption—which the Roman Church so often shows in dealing with human nature. It is in strange contrast; it should have become apparent by this stage of the exposition that the Roman Catholic Church exhibits many paradoxes. Among the things that the Roman Church at its worst has never relaxed are its standards of canonization. It is simply not true and never has been true that it can be bought; bribery may hasten the process, but it cannot insure it. The Roman Church does not apologize for any of its saints, in spite of some glaring cultural limitations. Jews remember Vincent Ferrer as anti-Semitic. Without a close examination no judgment is possible here; were the charge proved true, it would mean that the Roman Church believes that this cultural limitation need not inhibit the practice of heroic Christian virtue in Vincent's context. No one who left proved anti-Semitic utterances behind him could be canonized in the modern Roman Church. It was remarked that the standards have not been relaxed and also that the Roman Church does not pretend that its saints are flawless; what it does reject, one supposes, is any candidate who is proved to be small. They are a goodly company.

## 2. Education

In the Latin version and most English versions of Matthew 28:19, the risen Jesus gives his disciples a commission to go and teach all nations. The Greek text is more accurately translated "Go and make disciples," which does not mean quite the same thing. In Roman Catholic theology, this text is often used to support the teaching office of the church. It is not used to support the operation of formal school education, nor does formal school education appear in the early centuries of the Roman Church. Yet many Roman Catholics think of the church school system as a fulfilment of Matthew 28:19. Education has become an extremely important part of the Roman system and a major factor in retaining membership.

It is extremely difficult to find accurate statistics on the number of schools operated by the Roman Catholic Church. In the United States, the part of the world in which the system is strongest, education is easily the major operation of the Roman Church that is not strictly ecclesiastical.[1] The involvement of the Church in education is not a recent element in Romanism. In the centuries that followed the collapse of the Roman Empire and through the Middle Ages up to the Reformation, there were no European schools which were not conducted under church auspices. As we have noticed, almost all of the great European universities were ecclesiastical foundations. The modern ideal of universal education had not arisen, and schools existed for the learned professions of medicine, law, and divinity. In these early institutions, "ecclesiastical auspices" did not involve the kind of episcopal control that developed in modern times. The *universitas* stood with the *regnum* and *sacerdotium* as one of the pillars of medieval society. It vindicated its independence jealously and at times violently, but it was a member of the Roman Catholic community, and until the Reformation it had no thought of being anything else. It was not, however, an arm of the Roman Church any more than the *regnum* was an arm of the Church. It was involved only with those members of society who were educable, and this did not include all the clergy. While divinity was one of the learned sciences, not all the clergy were divines.

The emancipation of many European universities from the Roman Church did not at once mean their emancipation either from the *regnum* or from church control by other ecclesiastical bodies. The growth of educational freedom is a long story which is not our proper interest here. In the minds of many, this growth occurred not only outside the Roman Church, but against its opposition. The story is not that simple, but, until the last few years, the Roman Church has not exhibited academic freedom either in its laws or in its attitudes. Many think that its posture is still ambiguous, and in many parts of the Roman Church the ambiguity does remain. Yet schools and universities as the modern world knows them arose in the medieval community of Christendom, and even the ideal of academic freedom has its roots there.

Nor did universal education arise independently of the Roman Church. A large number of the religious communities in the Roman Church were instituted for the education of poor children. These children were not educated in preparation for the universities; they were taught the basic elementary subjects: reading, writing, arithmetic, the catechism. Almost all of these religious communities date from the seventeenth century and later; they are contemporary with the rise of universal education under other auspices, but they are older than the public education systems. In many European countries, public education still uses buildings constructed by agencies of the Roman Catholic Church; occasionally, by an unexpected paradox, the government uses these buildings for other purposes than education.

The attitude of the Roman Church toward what it calls *mixed* or *neutral* schools is frankly hostile. Education at any level should include religious instruction (CIC 1373), and Catholic students should not attend schools where this is not provided (CIC 1374). In many dioceses up to quite recent times this law was enforced by the penalty of excommunication of parents who sent their children to mixed or neutral schools. The Roman Church affirms its right to found universities (CIC 1374–1380). The administration of Catholic schools is committed to the ordinary (CIC 1381–1382). The candid hostility of the canon law to non-Catholic schools is tempered by some flexibility in the administration of the law of attendance, particularly where it is impossible to provide Catholic schools for all Catholic students. In modern times, this means nearly everywhere, but the hostile attitude often endures. It is more than coincidental that in so much nineteenth century European fiction the schoolmaster is the village atheist. The canon law reflects the "lay states" of the nineteenth century which removed education totally from the Roman Church in several countries. Mixed or neutral schools in such countries were often openly anticlerical and in some instances antireligious.

It seems to be one of the more interesting coincidences of history that the invention of printing and the subsequent rise of universal education were contemporary with the Protestant Reformation. One may say that it was the conjunction of these events that formed the Roman Catholic position about education which still endures. General education became an arm of the churches almost as soon as it appeared. Not only the Roman Church, but the Protestant churches as well, saw in elementary schools an opportunity to rear children in their confession. The Roman Catholic schools have always placed religious education as the primary purpose of the schools with no attempt to mask this under some other purpose. With the growth of the educational system, the elementary school has become the major agent of religious instruction rather than the home or the parish. In the United States during the nineteenth and early twentieth centuries, the years of massive European immigration and the fantastic expansion of Roman Catholicism in the United States, the school and the church stood together since the Third Plenary Council of Baltimore in 1884. This Council decreed the establishment of the parochial school system in the United States, and its motive was frankly the fear of perversion of Roman Catholic children in the public schools of the United States.[2] Indeed, the school was often built before the church; in many parishes temporary quarters were used for worship until the school was built. This might seem to be an inversion of values; whether it is or not, it expressed the Roman Catholic conviction in the United States that the parochial school was a vital element in the church.

A similar interest in schools has been manifested in the foreign missions. The situation in missionary countries was affected by the fact that in many countries missionaries were more welcome as educators than as churchmen. They furnished substantial assistance in education to underdeveloped countries, and in some of these countries they were the first to institute general education. Here also, however, it was believed that the child reared in the Roman Catholic faith was more likely to retain that faith in his adult life. The Roman Catholic belief in this principle is supported by those governments both in Europe and in missionary countries which finally removed education from church control.

The principle on which church education is conducted goes far beyond formal religious instruction. Children also learn the ways of worship; they are taught respect and reverence for prelates, clergy, and religious. They are daily reminded of their identity as Catholics. They grow up in an atmosphere of Roman Catholic traditions and attitudes which are communicated not so much by instruction as by prolonged close association under the direction of professional religious persons. The elementary school teacher has been for Roman Catholic school children for several generations the ultimate religious authority, even more than the clergy, who rarely instruct children. This authority carried over into adult life. "Sister says" has settled many religious disputes in Roman Catholic homes, in spite of the fact that only a generation ago sister's professional training may not have gone beyond high school. To refer again to the United States, the parochial school has the same sanctity in American Catholicism as "the little red school house," the public school where all children theoretically were equals and where they absorbed Americanism with their elementary instruction.

A number of questions have been raised recently about the Roman Catholic educational system. The celebrated dictum of George Bernard Shaw that a Catholic university is a contradiction in terms has been resurrected, this time by Roman Catholics. In the United States, Mary Perkins Ryan aroused intense discussion by publishing a book in which she asked whether parochial schools were necessary, and she concluded that they were not.[3] The primary question to be considered is certainly financing the enterprise. Roman Catholic schools have become much more expensive than they were when they were founded. In modern Western countries, and now in the developing countries, large portions of public funds go into education, and the state's share of education promises to continue growing before it declines. A generation ago, Roman Catholic schools, particularly the elementary schools, could be staffed by religious who were supported at a much lower cost than secular teachers. There are no longer enough religious to fill the posts; in addition to the cost factor, this raises in the minds of many Catholics a doubt whether schools staffed largely or even predominantly by secular teachers retain a character sufficiently "Catholic" to justify their retention. The doubt is in fact unfair to secular teachers, and it illustrates the peculiar veneration in which Roman Catholics hold professional religious persons. As long as the doubt remains, however, it may make Roman Catholics hesitate to make the large contributions which are necessary to sustain the system.

The second question is whether the Roman Catholic Church can or ought to attempt to furnish formal education for every Catholic student. Even in Roman Catholic countries this has never been achieved, and in countries where the Catholic school system cares for half or even less of the Roman Catholic students, it is asked whether a system ought to be retained which misses its objective by such a notable margin. In may parts of the United States, which has the largest Roman Catholic school system, the schools do not and cannot handle even half of the Catholic children. In Chicago, which has the largest diocesan school system in the United States, the largest "Catholic" high school in the city in terms of Catholic teachers and Catholic students some years ago was one of the public high schools. Thirty years ago the public schools of Boston were 75 per cent Catholic in the student population and 85 per cent Catholic in the teaching staff; this gave some wits occasion to remark that Boston did not really need a parochial school system.

Now the wits are asking whether Boston may not have been right. Failure to accommodate all Catholic students often leads to a distinction between the "haves" and the "have-nots," which does not make for unity and harmony in the Roman Catholic community. The situation in the United States is aggravated by the shrinkage of the Roman Catholic school system due to the financial problems mentioned above. Some schools have been closed or consolidated, others have eliminated some of the eight grades of the American elementary system.

The third question is the quality of instruction in the Roman Catholic system, and this can be subdivided into religious instruction and secular instruction. Concerning religious instruction, it is odd that there is no real evaluation of this effort for which the Roman Catholic system primarily exists. Two recent studies have not been conclusive in proving that the presence or absence of Roman Catholic schooling makes a substantial difference in the religion of adults, except that more of those who had Roman Catholic schooling continue to practice Catholicism,[4] but the ambiguity of the term *religion* makes such surveys uncertain. In a survey of the alumni of one of the largest and best-known Catholic universities of the United States, 53 per cent of those polled answered that it is more important to attend Mass on Sunday than to love one's neighbor, 38 per cent placed love above Sunday Mass, and 9 per cent had no opinion.[5] If this is what is meant by "practicing Roman Catholicism," then the success of the system is indeed questionable. Greeley and Rossi found that while those with Catholic schooling know their religion better and "practice" it more faithfully than those who were educated in public schools, they show no difference in their social attitudes or in their principles of Christian "charity."[6] Some would say that this in itself is enough to damn the system as a gigantic failure; others would say that the school does no more than it can and that the failure belongs to some other agency, but a system which is founded on the primary necessity of religious instruction cannot absolve itself from all responsibility in morality.

The quality of instruction in secular subjects varies with different parts of the educational system. In general, Roman Catholic schools are most successful at the elementary level, less successful at the secondary level, and least successful in higher education. Success at the elementary and secondary levels can be measured by further academic progress of the students, and here Roman

Catholic schools do as well as other schools. In some regions they enjoy special respect, because they maintain better discipline than other schools. Success in higher education is more difficult to measure, but there are some standards by which an estimate can be made. John Tracy Ellis precipitated a controversy by an article in which he noted the insignificant position of Roman Catholics among intellectuals in the United States.[7] Roman Catholic colleges and universities generally enjoy less respect than other institutions, and this is not merely a matter of prejudice. In those things which distinguished universities have—well-known scholars, publication of research, libraries, and laboratories—Roman Catholic institutions are deficient by comparison, sometimes notably deficient.

The inferiority of Roman Catholic higher education is due in large part to the problem of financing higher education; the cost of higher education is much greater than the cost of elementary and secondary education, and the standards of superior institutions at this level are in modern times much further above mediocrity than the standards of superior elementary and secondary schools. Unfortunately it is more than a problem of resources, and this leads to the basic question of Roman Catholic education, the role of the hierarchy and the clergy. The hierarchy and the clergy have yet to demonstrate that they really believe in those things which universities cherish, such as research and academic freedom. The incidents in which problems in these areas arise are too numerous to permit the simple affirmation that they believe in higher education as it is understood in most of the modern world. Since Roman Catholic higher education is still almost entirely under hierarchical and clerical control, these questions become important, not only in the minds of secular scholars, but also in the minds of Catholics who engage in higher education.

The attitude of the hierarchy and the clergy as a whole gives reason to ask whether they do not think of education at all levels as a tool of the Roman Church—that is, as an arm of the teaching office. A group of Roman Catholic educators in the United States has issued a statement in which this relationship is denied.[8] The group certainly spoke for most of those Catholics who are engaged in university work, but it is not clear that they spoke for the hierarchy. No Roman Catholic denies the supreme importance of religious faith. He does not thereby feel compelled to assert the supreme competence of religious authority in all fields of human endeavor. The difference between religious faith and theology as a learned discipline has already been discussed. If the competence of hierarchical authority does not directly involve theology, even less does it include secular learning. The Roman Catholic hierarchy can take the same position which some modern governments have taken, that learning must be an instrument of a higher cause—in one instance the state, in the other the church. That the cause of the church is noble does not mean that the church cannot distort learning; the nobility of the cause is conditioned by the integrity of the men in whose hands the cause is placed. The type of control which many of the hierarchy and the clergy seem to desire should not be granted to any one, because that type of control will render education impossible. Catholics who are engaged in educational work would be satisfied if the relationship of the medieval *universitas* to the *sacerdotium* were restored.

From these observations, one can conclude that the Roman Catholic educational system faces an uncertain future. Unless some totally unforeseen factor intervenes, the system will shrink further, and as it reaches fewer Catholics, it will be asked more frequently and more urgently whether it should be retained. Parallel to the shrinking, one can foresee rising costs to which no limit can be placed. As costs rise, some deterioration of the quality of the system can be expected. Already many Catholics speak of ways other than education by which the Roman Catholic Church can fulfil its mission. If education seems to interfere with other more urgent needs, it will receive less and less support.

If the Roman Catholic educational system were not to survive, the Church would have to recognize that the operation of schools is not included in its constitution. The gospel can be proclaimed without a system of schools. Possibly the existence of the school system has allowed clergy and parents to evade their own responsibilities in the education of the young. The success of the schools must be regarded as mixed at best. Child control may not be the best way to develop convinced adults, and there is reason to suspect that the conviction is often more shallow the greater the effort expended. Greater interest and participation by Catholics in general education in any country should have an effect on the educational system of that country, but it has to be understood that almost no modern nation would tolerate even the suspicion of clericalism in its educational system. It is regrettable that this attitude is not entirely without foundation. Where Roman Catholics enjoy the same rights as other citizens, however, they enjoy the same right to influence educational policy. Such influence does not mean that the general educational system should conform to the standards of the Roman Catholic educational system, but simply that the values which Roman Catholics cherish should be weighed on their merits by governments and educators.

The survival of the Roman Catholic system will probably depend on the degree to which the system passes from hierarchical to lay control—that is the degree to which CIC 1381–1382 becomes a dead letter. This forecast by no means implies that learning is exclusively the province of the laity; it is based on the fact that the laity have not learned—at least not yet—to desire that kind of control which has been characteristic of the hierarchy and the clergy. Totalitarianism can be lay or clerical, but the Roman Catholic system has not yet felt lay totalitarianism. The risk that lay control might prove as unfavorable to academic freedom and to research as clerical control is real, but if the Roman Catholic system is to survive at all, it seems that this risk must be run. If there are to be Roman Catholic schools, bishops and priests will be among those who are consulted and who have a voice in the determination of policy. All this means that a viable Roman Catholic educational system will be structured much like other public and private systems in which no single officer or board has the type of control which the hierarchy and the clergy have enjoyed. Whether the Roman Catholic system is flexible enough to modify itself to this degree cannot be predicted; it may seem unlikely, but it is not impossible.

## 3. Missions

The book of the Acts of the Apostles and the Epistles are the documents of the missionary enterprises of the church of the first century. The history of the church since the first century can be viewed as a history of its expansion by missionary work. In the nineteenth and twentieth centuries, this has become a vast Roman enterprise the size of which is not easily perceived because it is so scattered. Almost every European nation has its missionary patron who brought Roman Catholicism to the region—Augustine of England, Patrick of Ireland, Boniface of Germany, Cyril and Methodius of Eastern Europe, and many others. The Roman Catholic Church has always been conscious of the mandate to make disciples of all nations (Matthew 28:19). Protestant churches also have undertaken extensive missionary operations.

Roman Catholic expansion was conditioned by factors not under the control of the church. Missionary work among the Muslims has never been of any significance. The military posture of Christianity against the infidel, expressed to perfection in the Crusades, has left deep wounds which have not yet healed. Muslims, who sometimes show an astonishing knowledge of details of the Crusades, simply do not consider that Christianity can be a superior religion. From the conversion of Europe to Christianity by the tenth century to the age of discovery in the sixteenth century, Roman Catholicism conducted little missionary work. It may be one of the accidents of history that the first European nations to reach North and South America were the Catholic countries of Spain, Portugal, and France. The English were latecomers who achieved a remarkable success, and the other Protestant countries never founded a permanent colony of any importance. Christianity was brought to the natives of North and South America in its Roman Catholic form.

Less well known but hardly less impressive was the success of Roman Catholic missionaries in the countries of the Far East. Francis Xavier enjoyed the most sensational success, but he was only one of a large company. Before the seventeenth century was well advanced, Roman Catholicism was well established in India and the East Indies. A notable success in Japan was neutralized by the Japanese government, which nearly exterminated Christianity in the early seventeenth century. It was not very flattering to the United Kingdom that Jesuits of the sixteenth and seventeenth centuries ranked the Japanese mission and the English mission as equally perilous. A very promising beginning in China was ruined by a decision of a Roman congregation which historians now regard as a colossal blunder. Certain traditional Chinese family rites were defined by the Roman office as ancestor worship, and the mission ultimately came to an end.

Much of the nineteenth century missionary work was due to the French Society of the Propagation of the Faith, founded in 1822 with headquarters in Paris, an organization quite distinct from the Congregation of the Propagation of the Faith, an office of the Holy See. The society collected alms and distributed them to the missionaries. The precedent set by this society has been followed by many others; Roman Catholics in the nineteenth and twentieth centuries have been generous in their support of the foreign missions.

The methods of missionary work have changed notably since the New Testament, and the differences deserve more than passing attention. We gather from the New Testament that Paul and other missionaries moved to a new city, formed a group, resided there until the group was organized, and then departed for another new city. This meant that the fledgling community was fully a church, with its own officers elected by its members, fully capable of the ministry of the church (and of sending missionaries), and responsible to no high authority. Paul did not govern the churches to which he wrote letters. The establishment of modern missionary churches is much more complicated. As soon as possible, the parochial and diocesan structures are set up, and it has been noticed that Rome exercises a close supervision of missionary churches and dioceses, withholding from them certain liberties that belong to established dioceses. The structure means that churches and schools must be built, almost never with the support of the local population. This in turn means that the staff must be increased as the operation expands. What it has meant in missionary regions up to quite recent times is that the hierarchy, the clergy, and most professional religious persons are foreign to the country. The Roman Church has always desired the formation of a "native clergy" (the very term is patronizing), but only recently has the formation been successful on a large scale. Other factors, as will be seen, have entered into this development. Even where a native clergy was formed, they were not admitted to positions of responsibility. Missionary dioceses even now exist, founded several generations ago or even in the last century, that have a majority of native clergy but which have not yet had any but a foreign bishop. Nor are these dioceses in which a majority of the Catholics are savages. It is not surprising that in such regions Roman Catholicism remains a foreign religion.

This is the major problem which faces Roman Catholic missionary work. If one may speak in very broad generalities, apostolic Christianity was not a "foreign" religion; it was diffused in the Roman Empire by people of the Empire, and it was no more foreign than the mystery cults. When the barbarian peoples became Christian, they accepted the religion as a part of that Roman civilization which they desired to enter, although they wrecked the civilization in entering it. The missionary since the sixteenth century followed the explorer and the merchant; he came as a European as much as a Roman Catholic. The American historian Parkman exaggerated grossly when he wrote that not a cape was turned, not a river entered but a Jesuit led the way—besides leaving a quotation which does not please the Franciscans. There is hardly any region of North America which the fur trader did not reach before the missionary. Roman Catholicism since the sixteenth century has come to no country simply as a religious faith. It has come as an element of an invading culture, and the culture never failed to exploit the natives of the new countries. Many missionaries did what they could to hamper the exploitation, but what they could do was not much. Nor were they entirely indifferent to their own national loyalties. New Spain or New France should be like Spain or France, a country of Roman Catholic subjects of the king. New England should be a country of Protestant subjects of the king. Whether the missionary knew it or liked it, behind him always stood the musketeers. Nor could the missionaries distinguish between religious conversion and acculturation. The natives were to be civilized as they were Christianized, for they had become a part of Christendom, but naturally they were to be civilized at a level no higher than the European peasant. The only exception to this seems to have been the mission to China, where the missionaries attempted to interpret Catholicism in Chinese terms. It was the missionaries who were acculturated in China, not the natives; but in China the missionaries had no musketeers behind them. It may be significant that they also had no martyrs.

The vocation to the foreign missions has always been regarded as an heroic vocation by Roman Catholics, and most of the time it has been. Until quite recent times, the missionary left home with no prospect of ever returning. Furloughs are now granted missionaries, since it has been learned that they are helpful for survival. To become residents of a foreign country usually much more different from one's native land than America is from Europe, often to live in impoverished circumstances, and to present a message to a hostile or uncomprehending audience is not a career for one who loves ease. The missionaries and the explorers had much in common. It happens sometimes that the missionary feels uneasy and dissatisfied when the mission is so well established that the conditions of life at home can nearly be duplicated. He then feels that he might just as well be back home. But the greatest hardship of the foreign missions, not often real but frequent enough to be taken seriously, is the danger of violent death. Even here the Roman Church preserves the rigorous standards of canonization which we have discussed. It demands clear evidence that the missionary was killed "in hatred of the faith" and not merely as a foreign enemy. Very recently many missionaries in China and Africa have been killed with uncertainty as to the motive of the killing; but death was one of the hazards of the foreign missions just the same, even if it was a hazard shared with merchants, teachers, and civil servants.

The Roman Catholic religion remains a foreign religion in missionary countries until it ceases to be European. Since very few missions have followed the tactics of the Jesuits in China and of Roberto di Nobili (who actually became a Brahmin) in India, Roman Catholicism has not made itself at home in the missions.[2] The crude persecutions of earlier centuries have given way to more sophisticated means of suppression. In some countries, missionaries are informed that if they wish to remain they must become naturalized. Possibly this should have been done much earlier. Permission to enter or to remain is explicitly granted to them as educators with a prohibition of engaging in "religious propaganda." The foreign religion is not to be extirpated, but the governments will do what they can to see that it does not expand. They have concluded from past experience that the missionary is an agent of the foreign culture which has conquered and exploited them. This factor has hastened the formation of a native clergy and the appointment of native bishops.

This, however, does not solve the problem entirely. Most of the native clergy have been educated in Europe or in institutions conducted on the model of the European seminary. This writer remembers a missionary school where the staff was entirely native and entirely French in their education and outlook. They were an admirable group, but their ties with their fellow countrymen had been weakened by their education. It will take at least a generation for this condition to change, but a number of things indicate that it will. If I may appeal again to my own experience, I encountered in my own seminary teaching students from the foreign missions, both Americans and "natives." Almost to a man they were impatient with the time they were forced to spend learning material which, they assured me, would be of no use to them in the mission countries. If they are representative of the younger clergy in the mission countries, the necessary development will be more rapid than any one now expects.

The problem of the foreign missions is that they must proclaim *Roman*—that is, Western—Catholicism. An Indian or Chinese or African Catholicism has not yet come into being, and by this I mean a Catholicism which is no more Indian or Chinese or African than Roman Catholicism is European. For the *Roman* Catholic the very thought of such a Catholicism excites dismay, but the Roman Catholic does not reflect that his Romanism excites the same dismay in other cultures. These cultures are by no definition more in opposition to Catholicism than Hellenistic-Roman culture was, and the Catholic Church achieved a permanent identity with Hellenistic-Roman culture. Of course, the acculturation was mutual; the Western civilization which emerged included Catholic components. One might expect the same development in non-European cultures, as long as Catholicism can rid itself of its foreign character. It has to "go native."

The foreign missions raise the question whether the Roman Church is able and willing to achieve the fullness of the title *Catholic* which it claims. The institution of foreign missions in other countries does not make the church Catholic in a proper sense any more than the staff of the American Embassy in London become British by residing there. I have had to advert more than once to the modern Roman idea of uniformity. It is now manifest that this uniformity cannot be preserved in non-Western cultures. These cultures must develop their own Catholicism with the same freedom with which Europe developed its Catholicism. They can learn much from Europe, in particular how not to do a great many things.

In the age of discovery when most of the discoveries were made by the Portuguese, Spanish, and French, the new lands seemed to Roman Catholics a God-given opportunity to replace the Roman Catholics who had been torn from the church by the Reformation. The replacement was made by introducing the natives into European culture as hewers of wood and drawers of water, and in the twentieth century the missionary efforts are recognized as being much less than notably successful. The Roman Church could see in the developing countries only an opportunity to recover the losses to secularism. This view would be imperialistic. The Roman Church must return to the missionary ideal of the New Testament: proclaim the gospel, form a group of believers, and leave them with their church. There probably is no future for "the foreign missions" as we have known them. There can be a future only for the Catholic Church, Roman or something larger.

## 4. Benevolent Operations

Statistics again are not readily available for Roman Catholic benevolent enterprises. Like education, one does not like to dismiss them so briefly. They are vast, they engage an enormous number of persons and demand an enormous amount of money, and they are important. In some ways they represent the Roman Church at its finest. It is a simple fact of history that benevolent institutions for the care of the poor, the sick, the aged, children, and other helpless did not exist in the world before the Roman Catholic Church created them. There were no such institutions in the Roman Empire nor in earlier civilizations. The emphasis here is on institutions; not only the Old Testament, but some rare passages in Greek and Latin literature express sympathy for the dispossessed, and one of the crimes with which the prophets charged Israel was the oppression of the poor, but organized assistance is a form of Christian action.

Institutionalized benevolence was seen from its beginnings in Roman Catholicism as the fulfilment of several Gospel texts; one may mention in particular Matthew 25:31–46, the text from which "the seven corporal works of mercy" are derived. Benevolent institutions attempted to do these works not by the casual benevolence of the committed Christian, but by a permanent staff and regular procedure. Luke describes the primitive church of Jerusalem as electing officers with the specific responsibility of providing for the poor; and this may be seen as the earliest institutionalized charity in the history of Christianity (Acts 6:1–6). The precedent thus set was followed by the church of the early centuries, but the institution did not go beyond the appointment of officers. The legend of the deacon Lawrence relates that when he was commanded to show the treasures of the church he brought in the poor and infirm; it was to them that the treasures of the church had gone. The story expresses the attitude of the early church. Specialized institutions for benevolent works could not arise before the Peace of Constantine. Apart from specialized institutions, the legends of the saints are full of anecdotes of those who made sensational donations of their own possessions to aid the poor—bishops who sold off the sacred vessels, wealthy persons who renounced their wealth by a single gift, those who made the care of the sick poor a life's work. By the Middle Ages there were hospitals, almshouses, institutions for orphaned children. Benevolent assistance in those times was much less complicated than it has since become. Hospitals could not be much more than places where death was made a little more comfortable. Donations of food and clothing on a large scale could provide for many. Housing was bare shelter for most people, poor or others. These efforts of the Middle Ages made very little impression on the prevailing poverty; the Roman Catholic Church did not give most of its communicants a basic commitment to these works. They rather attest the survival of a Christian ideal in unfavorable conditions—if conditions have ever been favorable to the ideal.

A large number of Roman Catholic saints have been canonized for their dedication to institutional benevolence, especially for founding such institutions. A large number of religious orders have benevolence as their sole purpose or one of their principal purposes. Perhaps no more specialized benevolence was ever devised than the work of the Trinitarians and the Order of Our Lady of Mercy; these were founded to ransom prisoners taken by Muslims, with the understanding that the religious would pledge himself if funds were lacking. The number of benevolent religious communities has grown notably from what it was in the eighteenth century.

It is surprising that an operation so wholesome and so genuinely Christian should be faced with serious problems, but the problems exist, and they are of such magnitude that the Roman Church may be forced to seek some other way of continuing this Christian activity. The problems do not arise from the operations themselves; they are the result of the development of history and culture. The order in which they are mentioned is not the order of magnitude or urgency; no such order could be set forth at the present time.

The problem of finances is as acute here as it is in Roman Catholic education. Hospitals are no longer places in which the pain of death is assuaged. In a modern hospital the cost per patient has risen astronomically. Neither the Roman Catholic hospitals nor any other hospitals are able to furnish care to patients without charges. Where health insurance is common or provided by law, the hospitals do not hesitate to charge what the insurance will bear. The image of the hospital as a benevolent institution no longer exists. It has become a business—not a profitable business, but a business which must collect its charges just as a profitable business does. Only in missionary countries is the Roman Catholic hospital still able to act as a benevolent institution; there the people are not acquainted with Western standards, and the services are not equal to those of hospitals in Western countries. Similar rises in costs, although not as acute, afflict other Roman Catholic benevolent institutions. The immediate effect of such rises is that the institution is forced to restrict the number of persons it can serve. No principle of selection seems satisfactory. Other benevolent institutions, as well as Roman Catholic institutions, suffer from red tape, the administrative complications which become necessary as soon as the institution is no longer able to admit all applicants. Christian charity is seen dimly when it appears with an armful of forms to be filled out in quadruplicate. Yet survival for the benevolent institutions is better assured than it is for the schools because no other institutions are present to fill the vacuum their abandonment would create.

A second problem or set of problems arises from the part of public authority in benevolent operations. This is a legacy to the state from the Roman Catholic Church, even if the secular state accepts it as a humanitarian and not as a religious commitment. The relation between public and private benevolent institutions is similar to the relation between public and private schools. Public authority has more funds available; it also has the obligation of serving the entire population if it accepts the obligation at all. This suggests to many people that private institutions are unnecessary and will cease to exist. Where the state has adopted the principles of the welfare state, private institutions become part of the public establishment or close their doors. No value judgment is implied in this summary of the situation; it merely points up the novelty of the modern problem. Never before in history have so many states accepted benevolent operations as a public responsibility. When they accept it, one must think of benevolent operations in new terms. Roman Catholic operations are built and managed on the assumption that the state does not accept this responsibility in its totality. Should public authority succeed in rendering the services at a lower cost than the private institutions, the private institutions survive only as a refuge for those whose wealth permits them to seek something better than the public services. If this happens, the private operations cease to be charitable works in any sense of the term.

A third problem arises from the changing social structures of Western states, and this problem is of such complexity that a brief statement runs the risk of distortion. To put it briefly, Roman Catholic benevolent operations often do not succeed in reaching the really poor of modern society. Their services, even when founded for the poor and directed to the poor, may reach only the middle and upper classes. This can happen partly because the poor cannot afford these services, but partly also because in many countries the Roman Catholic Church is no longer the church of the poor. This bears no implication that Roman Catholic benevolent institutions render their services only to Catholics; it is to their honor that such restrictions are almost unknown. In the United States, benevolent institutions which as late as a generation ago served the urban poor now serve the urban and suburban middle classes. The poor are still there, but they are now a different ethnic and religious group. No one should think that this does not cause deep concern to those who administer the benevolent institutions, but they have not yet mastered the problem of giving increased and much more costly services to a more indigent clientele. This can be supported only by the kind of donations which the institutions no longer expect to receive. One may see again that the Roman Catholic Church has not given a profound commitment to benevolence to its members at large.

A fourth problem arises both from cultural changes in the Western countries and from political and cultural changes in other parts of the world. World poverty in the developing nations is far more degraded and far more helpless than urban poverty in the affluent societies of the West. No one is meeting this problem; apart from the somewhat threatening political implications of world poverty, authentic Christianity feels a compulsion to take some action. The existing benevolent institutions of the Roman Church are not equipped to deal with this problem, nor were they designed to deal with it. Foreign missions in some countries have directed their efforts to meet the problem on a local level; they can hardly do more, and this does not seem to be enough. World poverty can be attacked only by new institutions which have not yet arisen. Many young people who might at another time have engaged in benevolent work, dissatisfied now with public and private inaction, join such organizations as the Peace Corps of the United States. This puts them in direct touch with world poverty and gives them something tangible which they can do at once. They feel the same dissatisfaction with the failure of the institutions to cope with domestic poverty. In neither problem have the supreme Roman Catholic authorities yet presented an immediately practical program of action.

A fifth and final problem arises from the institutions as such, and it seems built into institutional benevolence. Institutional benevolence permits the individual Roman Catholic to feel that he has done his "duty of charity" if he contributes to institutions. He is excused from personal involvement and the gift of himself. This writer has elsewhere likened this to the old practice of purchasing a substitute when one was conscripted for military service. By itself institutional benevolence does not involve the individual Catholic, nor should it; this involvement is the work of some other agency of the church. The lack of this involvement has become all too apparent recently. For example, when some American Roman Catholics threaten to withhold their contributions from agencies which offer services to black and white, one sees that the original commitment to acts of benevolence was nearly zero from the beginning. This must be marked as a massive failure of Roman Catholicism in modern times.

When these problems are put together, they lead to the question whether Roman Catholic benevolent institutions can do what they must in the world in which they must live. The prognostication is not favorable. There will always be a place for the individual Christian to give a cup of water to the thirsty, to feed the hungry, to clothe the naked, to harbor the shelterless, and to visit the sick and imprisoned. Indeed there are more opportunities than most of us know. Since the Roman Church, however, like most of Western society, is long committed to the institutional treatment of these needs, the Roman institutions as they are cannot cope either with urban poverty nor with world poverty. There is a need of some one with the vision and imagination of Vincent de Paul and other founders of benevolent operations to find new institutions to meet new needs. The Roman Catholic Church has never been without such vision and imagination before, and one should not assume that they are missing now. Indeed people have appeared who may have these qualities; their problem has been to persuade the structure to accept some revolutionary propositions. I have mentioned the impatience of some of the young; the future, for better or for worse, rests with them. They are impatient at the funds and the personnel necessary to care for middle-class convalescents in suburban communities when in the same metropolitan area there are deaths each day from rat bites. They are impatient because in the standard modern hospital the staff outnumbers the patients by three or four to one, while in underdeveloped countries the proportion is inverted and heightened. If they have their way, they will close most of the existing benevolent institutions and let public authority provide the basic services. They say that the place for Roman Catholics to be found is the place where no one else will go. This, I think, is a degree of vision and imagination, but it still needs a structure within which to work.

## 5. *The Parish*

The parish is and has been for centuries the basis of the Roman Catholic structure; if the works of the Roman Church were mentioned in the order of importance, the parish should stand first. The parish is the successor of the local church which we find in the New Testament; it is the place where the Roman Catholic encounters the priesthood, the teaching office, and the sacramental system. It has also been the place where he most frequently encounters the other members of the Roman Catholic community. In an earlier day, the parish was nearly identical with all the groups with which a Roman Catholic was associated; that this is no longer true creates most of the problems of the modern parish.

The parish is administered by a pastor, with or without other priests appointed to assist him. It is a part of a diocese governed by an ordinary. Its physical plant includes at the minimum a church; in modern times, it often adds a rectory where the clergy reside, a school, a residence for the religious who teach in the school, and in well appointed parishes an assembly hall distinct from the church. As a rule the parish is defined territorially; all Roman Catholics within certain boundaries are attached to the parish church of the territory. The Roman Church insists as much as it can that the boundaries be respected, and it discourages the kind of ecclesiastical shopping not unknown in many Protestant churches. Respect for the boundaries makes it much easier to keep records, prevents pastoral rivalries and feuds, and assures each pastor the revenue he can expect from the parish. In the nineteenth century, United States immigrant groups were allowed to establish "national" parishes, on the ground that they had not yet learned English and that they would be happier with their own language group, as well as better protected from Protestant perversion. This could and did lead sometimes to five churches in as many city blocks, and it did not contribute to Roman Catholic unity. It was also in resistance to the process of Americanization and was viewed as slightly unpatriotic. Although some national parishes still exist, practically none have been built since the First World War. In some cities the members of national parishes were scarcely less hostile to other national parishes than they were to Protestant churches.

The modern parish is the successor of, the churches of the apostles, but it is more nearly the successor of the village church. In the village, the identification of the community and the parish was perfect. The parish was the place of baptisms, weddings, and funerals, and the entire village took part in these familial and ecclesiastical rites. Acquaintance of the pastor with the congregation and of the members with each other was as close as can be conceived. The village parish also exhibited the narrowness which is characteristic of the village. When the parish exists in a city, in particular in a large modern city, the village community no longer exists; if the parish is to be a religious community, it must find another form.

The parish has no ideal size, although the Roman Church prefers parishes to be smaller rather than larger; as has been seen, the ideal size is considered the size that enables the priests to know personally each member of the parish. Behind this is the belief that the pastor cannot be an effective spiritual leader unless he knows those whom he counsels. The parish should also be of a size sufficient to support itself. In countries in which church maintenance and priests' salaries are not furnished by the government, the parish has no revenue except the contributions of its parishioners. In these countries, the size and the regularity of one's contributions become one of the marks of the good parishioner; the "Sunday collection" is no longer left to casual generosity and a record is kept of the contributions of each wage earner.

The parish likewise has no set social structure. In cities the territory covers a neighborhood, and, in most modern cities, neighborhoods tend to be composed of people of the same economic status. But the mobility of urban populations can produce some startling diversities within a single parish. Under these conditions the priest find it difficult to serve a group which can range from the highest levels of wealth and education to the lowest. People of wealth and education tend to think of the parish as *their* parish and of the poor and uneducated as transients. A parish which exhibits great diversity is usually on the road to decline, if not to extinction.

The parish is normally the center of a certain number of benevolent and social organizations. These organizations are deliberately intended to keep the people together; unless there is a basis of real union without the organizations, the organizations are not remarkably successful in their purpose. Roman Catholics often express dissatisfaction with the way in which the Roman Church proliferates organizations for the different groups within the parishes—children, adolescents, young unmarried people, married people, husbands, wives, and finally widows. Many believe that the parish should be the single organization to which everyone belongs and in which everyone has a place.

The parish assembles only for worship on Sundays and holydays of obligation, and in large parishes it does not assemble even for this, since the church is not large enough to accommodate the entire parish. In large parishes, the celebration of Mass may be scheduled eight or ten times on a Sunday, and most of the parishioners do not meet each other at the church. Until a recent change in the rules governing the hours at which Mass may be celebrated, some parishes scheduled Mass on the hour all through Sunday morning, and the church resembled somewhat a large suburban railway station at the morning and evening hours. A certain expeditiousness, not to say haste, was desirable when the church was so crowded; and the mere fulfilment of the Sunday obligation of attending Mass became more important than the style and manner of the worship, or the participation of the laity in the worship, or the quality of preaching. The clergy in such parishes know to the second the time which is required to empty the church and to refill it.

The parish is often an educational agency, as has been seen. Where it is this, the school becomes the major operating expense, and it must all come from the parishioners where there is no government aid to religious schools. The funds do not come simply from the parents of the students; the practice is to charge a merely nominal tuition which even the needy members of the parish can meet and to make up the difference from the general funds. The Roman Catholic schools without government assistance cannot furnish education free of charge as the public institutions do, but they attempt to come as close to it as they can by distributing the expenses over the entire parish. The school is operated by professional teachers, up to recent years always members of religious communities, now more frequently supplemented by secular teachers. The administration of the school, however, does demand considerable time from the clergy, time which could be given to other activities more closely identified with the ministry. In addition, the pastor is not always trained and experienced in school administration—in fact, it is rarely that he is, and many local problems of the Roman Catholic system can be traced to this.

The modern parish priest may take comfort in the fact that Paul's church at Corinth had problems both in unity and in worship, areas where he too is likely to have problems. He may admire the way in which Paul handled the problems, but he may also wonder whether the solution was permanent. He will take less comfort from the fact that Corinth seemed to have no financial problems; at least Paul expected the Corinthians to furnish a generous contribution for the needy church of Jerusalem. This will remind the parish priest of the "drives" instituted by ordinaries and other ecclesiastical agencies for the "special collection." In many regions the favorite sermon topic, according to local wit and folklore, is money, but I have never met a priest who enjoyed talking about it. A statistical study which unfortunately is no longer available to me for reference reached the estimate that the average Roman Catholic in the United States contributes one half of one percent of his income to the church. The figure cannot be taken as entirely reliable and will be contested, but if it were five times less than the reality, which it can hardly be, the contributions óf Roman Catholics to the church in the United States are far from the point of pain. Priests need not feel so ashamed of mentioning contributions.

Both attendance at Mass and reception of the sacraments, the accepted tokens of "the practicing Catholic," are not well known. In one parish where I served temporarily, knowledge of the number of parishioners and the number of seats in the church made it clear that about half of the parishioners appeared at Mass on Sunday, even though the church was filled or near it seven times each Sunday. One may project a no more favorable figure for the reception of the sacraments. The parish was understaffed for its numbers, and it was impossible for the clergy to know the parishioners sufficiently well to form an idea of the attachment of the parishioners to the church. In such parishes, priests often wonder what they are accomplishing; the clerical idiom is "saving the saved." But since the priests are already occupied up to the limit of their time and endurance, they see no way in which they can do much about those Catholics whose membership is minimal. Presence at worship is not, of course, an adequate token of the quality of membership, but habitual failure to attend is taken as a sign of lack of interest, an assumption which is usually valid.

The problem of the modern Roman Catholic parish has become a problem of community, and the problem has become acute rather rapidly. The parish of a village or of a neighborhood with the character of a village exhibits the village vice of narrowness. The urban parish exhibits the urban vice of anonymity. In neither instance is a Christian community formed. Even in the village type of parish, the old identity of parish and community no longer exists. The modern Roman Catholic is a member of other communities besides his parish, and the other communities may have nothing in common with each other except his membership. In the United States recently, some parishes have acted to exclude "undesirable" ethnic groups from the neighborhood. The parish is not identical with the neighborhood, but in many of these neighborhoods the relationship is very close. This is village narrowness at its ugliest; and the fact that these people see nothing in their attitude which is contrary to their Roman Catholic belief suggests another massive failure of Roman Catholicism. Such a community moves toward its own dissolution.

The urban parish is no more faceless than the city as a whole, but the Roman Catholic Church has found no way to reach the faceless. In old village parishes in Europe, one may find his own family in the registers of baptisms, weddings, and funerals for four to six hundred years; in the modern urban parish many do not remain even long enough to register, and others do not register because the anonymity of the city pleases them. Such people can be pleasant and well mannered, they can be well educated and successful in their profession; they simply do not, in the modern phrase, wish to get involved. The city is their shell, and they are open to no new commitment which might break the shell. The parish church is their spiritual market or service station, but not the focus of community. Many would say that the large urban parish is not declining, it has already died. It is no longer a parish but simply a building which affords certain facilities to those who desire them.

Students of modern society have noticed that the absence of community is a widespread and unwholesome urban phenomenon, and the parish exhibits a lack which is found elsewhere also. Many Catholics wonder whether it is possible for the parish to be a center of Christian community. It has been suggested that in thirty years or even less the large churches typical of the cities will have disappeared. The parish base will be in a store, serving a very small neighborhood. The priest or priests, who by that time will have full-time lay assistants or deacons, will live in the rear of the store or in a loft. They will share fully in the life of the neighborhood, and they will not be distinguished from their fellows by distinctive garb or distinctive housing. Since they will serve fewer people, they will serve them more intensely, with no time demanded for schools or organizations. The parish will be of a size to allow a worshiping community of people who know each other to assemble. Worship will be conducted in homes as often as it is conducted in the church. The clergy and their assistants will spend much less time in offices and more time in religious and social action. They will mobilize the resources of the Roman Catholic community in such a way that the Catholics are full members of their neighborhood. One of the defects of the traditional parish is that it is for Roman Catholics. In the urban parish of the future, the parish will be open to all for whatever service the parish can render.

This dream may turn to reality. Until it does, certain experiments are being conducted with a nonparochial structure. The "floating parish" abandons territorial lines and is formed by a small group of people with common interests. It has no set place of worship, but moves about the city inviting people from the neighborhoods which it visits to join the worship. A part of the rite of the assembly is the recital of social needs and services which the group is doing or ought to undertake, all of which are assigned on a volunteer basis. The liturgy is as informal as the ordinary permits it to be. The few groups which have been allowed to attempt this seem to be well aware of the danger that they may form an exclusive group of people with common educational and economic backgrounds, and they spare no effort to make their groups open to anyone, but they cannot attract anyone until they have become diversified enough to authenticate their openness. The "floating parish" does not seem to indicate the structure of the future parish; it is rather an attempt to find out how much diversity is possible in structure with a genuine worshiping community retained. What they have found is that the worshiping community that is merely a group assembled for ritual cult is not a community. This was recognized in the traditional parish, as the parish organizations attest. The floating parish shows that action is necessary to form and sustain the community and that the action must be directed to the "neighbor" in the etymological sense—that is, the people who are nearest. And it must not be a closed Roman Catholic group either in membership or in its outlook.

It may perhaps be merely a question of size; whatever *community* is thought to mean, there seems to be a maximum beyond which a community comes apart. One must remember that the idea and the reality of Christian community arose in the Hellenistic-Roman world in a population as rootless as the people of the modern cities. The experimental or the ideal parishes are candid returns to the New Testament community and to the techniques of the apostolic church. There is a danger of archaism in such restorations; but no one has found a superior technique, and this is something which technique cannot achieve. Modern communications make it much easier to reach one's fellow man, but they have not created community; they can be used by a community, but they cannot form it. They have not overcome the tribalism, also archaic, which seems to be the earliest and in a way the most natural form of human community. The word "tribal" could be used accurately of many Roman Catholic parishes.

That the search for community should have arisen so suddenly and so spontaneously in diverse areas is itself one of the most interesting phenomena of contemporary Roman Catholicism. The search is spontaneous, for neither recent theological writing nor the acts of the Second Vatican Council stimulate such a search. It is rather that the Council's view of the church made many Catholics aware that they do not have the community necessary to realize the kind of church which the Council described. There has been a structural failure; and the interest in repairing the structure comes from the learning church, not from the teaching church. The danger implicit in this search is that the community may form itself without including the hierarchy and the clergy; such a community would not be the Roman Catholic Church, nor could it hope to realize the potential of the Roman Catholic Church. Yet the uncooperative attitude of many prelates and clergymen to the efforts to establish community must be recognized. Possibly this may be a problem which the passage of time will help to solve, but no problem is really solved just by the passage of time. The Roman Church, as was noticed several times, is sensitive to the desires and the pressure of the laity, but the structure does not have channels through which the laity may speak. There are in fact many more experimental groups than the bishops have authorized, and more than the bishops know about; a few such groups have been suppressed by episcopal decree. Suppression seems only to multiply the groups. Certainly clandestine meetings seem out of character in the Roman Catholic Church, and it should not be necessary to form a church of the catacombs against the bishops. Yet in the United States the name given to the movement is "the underground church." The dissatisfaction with the traditional parish as a business organization and a spiritual pharmacy must be acknowledged. No firm steps can be taken to change the parish into a Christian community without episcopal leadership. It is not a question of whether the demand for such leadership will be met, for it will be met; it is a question of how much loss the Roman Catholic Church must suffer before episcopal leadership responds to the demand.

## 6. Preaching

Preaching, certainly one of the most important functions of the pastoral ministry, could have been included in the preceding section, but it deserves separate discussion. Several have said that the quality of preaching has more to do with the state of religion in the Roman Catholic Church than any other single factor.[1] The remark frightens at first, and the observation is disputable, but no other single factor can be much more important. The Protestant churches since the Reformation have placed greater emphasis on the ministry of the word than the Roman Catholic Church and it is probably true to say that the Protestant churches generally have a higher grade of preaching than the Roman Catholic Church. Protestants often choose a church simply because its minister is a respected preacher. This has nothing to do with appointments or promotion or attendance in the Roman Catholic Church. Whether a priest preaches well or poorly is not a factor which is weighed in his evaluation.

Yet the Roman Church is not without its tradition of great preachers. The collected sermons and homilies of the Fathers of the Church run into hundreds of volumes. The Roman Church venerates preachers like Bernardine of Siena, Vincent Ferrer, and Francis de Sales, all of whom enjoyed unusual success in reclaiming lapsed or misbehaving Catholics. In the modern Roman Church, as for several centuries previous, preaching and singing a high Mass are two things which each priest is expected to do. He will get training and exercise in both and he will do them both, whether his performance is good or bad.

It is impossible to generalize about the quality of Roman Catholic preaching throughout the world. I can say only that I have never been in a place where the preaching was praised or met anyone who came from a place where the preaching was praised. The observation quoted at the beginning of this section is verified for many people by some of the more notable failures of Roman Catholicism in some vital moral areas; the failure is not so much in dissuading people from doing wrong as it is in persuading them that it is wrong. If the observation is accurate, the Roman Church has its task clearly defined; the methods of doing the task are not so clearly defined.

What is a good sermon? Or what is a bad sermon? After one weighs the question and eliminates such obviously false answers as those which would distinguish the quality of a sermon by orthodoxy or eloquence or persuasion, one comes down to the simple statement that a good sermon is one in which something is said. What that something should be is a further question. We are dealing with a religious act that is performed in every church weekly, and it is absurd to expect something like Bossuet every Sunday—in fact, the modern audience would not tolerate Bossuet. On this basis, the quality of preaching, which must be judged rather low generally, means that the preachers have nothing to say much of the time.

The problem is too complex for the preachers themselves to solve. In the nineteenth century, two hours were regarded as not too much time for a really good sermon—and they were not all good. One of Paul's Christians is the first recorded instance of a Christian churchgoer who fell asleep during the sermon; and it is surprising that more churches are not dedicated to St. Eutychus

(Acts 20:9–12). The modern audience will not give the preacher even one hour. The preacher, who may feel that he has nothing but a bad sermon in any hypothesis, prefers to give a short bad sermon rather than a long bad sermon and abbreviate the pain for both speaker and audience. A good sermon need not take an hour, but it can hardly be delivered if the speaker must watch the clock like a dispatcher of aircraft. It has been noticed that many parishes leave little time for the sermon.

The modern preacher must compete with forms of entertainment which older preachers and audiences did not know. One should not think of sermons as entertainment, but in the nineteenth and early twentieth centuries there was nothing to do on Sunday except go to church, especially in strongly Sabbatarian communities. A good sermon, or two of them, helped to pass the time on the only day of the week free from work. The modern preacher faces an audience which is familiar with the moving pictures, radio, television, or fast, easy transportation to spectator sports or clean outdoor exercise. This is not to say that the quality of moving pictures or television is much higher than the quality of sermons; it is not, but these media are much more costly and pretentious, have a much larger potential variety, and they always present the viewer with the hope that this time will be better than the last. The hearer of the sermon usually has no such hope. For him the possibilities of the sermon are exhausted. It is known that over-exposure on television forces performers to retire after a season or two. The preacher, also exposed weekly, remains at his post with his captive audience until he is reassigned. He too may have used all his material, but he cannot retire or seek another network. The modern audience, accustomed to the mass media, is jaded with novelty and with stunts. There is an anecdote of a famous Dominican preacher named Thomas Burke who began a sermon with the startling sentence, "To hell with the Jesuits." This would not surely startle a modern audience, and it should be added that Father Burke went on to deliver a eulogy of the organization which he had named.

The Roman Catholic seminaries have not been indifferent to the preparation of preachers; if one may judge from the curricula, they do not lag notably behind the Protestant seminaries in formal preparation. But the Roman Catholic seminarian does not have that stimulus which the Protestant seminarian has in the prospects of success for a good preacher. In addition, he is trained in the

Roman emphasis on doctrine. In my experience, most seminarians gave little time and interest to the formal training for preaching. This can lead to some nearly disastrous results even in the basic mechanics of speech. When Catholics praise a sermon, inquiry will often disclose that the greatest merit of the sermon was that it was audible. There is something which is universally recognized as "the preacher's tone," which means more than inflection. It means that the preacher uses a vocabulary and style which he never uses elsewhere. If the audience knows him at all, it knows that he is not speaking to them; he is reciting a piece which may be his own, but which probably is not.

The question of content has become more urgent since the liturgical reforms of the Second Vatican Council restored the homily to its position as a part of the liturgical worship. Before the Council, very little excuse was needed for the priest to omit the sermon. That content alone can make a sermon successful is seen in Newman's sermons, solid and well written and esteemed when they were uttered as they are by readers; it seems well established that his delivery was one of the worst ever heard in St. Mary's Church. Dioceses often meet the problem of content by publishing schedules of sermon topics to which the clergy are expected to adhere, and they usually do; selection of a topic can be such a desperate task that any suggestions are welcome. The schedules favor a traditional Roman Catholic type of sermon, the doctrinal sermon; the peculiar Roman esteem of doctrine has been noted. Since adult Catholics are not likely to be instructed by any other means than the pulpit, such doctrinal instructions are quite frequent, at least up to the present. As pulpit oratory they are usually glaring failures. The doctrinal exposition echoes the textbook treatment in seminaries and is at least equally dull; only a brilliant preacher can relate these expositions to Christian life and belief. The homily, as its name indicates, is an exposition of the biblical texts employed in the liturgy of the day, and these are more likely to present a challenge to the audience, but the liturgical selections are not always felicitous. The writer remembers the displeasure with which he once found that he had fallen on the Sunday Gospel of which the climactic line is "He spoke right." One would almost prefer to expound the text, "I see men like trees walking."

Yet if the ambitious young preacher studies the techniques of modern political orators, he may conclude that the preacher is no worse off; he may even conclude that speaking has become a lost art in modern times. That this is untrue is evident from the enthusiasm which a genuinely good speech never fails to arouse, whether it be political or homiletic. If he studies the sermons and homilies of the Fathers, Bossuet, Newman, and other esteemed preachers ancient and modern, he will learn only how they did it, not how he should do it. He has not the same audience, nor can he use the same material and style. Roman Catholic preaching will improve when all who engage in it realize that each sermon is a new creation.

That a good speech is a dialogue with the audience is now literally realized in many Roman Catholic churches where the *dialogue homily* appears. The Roman Catholic, who was trained never to speak in church, may ask questions of the preacher, suggest further developments, approve and expand the statement, or say, "That is not right." Whether this is the key to improved preaching is uncertain; one sees that without proper handling the dialogue could degenerate into confusion, but it helps the preacher to solve the problem of overexposure, and it makes him much more certain that he is speaking to the people who sit before him. In some other experimental forms of worship, the congregation expresses a primitive faith in the spirit by inviting some one from the congregation to speak. These practices are familiar to certain Protestant Churches, and they have a very ancient precedent.

Since the preacher rightly hesitates to become political, he may also hesitate to become urgent or even contemporary. When one adds up the list of defects in preaching, timidity stands well near the top of the list. Young priests are instructed both in the seminary and after they leave it that they should never become controversial in the pulpit. This principle would make it impossible to deliver the Sermon on the Mount in a Roman Catholic pulpit. It leads to quite bland discourses which present the congregation with no moral challenge. Nor is the principle entirely honest. No priest will be questioned for speaking against contraception, which is certainly a controversial topic; he may be questioned if he speaks against segregation, which is also controversial; and he will certainly be questioned if he speaks against war. It was observed that the ordinary is fully within his powers when he supervises preaching; there is nothing but his personal integrity to prevent him from abusing these powers. In some cases, it may be abuse of the power of episcopal supervision which leaves priests uninterested in the work of preaching. There are too many things which they feel they cannot say.

The quality of preaching is one church activity about which the laity can and ought to speak, for ultimately the quality of preaching will be as good as the laity insist that it be. The Roman Catholic laity is so accustomed to preaching that ranges from mediocre to poor that it probably thinks nothing else is possible. A vigorous demand would certainly have results, but improvement must come from the clergy itself. It is more than lack of preparation, which happens often enough. Priests do not have faith in the spoken word as a word of power. Unless they can see the sermon as an opportunity and a challenge, a personal encounter between the people and themselves in which the reality of the church lives, they will not have the spark which even a routine good sermon demands. It is hardly necessary to add that good preaching means that the priest is what he utters, and this is more than the conventional "good example." The priest can communicate only the faith which he has. One can say that renewal and reform within Roman Catholicism will march as far and as fast as good preaching will take it.

# EPILOGUE: NEW DIRECTIONS

At the beginning of this book, I said there was scarcely any period in the history of the Roman Catholic Church when its future was more difficult to predict than it is now. In every topic surveyed, change can be seen, and more changes can be foreseen. In earlier history, those who bore authority in the Roman Church were in the best position to predict its future, since its future would be largely determined by their decisions. One of the most remarkable changes is that they no longer have this certainty.

In planning this book, which was difficult, it occurred at one time that the work might be planned in terms of the heritages of the Roman Catholic Church: its legacies from Greece, from Rome, from Judaism, from the Middle Ages, from the Renaissance, and from any source which has contributed to its historical reality. The plan was quickly dismissed as unsatisfactory; it was almost certain to be disorderly, to suffer from overlapping and omission, and much less likely to give a clear picture than a topical description. Even the topical description suffers from compression and distortion; the Roman Church is viewed from a certain perspective, and the view may be the same as one gets through inverted binoculars. Probably no two writers would choose the same emphases. The Roman Catholic Church is an old and a large organization, and almost any generalization about it is likely to be false. At the conclusion of the book, one is aware of the omissions, but since omissions and compressions were inevitable, one must hope that one's judgment of what should be compressed and omitted is defensible.

One need not even read the book to discover that structure is treated more fully than any other aspect of Romanism; the table of contents makes this clear. No doubt some readers will regard this as distortion. Yet the objective from the beginning was to dwell on those features of Romanism which are most Roman, and structure certainly has the first place in this ranking. There is not and never has been another ecclesiastical structure like it. It is not the only thing which gives Romanism its character, and one may argue whether it is the most important determinant, but no other factor can be much more important. The liturgical cult of Romanism has received the next most extensive treatment because Romanism is the most liturgical of the Christian churches and because Romanism attaches an efficacy to liturgical worship given by no other Christian church.

Roman beliefs could not be treated adequately within the scope of this work, as was noted, and it proved difficult to set forth the Roman understanding of faith and the Roman conception of the teaching office. These again are peculiarly Roman features, and to understand Romanism it is perhaps less important to know Roman beliefs than to know what Roman belief is. In fact, most Roman Catholics are not fully instructed in their beliefs, but they have a definite idea of what it means to believe.

The final section on the works of the Roman Church is the least satisfactory, again because the magnitude of the material goes far beyond the available space. This section might have been omitted in order to treat belief at greater length, in particular some Roman problems in the area of morality which have only been touched under other headings, but a picture of the Roman Church which presents its government, its cult, and its belief simply fails to present its life; and it is alive. How is one to capture in words the life of a worldwide church? Perhaps one can do no more than affirm one's belief that it does live.

The preceding paragraphs are not intended to do the work of the reviewers of this book for them, but simply to indicate why the work has the form and shape that emerged. It is in these areas that my view of new directions must be summarized, for new directions have been seen under nearly every heading in the book. It has been our effort to point out the historical roots of Roman institutions, beliefs, and practices as much as possible; the scope of the work again did not permit a thorough historical study of each element. One must understand that Romanism is highly conscious of its history and much attached to its traditions. In modern times it has projected the image of a body that resists change simply as such. This is not a true image of Romanism either in the present or in the past, although if one must find a single word for the Roman position, the word would be conservative rather than radical. Romanism often shows a hypersensitivity toward what it suspects is a betrayal of its traditions. Its identity depends on its continuity with its traditions, and this is true of any society. No society can abandon its past without ceasing to be. It was the intention of the revolutionaries in France to destroy the old France and create an entirely new France. Even they could not abandon the past of France, however. A society can cease to be also by refusing to move out of its past. Romanism has sometimes threatened to do the second; it has never threatened to do the first.

Roman conservatism has meant, in other junctures than the present, that when Rome does move to change, it moves when accumulated forces produce a more rapid and intense rate of change than one finds in a society which is better organized for a regular rate of growth and development. The changes which occur create problems simply because they come in too great numbers and at too rapid a pace for many Roman Catholics to assimilate. I have speculated that had the Roman Church moved in the early sixteenth century at the rate at which it has moved in the mid-twentieth century, the Protestant Reformation may very well not have happened. The forces that worked for change—and they were many and strong—could have been channeled within the structure of the Roman Church. In saying this, one risks too optimistic a view of the work of the Second Vatican Council; unfavorable developments could make this writer a false prophet before the manuscript reaches the printed page. The reason for optimism is that the historic Roman Church has often suffered from changing too little and too slowly, but never from changing too much and too rapidly. Many Roman Catholics fear that even the changes made and opened by the Second Vatican Council are too little and too late. One must realize that none of the earlier twenty ecumenical councils accomplished anything like this Council.

The only safe prediction at the moment is that changes will continue before the Roman Church stabilizes itself anew. It is probably too much to expect that it will rid itself of its excessive attachment to tradition as such. On the other hand, the first twenty ecumenical councils all had as their purpose to stabilize some positions. The Second Vatican Council did not stabilize positions. It issued no dogmatic definitions, and its desciplinary directions were calculated to leave room for further modifications. The Council did not abandon tradition, but it did not choose to make the affirmation of tradition its major purpose. Hence a change in the Roman attitude toward tradition, already perceptible in the laity, many of the clergy, and even in some of the hierarchy, may be the sign of the future.

It can, it seems, be safely predicted that the relations of authority and freedom in the Roman Church will not retain the character which they have had. The Roman Church may have recognized that an excess of authority is as much a danger to the mission of the Roman Church as an excess of freedom; to put it another way, that authority too needs restraints other than those which the bearers of authority place upon themselves. The image of the Roman Catholic as a passive, sheeplike subject of his prelates is already passing into the museum of history. The image of the Pope and the bishops as absolute monarchs is changing, but the new image has not yet emerged clearly. Some will find this description too optimistic; it is a question whether a trend has been set in motion which cannot and will not be reversed. I am convinced that this has happened.

It was observed that the most evident changes have occurred in liturgical worship and that these changes have been directed to renew, or if necessary to create, an authentic worshiping community. In our treatment of the parish, it was seen that the parish is faced with an identity crisis. A religious community must be a worshiping community; whether the moves which have been made will achieve this is less important than the fact that the attempt has been made. Should these moves prove ineffective, the official position of Romanism now is that experiment may continue. Worship alone will not create a Christian community, but it would not be a Christian community without worship.

Belief probably shows the least possibility of change, which may be surprising and should be comforting to those who fear that basic Roman Catholic beliefs are imperiled by the present mood of change. The change here is rather in the direction of openness to further study and research, to more sympathy to bold new efforts to proclaim Roman Catholic belief in modern language. The teaching office will be seen in its true reality as the office of proclaiming belief and not as a supercensor of thought and speech. In this as in other areas, the most significant change would be the development of implicit mutual confidence between all members of the Roman Church.

The works of the church will continue, for the Roman Church could not claim to be a Christian church without its works; but it was observed here that every one of the works is threatened with extinction in the form which they now have. This is disturbing, for the Roman Church has not yet developed new forms in which the works may be done. Optimism about the capacity to develop new forms is justified both by the history of Romanism and by its present reality, but the optimism has to be tempered with a dash of pessimism based on some of the more outstanding past failures of Romanism to rise to the occasion. A church which could have a bureau capable of suppressing the Chinese mission has a capacity of blundering to which it is difficult to assign a limit. Perhaps such bureaus no longer exist; one hopes not, but one would like more complete assurance than the history of recent theological censorship will allow.

Will the changes, those already made and those which can be projected, make the Roman Church really Catholic, as we have asked earlier? Those who are convinced believers in Romanism have no doubt that the Roman Church must move toward its Catholic destiny, and that it will reach it. Not all of these convinced believers yet recognize that it is the task of Roman Catholics themselves to accomplish this completeness. This impinges upon the contemporary ecumenical movement, as well as on the Roman Church outside Europe—which I distinguish from European extensions of Romanism on other continents. It was seen that the Roman Church has made its first gesture of reconciliation toward the Protestant churches since the Reformation. This is a basic change of attitude, and the laity seem to be moving more rapidly than the hierarchy and the clergy. Does this decision imply that the Roman Church envisages changes of sufficient magnitude to permit the emergence of an ecumenical Christian church, a church which would be truly Catholic in the etymological sense of the word? This would be the most radical change which the Roman Church could make, and it will not be made as long as such a change is viewed as a renunciation of the identity of the Roman Church.

The Roman Church may be entering upon its own identity crisis, however, or perhaps may have entered it already. What is it really, and what is its place and its mission in the world? As long as the Roman Church lives and moves in history, the question must be constantly asked and constantly answered. The Roman Church cannot be simply what it has been; this is a fossil by definition. It must find, indeed it must assert its place in the world. The most significant of the documents of the Second Vatican Council may not be "The Church in the Modern World," but this is certainly the most significant title; the Roman Church has never asked itself this question before. From such a change almost any development is possible. Up to this time the Roman Church has judged the world.

Believing Roman Catholics have never had any uncertainty about the identity of the church and its mission; they believe that it is the body of Christ present in the world and saving the world. It will take a great many ecumenical discussions before this belief is assimilated by the Protestant churches, but let it be understood that this is Roman Catholic belief, and that it explains nearly everything Roman Catholics say and do about their church. How, then, can there be an identity crisis? Since the modern term *image* has been used rather frequently, let me use it again and say that the identity is obscured when the Roman Church does not seem to project the image of Christ, the savior. If it is the pilgrim church, as the Second Vatican Council called it, it is unable to project the image of the eschatological Lord.

Yet to many eschatological lordship is the image Romanism projects, and they do not accept it. No change in the Roman Church can be meaningful unless the image is seen clearly. It can be seen in any given time and place only in those Roman Catholics who exist in that time and place. No one is capable of seeing the Roman Church in the whole of time and space, and, if he did, he could find areas where the image is dimmed. The Roman Church, however, knows that it has no other credible image to project. Ultimately this is the direction in which the changing Church of Rome is moving.

# NOTES

---

## INTRODUCTION

1. Michael de la Bedoyere, ed., *Objections to Roman Catholicism* (Philadelphia: J. B. Lippincott Company, 1965).

2. Charles Davis, *A Question of Conscience* (New York: Harper & Row, Publishers, 1967).

## I. THE STRUCTURE OF ROMAN CATHOLICISM

### 1. THE STRUCTURE OF RELIGION

1. H. W. T. Saggs, *The Greatness That Was Babylon* (New York: Hawthorne, 1962), pp. 157–169.

2. M. Rostovtzeff, *Greece* (New York: Oxford University Press), pp. 185–186.

### 2. APOSTOLIC SUCCESSION

1. G. Kittel, *Theological Dictionary of the New Testament* (Grand Rapids, Mich.: Wm. B. Eerdmans Publishing Company, 1964), Vol. I, pp. 428–437.

### 3. THE PAPACY

1. Oscar Cullmann, *Peter: Disciple, Apostle, Martyr* (Philadelphia: The Westminster Press, 1962), pp. 228–242.
2. H. Strack-P. Billerbeck, *Kommentar zum Neuen Testament* (München: Beck, 1965), Bd. 1, pp. 738–741.
3. Oscar Cullmann, *op. cit.*, pp. 25–57.
4. *The Vatican Council from Its Opening to Its Prorogation* (London: Burns, Oates & Washbourne, Ltd.), pp. 112–115.

5. Clement of Alexandria, in Eusebius, Hist. Eccl., vi, 14; Origen, *Commentary on Genesis*, in Eusebius, Hist. Eccl., iii, 1; Tertullian, *De Praescriptione* 36 and *Adv. Marcionem*, iv, 5; Irenaeus, *Adv. Haereses*, iii, 1; Eusebius, Hist. Eccl., ii, 25.
6. Philip Hughes, *A History of the Church* (New York: Sheed and Ward, Inc., 1959), Vol. I, pp. 66–156.
7. M. Rostovtzeff, *The Social and Economic History of the Hellen-*

*istic World* (Oxford: Clarendon Press, 1940), pp. 268–271.

8. *Ibid.*, pp. 271–274.

9. Philip Hughes, *op. cit.*, Vol. II, pp. 239–248.

10. Philip Hughes, *A Popular History of the Reformation* (Garden City, N.Y.: Hanover House, 1956).

11. Philip Hughes, *A History of the Church*, Vol. II, pp. 191–201.

12. Xavier Rynne, *The Second Session* (New York: Farrar, Straus & Giroux, 1964), p. 182.

13. W. E. Addis and T. Arnold, *Catholic Dictionary* (London: Routledge and Kegan Paul, Ltd., 1960).

14. Walter M. Abbott and Joseph Gallagher, *The Documents of Vatican II* (New York: The America Press, 1966), p. 438.

15. Xavier Rynne, *The Third Session* (New York: Farrar, Straus & Giroux, 1965), pp. 95–108.

16. Xavier Rynne, *The Second Session*, pp. 338–346.

## 4. THE COLLEGE OF CARDINALS

1. Philip Hughes, *A History of the Church*, Vol. III, pp. 229–246.

## 5. THE EPISCOPACY

1. C. C. Richardson, ed., *The Library of Christian Classics*, Vol. I (London: SCM Press, Ltd., 1953).

2. Addis and Arnold, *Catholic Dictionary*.

3. Adolf Harnack, *Sources of the Apostolic Canons* (London: Norgate, 1895), pp. 35–37.

4. Philip Hughes, *A History of the Church*, Vol. II, pp. 226–233.

5. With reference to 1 Corinthians 7:27, the Council of Alexandria said in its encyclical letter of 338: "For if this expression applies to a wife, how much more does it apply to a church, and to the episcopate itself, to which whosoever is bound ought not to seek another, lest he prove an adulterer according to Holy Scripture" (Athanasius, *Apol. contra Arianos*, 6). Whatever is to be said about the sentiments of the Council, its exegesis is a bit of typological fancy of the type known as Alexandrian.

6. Peter Canisius van Lierde, *The Holy See At Work* (New York: Hawthorn, 1962), p. 548.

7. Abbott and Gallagher, *The Documents of Vatican II*, p. 417.

8. Donald Attwater, *A Catholic Dictionary* (New York: The Macmillan Co., Inc., 1949).

9. Addis and Arnold, *Catholic Dictionary*.

10. Joseph H. Fichter, *America's Forgotten Priests* (New York: Harper & Row, Publishers, 1968).

11. Abbott and Gallagher, *The Documents of Vatican II*, pp. 396–430.

## 6. THE PRIESTHOOD

1. James J. Kavanaugh, *A Modern Priest Looks At His Outdated Church* (New York: Trident Press, 1967); Charles Davis, *A Question of Conscience.*
2. James M. Lee, ed., *Seminary Education in a Time of Change* (Notre Dame: Fides Publishers, 1965).
3. *The Worker-Priests: A Collective Documentation*, John Petrie, tr. (New York: The Macmillan Co., Inc., 1956).
4. 1 Corinthians 7:25–39; 9:5.

## 7. THE LAITY

1. Daniel Jenkins, *Congregationalism: A Restatement* (New York: Harper & Brothers, 1954).
2. Philip Hughes, *A History of the Church*, Vol. II, pp. 227–239.
3. Stanley and Evans, eds., *Return to Reality* (London: Zeno, 1954), pp. 192–210; Ignace Lepp, *The Christian Failure* (Westminster, Md.: The Newman Press, 1962).
4. Gordon Zahn, *German Catholics and Hitler's Wars* (New York: Sheed & Ward, Inc., 1962).
5. Michael de la Bedoyere, ed., *Objections to Roman Catholicism*; Donald Thorman, *The Emerging Layman* (New York: Doubleday & Co., Inc., 1962); Thorman, *The Christian Vision* (New York: Doubleday & Co., Inc., 1967); Daniel J. Callahan, *The Mind of the Catholic Layman* (New York: Charles Scribner's Sons, 1963); Callahan, *The New Church: Essays in Catholic Reform* (New York: Charles Scribner's Sons, 1966); Andrew M. Greeley, *The Hesitant Pilgrim* (New York: Sheed & Ward, Inc., 1966).
6. Abbott and Gallagher, *The Documents of Vatican II*, pp. 489–522.
7. *Ibid.*, p. 205.
8. *Ibid.*, p. 243.
9. *Ibid.*, p. 270.
10. *Ibid.*, p. 515.
11. *The New York Times*, Oct. 22, 1967, Section E, p. 6.

## 8. RELIGIOUS COMMUNITIES

1. John A. Hardon, *Religions of the World* (Westminster, Md.: The Newman Press, 1963); R. C. Zaehner, ed., *The Concise Encyclopedia of Living Faiths* (New York: Hawthorn, 1959).
2. John A. Hardon, *The Protestant Churches of America* (Westminster, Md.: The Newman Press, 1957), pp. 98–107; Peter F. Anson, *The Call of the Cloister: Religious Communities and Kindred Bodies in the Anglican Communion* (London: S.P.C.K., 1958); *The Rule of Taizé*, Communité de Taizé, 1961.
3. Owen Chadwick, *John Cassian* (Cambridge: Cambridge University Press, 1950), pp. 13–26.
4. M. Rostovtzeff, *Social and Economic History of the Roman Empire* (Oxford: Clarendon

Press, 1957), Vol. I, pp. 274–275, 488; Vol. II, p. 677.

5. Philip Schaff and Henry Wace, eds., *The Nicene and Post-Nicene Fathers* (Grand Rapids, Mich.: Wm. B. Eerdmans Publishing Company, 1952), Vol. VIII, pp. lii–liv.

6. Ruth J. Dean and M. Dominica Legge, eds., *The Rule of St. Benedict* (Oxford: Basil Blackwell, 1964).

7. Philip Hughes, *The Reformation in England* (New York: The Macmillan Co., Inc., 1963), Vol. I, pp. 37–86.

8. *The Shorter Cambridge Medieval History* (Cambridge: Cambridge University Press, 1952), Vol. I, pp. 283–289; H. Daniel-Rops, *The Church in the Dark Ages* (New York: Doubleday & Co., Inc., 1962), Vol. I, pp. 353–367; Norman F. Cantor, *Medieval History* (New York: The Macmillan Co., Inc., 1963), pp. 182–192.

9. B. S. James, *The Life of St. Bernard of Clairvaux* (Chicago: Henry Regnery Company, 1953), p. 417.

10. *The Canterbury Tales* (New York: Random House, Inc., 1929), pp. 259–277.

11. Michael de la Bedoyere, *The Greatest Catherine* (Milwaukee: The Bruce Publishing Company, 1947), pp. 100–233.

12. Pierre Coste, *Life of St. Vincent de Paul* (London: Burns, Oates & Washbourne, Ltd., 1934), Vol. I, pp. 346–348.

13. Matthew 19:10–12; 1 Corinthians 7:25–40.

14. Maurus Wolter, *The Principles of Monasticism* (St. Louis: B. Herder Book Company, 1962), p. 464.

15. Manuel Espinosa Polit, *Perfect Obedience* (Westminster, Md.: The Newman Press, 1947), p. 28.

16. Wilfrid Ward, *The Life of John Henry Cardinal Newman* (London: Longmans, Green & Co., Inc., 1913), Vol. I, pp. 124–125.

17. Philip Hughes, *A History of the Church*, Vol. III, p. 130.

18. Inaccurate use of the terms clergy-laity and religious-secular is so common that this pompous truism seems necessary.

19. Compiled from *Annuario Pontificio 1965* (Citta del Vaticano, 1967).

## 9. ECUMENICAL COUNCILS

1. Paul G. Sigmund, *Nicholas of Cusa and Medieval Political Thought* (Cambridge, Mass.: Harvard University Press, 1963), pp. 11–20, 304–314.

2. Philip Hughes, *A History of the Church*, Vol. III, pp. 282–305.

3. *Ibid.*, pp. 321–340.

4. Colman J. Barry, ed., *Readings in Church History* (Westminster, Md.: The Newman Press, 1965), Vol. III, pp. 74–79.

5. Philip Hughes, *The Church in Crisis* (New York: Image Books, 1964), pp. 33–34.

6. *Ibid.*, pp. 122–132.

7. Philip Hughes, *A History of the Church*, Vol. III, pp. 346–350.

8. Carlo Falconi, *Pope John and The Ecumenical Council* (Cleveland: World Book Company, 1964), p. 18.

9. Philip Hughes, *A History of the Church*, Vol. III, pp. 478–485.

10. Xavier Rynne, *Letters from Vatican City* (New York: Farrar, Straus & Giroux, 1963), pp. 1–3, 44–47.

11. Abbott and Gallagher, *The Documents of Vatican II*, pp. 424–426.

## 10. CHURCH AND STATE

1. John Courtney Murray in a series of articles in several journals: *Theological Studies*, Vol. VI (1945), pp. 230–232; "The Problem of State Religion," Vol. XII (1951), "The Church and Totalitarian Democracy," Vol. XIII (1952); "Leo XIII on Church and State," "Leo XIII: Separation of Church and State," "Leo XIII: Two Concepts of Government," Vol. XIV (1953); "Leo XIII: Two Concepts of Government," Vol. XV (1954); "For the Freedom and Transcendence of the Church," *American Ecclesiastical Review*, Vol. CXXVI (1952); "Church and State," Vol. CXXVII (1953). E. A. Goerner, *Peter and Caesar* (New York: Herder and Herder, 1965).

2. Martin Dibelius, *Botschaft und Geschichte* (Tübingen: Mohr, 1956), Vol. II, 177–228.

3. Philip Hughes, *A History of the Church*, Vol. I, p. 213.

4. *Ibid.*, pp. 191–198.

5. Marcus Dods, ed., *The Works of Aurelius Augustine* (Edinburgh: Clark, 1872), Vol. III, pp. 479–521.

6. E. G. Weltin, *The Ancient Popes* (Westminster, Md.: The Newman Press, 1964), pp. 178–179.

7. Philip Hughes, *A History of the Church*, Vol. II, pp. 135–137.

8. Louis de Wohl, *Founded on a Rock* (Philadelphia: J. B. Lippincott Company, 1961), p. 85.

9. Fernand Mourret, *A History of the Catholic Church*, trans. by Newton Thompson (St. Louis: B. Herder Book Company, 1957), Vol. XIII, pp. 567–577; E. E. Y. Hales, *Pio Nono* (New York: P. J. Kenedy & Sons), pp. 255–273.

10. *Church and State in Spain* (Madrid: O. I. I., 1962).

11. Abbott and Gallagher, *The Documents of Vatican II*, pp. 238–247.

## 11. THE ONE TRUE CHURCH

1. Philip Hughes, *A History of the Church*, Vol. I, pp. 98f.

2. 1 Corinthians 6:15.

3. Philip Hughes, *A History of the Church*, Vol. I, pp. 54–56.

4. *Ibid.*, pp. 224–228.

5. *The Work of St. Optatus against the Donatists* (London: Longmans, Green & Co., Ltd., 1917), pp. 58–62.

6. Augustine, *Contra epistolam Parmeniani*, iii, 24; John Henry Newman, *Apologia Pro Vita Sua* (Cambridge: Riverside, 1956), pp. 123–124.

7. Abbott and Gallagher, *The Documents of Vatican II*, p. 346.

8. *Ibid.*, p. 245.

## II. WORSHIP

### 2. THE SACRAMENTS

1. Maurice de la Taille, *The Mystery of Faith and Human Opinion* (London: Sheed & Ward, Ltd., 1930), pp. 30–37.

2. *Summa Theologica* III, q. 60, a. 6–7.

### 3. BAPTISM

1. Ludwig Ott, *Fundamentals of Catholic Dogma* (St. Louis: B. Herder Book Company, 1964), pp. 353–354; F. L. Cross, ed., *Oxford Dictionary of the Christian Church* (London: Oxford University Press, 1963).
2. *Ibid.*
3. The material is abundant; one may consult Tertullian, *Adversus Praxeam*, 26, and *De Bap-*

*tismate*; Ambrose, *De Mysteriis*; Hippolytus, *Apostolic Tradition*.
4. Irenaeus seems to be the first witness to infant baptism; J. Quasten, *Patrology* (Westminster, Md.: The Newman Press, 1950), Vol. I, p. 311; L. Ott, *Fundamentals of Catholic Dogma*, pp. 359–360.

### 4. CONFIRMATION

1. Ludwig Ott, *Fundamentals of Catholic Dogma*, pp. 362–363; *Oxford Dictionary of the Christian Church*.

2. John A. Hardon, *The Protestant Churches of America*.

### 5. THE EUCHARIST

1. *The Church Teaches* (St. Louis: B. Herder Book Company, 1955), Nos. 756–759.
2. Matthew 26:26–29; Mark 14:22–25; Luke 22:15–20.
3. Maurice de la Taille, *The History of Faith and Human Opinion*, Book II.
4. Leviticus 3.
5. Joseph M. Powers, *Eucharistic*

*Theology* (New York: Herder and Herder, 1967), pp. 170–179.
6. *Dictionnaire Théologique de la Foi Catholique*, Vol. III, col. 565; Philip Hughes, *A History of the Church*, Vol. III, pp. 306–316.
7. 1 Corinthians 10:14–17; 11:17–33; 12:13; Ephesians 5:30.

### 6. PENANCE

1. Michael de la Bedoyere, ed., *Objections to Roman Catholicism*, pp. 44–45.

2. S. L: Greenslade, ed., *Tertullian: De Pudicitia* (Philadelphia: The Westminster Press, 1957), pp. 74–77.

### 8. ORDERS

1. Ludwig Ott, *Fundamentals of Catholic Dogma*, p. 456.

2. *The Church Teaches*, No. 839.

### 9. MATRIMONY

1. Matthew 5:32; 19:1–12; Mark 10:1–13; Luke 16:18; 1 Corinthians 7:10.

### 11. MYSTICISM

1. E. H. Gilson, *The Mystical Theology of St. Bernard* (New York: Sheed and Ward, Inc., 1940); D. T. Suzuki, *Mysticism: Christian and Buddhist* (New York: Harper & Brothers, 1957); R. E. Whitson, *Mysticism and Ecumenism* (New York: Sheed and Ward, Inc., 1966); Sidney Spencer, *Mysticism in World Religion* (Baltimore: Penguin Books, Inc., 1963).

2. John J. Burke, ed., *St. Teresa of Jesus* (New York: Columbus, 1911), pp. 188–198, 323–334.

3. *Ibid.*, pp. 120–129.

## III. THE BELIEFS OF THE ROMAN CATHOLIC CHURCH

### 1. FAITH

1. George D. Smith, ed., *The Teaching of the Catholic Church* (New York: The Macmillan Company, Inc., 1949).

2. Thomas Aquinas, *Summa Theologica*, II.II., qq. 1–7; *The Church Teaches*, Nos. 63–85.

3. *The Church Teaches*, Nos. 8–14, 88–90.

### 2. THE TEACHING OFFICE OF THE CHURCH

1. J. J. Langford, *Galileo, Science and the Church* (New York: Desclée Company, 1966); Pio Paschini, *Vita e opere di Galileo Galilei* (Vatican City: Vatican Press, 1964). One bishop in the

Second Vatican Council asked for an official rehabilitation and amendment of the Galileo case. This does not appear in the acts, but the tone of the *Constitution on the Church in the Modern World*, No. 36, is not in sympathy with the type of process used in the Galileo case (Abbott and Gallagher, *The Documents of Vatican II*, pp. 233–234).

2. N. C. Eberhardt, *A Summary of*

*Catholic History* (St. Louis: B. Herder Book Company, 1962), Vol. II, pp. 212, 240.

3. *The Church Teaches*, Nos. 212–220.

4. Denzinger-Schönmetzer, *Enchiridion Symbolorum* (Freiburg: Herder, 1963), Nos. 2901–2980. It may be of interest that the complete collection of the syllabus is quite difficult to find in modern languages.

## 3. TRADITION AND SCRIPTURE

1. *The Church Teaches*, No. 95.
2. Josef Geiselmann, *Die Heilige Schrift und die Tradition* (Freiburg: Herder, 1962); G. H. Tavard, *Holy Writ and Holy*

*Church* (London: Burns, Oates & Washbourne, Ltd., 1959).

3. J. H. Newman, *An Essay on the Development of Christian Doctrine* (New York: Doubleday & Company, 1960).

## 4. THEOLOGY AND DOCTRINE

1. J. Waterworth, *The Canons and Decrees of the Council of Trent,* pp. 187–192.

## IV. THE WORKS OF THE CHURCH

### 1. THE SAINTS

1. James Brodrick, *Robert Bellarmine* (Westminster, Md.: The Newman Press, 1961), pp. 172–173.
2. Philip Hughes, *A History of the Church*, Vol. III, pp. 277–280.
3. *Ibid.*, Vol. I, pp. 217–220.
4. C. C. Martindale, *The Vocation of Aloysius Gonzaga* (New York: Sheed and Ward, Inc., 1945), pp. 88–89.

5. Francis de Sales, *Introduction to the Devout Life* (Westminster, Md.: The Newman Press, 1956).
6. Teresa of Avila, *The Book of the Foundations* (London: Burns, Oates & Washbourne, Ltd., 1871).
7. I regret that I am unable to trace the reference to this exchange.

## 2. EDUCATION

1. *The Catholic Directory, 1967*, reports 4,369,845 students in 10,927 elementary schools, 1,103,761 students in 2341 secondary schools, and 431,070 students in 305 higher institutions. The same source in 1965 reported 4,566,809 students in 10,931 elementary schools, 1,095,519 students in 2465 secondary schools, and 384,526 students in 304 higher institutions. Even this sample illustrates the trend in the United States: abandonment of elementary schools, consolidation of secondary schools, and increase of college and university enrollment.

2. P. K. Guilday, *A History of the Councils of Baltimore* (New York: The Macmillan Company, 1932).

3. Mary Perkins Ryan, *Are Parochial Schools the Answer?* (New York: Holt, Rinehart and Winston, 1964).

4. Andrew Greeley and Peter Rossi, *The Education of Catholic Americans* (Chicago: Aldine Publishing Co., 1966); R. A. Neuwien, *Catholic Schools in Action* (Notre Dame: University of Notre Dame Press, 1966).

5. *Notre Dame Alumnus*, Sept.-Oct. and Nov.-Dec., 1967; Jan.-Feb., 1968.

6. Greeley and Rossi, *The Education of Catholic Americans*, pp. 66–67, 72–76.

7. John Tracy Ellis, *American Catholicism and the Intellectual Life* (Chicago: Heritage Foundation, 1956).

7. *The Idea of the Catholic University* (Notre Dame: University of Notre Dame Press, 1967).

## 3. MISSIONS

1. T. J. Campbell, *The Jesuits 1534–1921* (New York: Encyclopedia Press, 1921), pp. 255–267.

2. *Ibid.*, pp. 228–267; Theodar Griesinger, *The Jesuits* (London: W. H. Allen, 1903), pp. 85–140; L. J. Gallagher, *China in the Sixteenth Century: The Journals of Matthew Ricci 1583–1610* (New York: Random House, Inc., 1953).

## 6. PREACHING

1. "What are the causes of the de-Christianization of our present-day world? Canon Boulard, following Abbé Godin, emphatically asserts that the greatest blame is to be borne by inadequate preaching"; Y.-B. Tremel in *The Word* (New York: P. J. Kenedy & Sons, 1964), p. 171.

# INDEX